D0167777

THE EVERYTHING

DEALING

Dear Reader,

I like to think of myself as an educated and enlightened mom. I do everything I can to keep my kids safe. I get my kids vaccinated, have them wear helmets, sign them up for swim lessons, and make them ride in booster seats. I taught them to be wary of strangers and to look both ways before crossing the street. But I failed to teach them about one very real danger—bullies.

I had no idea my four-year-old son was dealing with a bully until the day I asked him to identify his preschool classmates in the class picture. As he pointed from one smiling child to the next, my son said, "This is Jenny, this is Thomas, and this is my bully. . . ."

I was taken aback because I hadn't realized that bullying existed in kids so young. I've since discovered that bullying exists in every school and in every classroom from preschool through college. In researching and writing this book, I feel incredibly lucky to have learned the specific skills and strategies that will help keep my kids safe from bullies (or from behaving like a bully themselves) early on. I hope reading it does the same for you and your children.

Deborah Carpenter

Welcome to

THE

EVERYTHING®

PARENT'S GUIDES

Everything® Parent's Guides are a part of the bestselling *Everything*® series and cover common parenting issues like childhood illnesses and tantrums, as well as medical conditions like asthma and juvenile diabetes. These family-friendly books are designed to be a one-stop guide for parents. If you want authoritative information on specific topics not fully covered in other books, *Everything*® Parent's Guides are your perfect solution.

Alerts: Urgent warnings

Essentials: Quick handy tips

Facts: Important snippets of information

Questions: Answers to common questions

PUBLISHER Karen Cooper

DIRECTOR OF ACQUISITIONS AND INNOVATION Paula Munier

MANAGING EDITOR, EVERYTHING SERIES Lisa Laing

COPY CHIEF Casey Ebert

ACQUISITIONS EDITOR Katie McDonough

SENIOR DEVELOPMENT EDITOR Brett Palana-Shanahan

EDITORIAL ASSISTANT Hillary Thompson

Visit the entire Everything® series at *www.everything.com*

THE
EVERYTHING®

PARENT'S GUIDE TO

DEALING
WITH
BULLIES

From playground teasing to cyber
bullying, all you need to ensure
your child's safety and happiness

Deborah Carpenter with Christopher J. Ferguson, PhD

Aadamsmedia
Avon, Massachusetts

This book is dedicated to my children, Kaylin and Kevin.

• • •

An Everything® Series Book.
Everything® and everything.com® are registered
trademarks of F+W Media, Inc.

Published by Adams Media, a division of F+W Media Inc.
57 Littlefield Street, Avon, MA 02322 U.S.A.
www.adamsmedia.com

ISBN 10: 1-60550-054-2
ISBN 13: 978-1-60550-054-6

Printed in the United States of America.

J I H G F E D C B A

Library of Congress Cataloging-in-Publication Data
is available from the publisher.

*All the examples and dialogues used in this book are fictional, and
have been created by the author to illustrate disciplinary situations.*

▶**bul·ly** (bŏŏl´ ē) n.
1. An individual who is consistently cruel, overbearing, and often abusive, especially to those persons who are perceived to be weaker. Also known as *Canis Canem Edit* (Latin for "dog eat dog")

Acknowledgments

I'd like to thank my family (especially my husband, Jeff) and friends for all the support and encouragement given to me during this project. The encouraging e-mails, babysitting services, and coffee dates were greatly appreciated. And many thanks to Bob Diforio, Katie McDonough, and Brett Palana-Shanahan for their kind guidance through this process.

During the researching and writing of this book, I read far too many heartbreaking stories of children suffering at the hands of bullies. No child deserves to be bullied. And no child should be allowed to bully. To all you parents, teachers, school personnel, and professionals who work tirelessly day in and day out to protect children from harm—thank you. You are the people who truly make a difference.

Contents

INTRODUCTION. XIII

CHAPTER 1 **What Is Bullying?** 1
Definition of Bullying 1
History of Bullying. 2
Facts and Statistics 5
Common Markers of Bullying 8
Bullying Versus Normal Conflict 10
Why Most People Underestimate the Impact of Bullying 11
The Triad: The Bully, the Bullied, and the Bystander 11

CHAPTER 2 **Types of Bullying** 15
Verbal Bullying 15
Physical Bullying. 19
Social, Relational, and Emotional Bullying 20
Extortion 23
Direct Bullying Versus Indirect Bullying. 24
Cyber Bullying. 26

CHAPTER 3 **Types of Bullies** 32
Confident 32
Social 33
Detached 34
Hyperactive 35
Bullied Bully. 36
Bunch of Bullies 38
Gang of Bullies 38

CHAPTER 4 **The Bully** 40
Characteristics of a Bully 40
Why Do Some Kids Bully? 43

The Bully's Role in the Triad. 47
The Stereotypical Bully. 47
Common Places Bullying Occurs 48
The Mean Bully 49
The Meaner Bully 51
The Meanest Bully. 52

CHAPTER 5 **The Bullied** 53
Characteristics of a Bullied Child 53
The Bullied Child's Role in the Triad. 55
The Making of a Victim: F-E-A-R 56
Why Me?. 59
Why Victims Don't Tell 61
The Victim Who also Becomes a Bully. 63

CHAPTER 6 **The Bystander** 64
Characteristics of a Bystander. 64
The Bystander's Role in the Triad 65
Bystander Roles. 65
Why Bystanders Don't Tell 68
Why Bystanders Aren't Innocent 69
How Bystanders Can Stop Bullying. 70

CHAPTER 7 **Factors That Lead to Bullying Behavior** . . . 73
Violence in the Family 73
Lack of a Positive Role Model 78
Violent Television 79
Violent Video Games 82
Prior Victim of a Bully. 84
School Failure 85
Peer Rejection 86
School Climate. 86

CHAPTER 8 **Common Bullying Myths** 88
Myth 1: Bullying Is a Normal Rite of Passage 88

Myth 2: Kids Need to Learn to Defend Themselves. 90

Myth 3: Children Who Are Bullied Always Tell an Adult. 92

Myth 4: People Are Born Bullies 95

Myth 5: Bullying Doesn't Happen at My Child's School. 96

Myth 6: Bullies Are Loners with No Social Skills 97

Myth 7: Bullying Is a School Problem 98

CHAPTER 9 **Warning Signs That Your Child Is Being Bullied** 100

Physical Clues 100

Psychological Clues 102

Educational Clues 103

Most Likely Targets 104

How to Respond (Dos and Don'ts) 105

Steps to Take if Your Child Is Being Bullied 107

CHAPTER 10 **The Consequences of Bullying**. 111

Physical 111

Emotional. 113

Educational 114

Short-Term Effects of Being Bullied 115

Long-Term Effects of Being Bullied 117

How Parents Can Help 118

CHAPTER 11 **Boy Bullies**. 119

The Boys-Will-Be-Boys Myth 119

The Danger of Stereotypes. 122

Physical Aggression 123

Boys Bullying Girls 126

Why Boys Bully Other Boys 127

How Parents Can Help 128

CHAPTER 12 **Girl Bullies** 129

Verbal Bullying 129

When Girls Get Violent 132

Group Bullying. 134
Why Girls Bully Other Girls 136
The Good-Girl Persona 137
How Parents Can Help 137
The Ophelia Project 140

CHAPTER 13 **How to Bully Proof Your Child** 142
Teaching Social Skills. 142
Ways to Improve Your Child's Self-Esteem 144
Teach Your Child How to Be a Friend. 154
Encourage and Foster One Good Friendship. 157
Allow Your Child to Join a Group 158
Enroll Your Child in a Self-Defense Class 158
Teach Basic Prevention Skills 159

CHAPTER 14 **Social Skills and Assertiveness
Training**. 160
Why Your Child Needs Social-Skills Training. 160
The Most Essential Social Skills For Kids 161
Body Language 163
Voice Quality 166
Conversational Skills. 167
Friendship Skills 168
Assertiveness Skills. 170

CHAPTER 15 **Parental Responsibility and Why Getting
Involved Can Help Enact Change** 173
Fear of Making the Situation Worse 173
Embarrassed by a Bullied Child 174
Kids Beg Parents Not to Tell. 175
Parents Fear Being Seen as Overprotective 176
Parents Want the Child to Stand Up for Herself. 177
Reasons Why Bullying Should Always Be Reported 177
What Works in Bullying Prevention?. 178

CHAPTER 16 **Cyber Bullying**. 186
Types of Cyber Bullying 186
Why Cyber Bullying Has Become such a Problem 193
You Can't See Me, I Can't See You 195
Impact of Cyber Bullying 195
Signs of Cyber Bullying. 197
Ways to Protect Your Child. 198
Responding to Cyber Bullying 200
Prevent Your Child from Being a Cyber Bully 202

CHAPTER 17 **What if My Child Is a Bully?** 204
Signs that Your Child Might Be a Bully 204
Keep an Open Mind 205
Intervention 206
Teaching Your Child Friendship and Interpersonal Skills. 212
Create More Feel-Good and Do-Good Opportunities 213
Engage in Constructive, Supervised Activities and Sports. 214
Limit Exposure to Violent Media. 215

CHAPTER 18 **Bullying Among Children with Special
Needs**. 217
Are Schools Protecting Your Children?. 217
Is Your Child Vulnerable? 218
New Threat to Kids: Food-Allergy Taunts 220
What Is Disability Harassment? 224
What You Can Do if It Doesn't Stop. 225
What to Do if Your Child Is Being Bullied. 225
Is Legal Action Necessary?. 227

CHAPTER 19 **When Bullying Becomes a Crime**. 229
Do You Know the Law in Your State? 229
Directives in Bullying Laws 232
Definition of Bodily Injury or Threat of Bodily Injury 233
Dealing with Uncooperative School Officials 234

Filing a Complaint 236
Resolution 238
Bullying Prevention Programs 239

CHAPTER 20 **Why Zero Tolerance Policies Don't
Work** 240
What Is a Zero Tolerance Policy? 240
Why Zero Tolerance Actually Decreases Reports 242
Student Exclusion Policies 244
Bullies Need Intervention and Positive Role Models 245
Other Misdirected Policies 246
What Policies and Programs Should Be Implemented? 247

CHAPTER 21 **How Students, Parents, Schools, and
Communities Can Work Together** 250
Identify the Extent of the Problem 250
Create an Awareness Campaign 251
Implement Educational Programs 252
Start a Peer-Counseling Program 254
Specify Classroom Rules 255
Practice Cooperative Learning Activities 257
Increase Supervision in High-Risk Areas 258
Whole-School Policies 259

APPENDIX A **Glossary** 261

APPENDIX B **Resources** 271

APPENDIX C **Existing Anti-Bullying Education and
Prevention Programs** 275

APPENDIX D **Anti-Bully Pledge for Use in the
Classroom** 279

INDEX 281

Introduction

Your first inkling that something is wrong might be when your kindergartner says, "I hate school and I don't want to go anymore!" Or maybe your school-loving second grader suddenly develops mysterious bellyaches every weekday morning. Perhaps it's the dark bruise on your seventh grader's upper arm and his sudden desire to quit the soccer team.

No matter how a child's bullying comes to light, the knowledge is likely to ignite powerful and often conflicting emotions. You may be furious at the bully and have the desire to march right over to school to give "that kid" a taste of his own medicine. You may feel sad that your child has endured cruelty at the hands of one or more of his classmates or feel frustration that your child isn't able to stick up for himself. On top of all that, you may feel completely unsure of what to do next.

It's natural to want to protect your child from bullies. But the unfortunate truth is that many parents don't know what to do to help. Should you let your child handle it? Do you complain to the teacher? Call the parents of the abusive child? The last thing you want to do is make it worse for your child.

No doubt those of you who have a few unpleasant memories of being bullied as kids remember that sick-to-your-stomach feeling of anxiety at what awaited you on the bus, at school, or in the neighborhood play yard. The thought that your child may currently be experiencing similar pain and humiliation can be difficult to bear.

One of the reasons bullying has been able to thrive for so long is that it continues to remain under the radar of most parents and school personnel. When bullying behavior is discovered, it's often dismissed with the attitude that boys will be boys or that it's no big deal. That attitude is harmful and leaves your child feeling like he's all alone. But he's not alone—he has you.

Bullying can be stopped. And this book will teach you, the parents, how to stop it. The more you learn about what bullying is—how, where, and why it happens, why it happens to specific groups of kids, the difference between bullying among boys and girls, why cyber bullying is a growing problem, what to do if you suspect your child is being bullied (or is bullying), and why bullying continues on every playground, in every lunchroom, and in every neighborhood play yard despite a growing awareness of the tragic personal and societal ramifications—the better prepared you will be to help your child.

The good news is that researchers and public policy makers are beginning to see bullying for what it is—peer abuse. When normal, good-natured childhood teasing and taunting escalates into constant mocking that is hurtful and unkind or turns physically aggressive, it crosses the line into bullying and needs to stop. It's abuse—plain and simple. And regardless of whether the bullying is verbal, physical, or emotional, it needs to stop.

Regardless of whether your child is being bullied, is the one engaged in bullying behavior, or is a bystander, this book will help you stop the mistreatment by providing effective, practical tips and suggestions that will give all kids and parents hope for a bully-free future.

CHAPTER 1

What Is Bullying?

According to the National Youth Violence Prevention Center, "Almost 30 percent of youth in the United States (or over 5.7 million) are estimated to be involved in bullying as either a bully, a target of bullying, or both." This means that bullying likely exists in almost every classroom and in every school in the United States. It's a reality in the lives of all children, whether they are bullies, bullied, or bystanders.

Definition of Bullying

Bullying is intentionally aggressive behavior that can take many forms (verbal, physical, social/relational/emotional, or cyber bullying—or any combination of these); it involves an imbalance of power, and is often repeated over a period of time. The bullying is generally unprovoked and can consist of one child bullying another, a group of children ganging up against one lone child, or one group of kids targeting another group.

Common behaviors attributed to bullying include put-downs, name calling, rumors, verbal threats, menacing, harassment, intimidation, social isolation or exclusion, and physical assaults. Bullying can happen anywhere, but occurs primarily in places with little adult supervision such as at the bus stop, on the bus, in the school bathroom, hallway, cafeteria, and on the playground. It also happens when groups of children play unsupervised at a friend's house or in a neighboring yard.

Don't be reluctant to discuss bullying with your young child; you won't frighten her. Studies show that by kindergarten, most children can identify the class bullies and can tell you exactly what they do to hurt other kids. A great way to bully proof your child is to talk with her (early and often) about bullies, read age-appropriate bully related books together, and role play ways to ignore or confront another child who attempts to bully her.

Alert!

According to a 2001 study done by the Kaiser Family Foundation & Children Now, "Teasing and bullying were first on the minds of children when asked what threatens their safety and emotional well-being." With bullying first on the minds of children, it should be first and foremost on the minds of the adults who care for them.

History of Bullying

Bullying isn't a new problem, but people are becoming more and more aware of its negative impact on kids. In the past, bullying was seen as a harmless rite of passage, a normal, unavoidable part of growing up. Taunts, social isolation, rejection, gossip, pushing, shoving, and tripping were often dismissed as child's play or simply kids being kids. Bullied children were told, "Don't let it get to you," "You're too sensitive . . . toughen up," or that bullying builds character.

The problem with this approach is that while some children have the confidence and social skills to stop bullying when it happens, many do not. Bullying is abuse, and expecting a victim of abuse to handle it on their own is unrealistic. After all, we don't tell victims of traditional child abuse or domestic violence to toughen up or just not let it get to them.

The Bully in Books

In literary works, children have been singled out and systematically harassed since the beginning of time. *Oliver Twist* is likely one of the most memorable examples. Written by Charles Dickens and published in 1838, *Oliver Twist* was one of the first novels in the English language to focus on the bullying and criminal mistreatment of a child protagonist.

Lord of the Flies, another memorable novel, written by William Golding and published in 1954 (a book that is required reading in some middle school English classes), describes the actions of a group of young children who, in the absence of adult supervision, make a swift descent from civilized to barbaric after being stranded on a deserted island.

S.E. Hinton's well-known 1967 novel *The Outsiders* is the coming-of-age story of a fourteen-year-old boy who is bullied and victimized by rival high school students. And *Blubber*, written by Judy Blume in 1974, tells the story of the mean-spirited and cruel bullying of an overweight fifth-grade girl.

Granted, these books are extreme examples of bullying behavior, but in the broader cultural picture, the bully/target, perpetrator/victim, predator/prey experience is deeply entrenched in our nation's subculture. Just when did it become acceptable, even expected, to have a bully included in the cast of characters of almost every book, movie, and television show?

Defeating the Bully

Often the bullying in movies is viewed as a challenge to the character of the kid being bullied. The entire outcome of the movie depends on how the kid being bullied eventually deals with the bully. This usually means one of three things: the bullied child can stand up to the bully, like when Michael J. Fox travels back in time and helps Marty McFly's father stand up to the class bully in the film *Back to the Future*; the bullied child can "take it like a man," as in the movie *Stand by Me*, where the older boys beat up the younger boys and the younger boys do their best to fight back; or the bullied kid must defeat the bully or bullies, as in *The Karate Kid*, where Daniel, a bullied boy, learns karate in order to fight and defeat his tormentors.

In each of these examples, you root for the bullied kids to fight back and win; and when they do, you feel that all is right in the world. Unfortunately, real-life bullying situations rarely end with this type of Hollywood cinematic victory. The majority of children who are being bullied can't or just don't know how to fight back on their own. They need help, support, and, most importantly, intervention. All children have the right to feel safe from bullying, and not one of them should be forced to face it alone.

The First Bully Related Research Study

Prior to the 1970s, bullying wasn't considered a significant social problem. It wasn't until Swedish researcher Dan Olweus, a psychology professor at the University of Bergen in Norway, completed the first large-scale, scientific study of bully/victim problems among school children and youth that the public was alerted to the magnitude of the problem. Olweus's study was published as a book in Scandinavia in 1973, and was published again in 1978 in the United States under the title *Aggression in the Schools: Bullies and Whipping Boys*.

The findings of Olweus's study opened the eyes of researchers and demonstrated that bully/victim problems were quite prevalent in school settings. In the 1980s, Olweus conducted the first systematic intervention study that highlighted the positive effects of his "Bullying Prevention Program." Since then, several more large-scale intervention projects have been conducted in schools, most with good results.

In 1993, Olweus wrote *Bullying at School: What We Know and What We Can Do*, and is now widely considered to be the world's leading authority on bullying behavior. Olweus's groundbreaking research and intervention programs have played a significant role in increasing awareness that bullying is a growing social problem, one that must be taken seriously by researchers, educators, lawmakers, parents, students, and society in general.

Today, slow but steady progress is being made. Schools are beginning to adopt anti-bullying intervention and education programs, and states are starting to pass comprehensive anti-bullying laws. By 2003, fifteen states had enacted anti-bullying laws, most in direct response to the school shootings that occurred between 1997 and 2001. And as of June 2007, a total of thirty-five states had laws that address harassment, intimidation, and bullying at school. With a clear definition of bullying, schools will be required to enforce uniform standards of conduct.

Facts and Statistics

If your child is being bullied (or is bullying), he's not alone. A recent national survey of students in grades 6 through 10 reported that 13 percent of students bullied others, 11 percent had been bullied, and 6 percent reported both being bullied and bullying others. Bullying generally begins in the elementary grades, peaks in the sixth through eighth grades, and persists into high school.

 **Fact**

When examining statistics and survey results, it is important to remember that different surveys may use different measures and definitions of bullying, and the focus of the survey may be on a specific age group or on school-age children in general. This variability can cause statistical results to differ significantly from one study to the next.

In 2001, *The Journal of the American Medical Association* reported that more than 160,000 students skip school every day because they are anxious and fearful of being bullied by other students. School is supposed to be a safe haven for students, but adults who did not experience bullying or don't fully understand it may inadvertently downplay and devalue the experience. This is mainly caused by confusion among parents, teachers, and administrators about what the definition of bullying is and how they should deal with it when it occurs.

The Youngest Targets

According to a 2001 national survey of parents and kids by the Kaiser Family Foundation and Nickelodeon, 74 percent of eight- to eleven-year-old students said teasing and bullying regularly occur at their schools, while only about half of parents in this survey saw bullying as a problem for their children. This discrepancy may be because young kids believe that since teasing and bullying happens so frequently it's normal or to be expected. Or it could be that kids who are teased or bullied are afraid to tell anyone about it, even their parents.

 Essential

"Being bullied is not just an unpleasant rite of passage through childhood," said Duane Alexander, MD, director of the National Institute of Child Health and Human Development (NICHD) in an NIH news release. "It's a public health problem that merits attention. People who were bullied as children are more likely to suffer from depression and low self-esteem, well into adulthood, and the bullies themselves are more likely to engage in criminal behavior later in life."

Recent playground statistics show that when a child is bullied, a whopping 85 percent of the time no one intervenes. This just proves that most school bullying continues to be carried out under the radar of teachers and school personnel. A 2001 Kaiser Family Foundation study confirmed this when 71 percent of teachers reported that they intervened often or almost always, whereas only 23 percent of children agreed.

Middle School Bullying

According to the Josephson Institute of Ethics, bullying peaks in the eleven- to twelve-year-old age group, so it isn't surprising that 39 percent of middle school students say they don't feel safe at school.

In a 1999 study involving middle schools, Bosworth reported that 80 percent of the students engaged in some form of bullying for the past thirty days. Students report that, "bullying takes place during times when the attention of the teacher is focused elsewhere, such as, when a teacher's back is turned to help another student or perhaps to write on the board."

High School Violence

In a 2001 Kaiser Family Foundation study, 86 percent of children between the ages of twelve and fifteen reported that they get teased or bullied at school. This means that bullying is more prevalent than smoking, alcohol, drugs, or sex among this age group. And while a large percentage of these incidents likely fall into the teasing/taunting side of things rather than vicious, violent bullying, it's unnerving to realize that so many of our kids are dealing with bullying on some level on a daily basis.

Tragically, investigations of the student shootings at Columbine High School and other U.S. schools have suggested that bullying was a factor in many of the incidents. In 2002, a report released by the U.S. Secret Service and the Department of Education concluded that bullying played a significant role in many school shootings. In fact, one key finding was that in thirty-seven incidents involving forty-one school shooters, "many of the attackers felt bullied, persecuted, or injured by others prior to the attack."

Bullying is now recognized as an important contributor to youth violence, including homicide, suicide, and "bullycide"—the label now applied to children who kill themselves to escape being bullied. The term "bullycide" was coined by authors Neil Marr and Tim Field in their book *Bullycide: Death at Playtime*, which explores stories of children who have committed suicide as a result of having been bullied.

The New Cyberthreat

Thanks to modern technology, bullying is no longer "just" a schoolyard problem. Unlimited and often unsupervised access to instant messaging, e-mail, chat rooms, and websites created specifically to insult and humiliate peers are changing the face of the traditional bully. Cyber bullying is the ever-increasing phenomenon of twenty-four hours a day, seven days a week online peer bashing. And even without the tell-tale physical signs of conventional bullying (black eyes, torn clothes, missing lunch money), the potential for psychological damage is alarming and no less real.

Fact

According to the 2004 i-SAFE survey of 1,500 students: 58 percent of kids admit someone has said mean or hurtful things to them online; 53 percent of kids admit having said something mean or hurtful to another person online; and 58 percent have not told their parents or an adult about something mean or hurtful that happened to them online.

Common Markers of Bullying

When one child accidentally collides with another child on the playground, apologizes, and helps him up, it's not bullying. But let's say a third grader trips a first grader every day as he runs to line up at the end of recess. The younger boy is being bullied. Bullying behavior should not be confused with horseplay, occasional good-natured teasing, or the sudden but brief clash between children on the school playground. Kids are active, impulsive, and they are going to have scuffles. Friendship troubles, squabbles between classmates, and the all-in-good-fun wrestling match that gets a little out of hand are normal; sticking a foot out to intentionally trip (and possibly hurt and humiliate) a younger child is not. If you suspect your child is being bullied, be on the lookout for these three common markers of bullying: an imbalance of power, the intent to harm, and the threat of further harm.

An Imbalance of Power

Sam and Josh are playing dodge ball in gym. They are the two strongest athletes in the fifth grade, and after ten minutes of play are the only ones left in the game. Sam hurls the ball at Josh and accidentally hits him in the face. Josh is hurt and angry, and he lunges forward to shove Sam. While this behavior is aggressive and unacceptable, it is not bullying. Sam and Josh normally get along; this was a one-time event, and Sam did not intend to hit Josh in the face with the ball.

If Sam were a bully, he would have targeted someone he was sure he could dominate—preferably someone younger, smaller, less popular, less outgoing, or less able to defend himself. He would have intended to hurt Josh, and he would be looking forward to doing it again. A bully takes pleasure in hurting others and intentionally seeks out targets he can control.

Alert!

A shocking new trend has bullies taunting allergic kids with food. Putting a peanut on an allergic child's desk or in her lunchbox is not a prank; it can put her life in danger. When bullies target food allergies, kids and schools face a serious, not to mention potentially lethal, problem. This is especially concerning, as the number of reported peanut allergies has doubled in recent years.

Intent to Harm

A bully wants to inflict harm emotionally or physically. He intends to make the other child miserable. It's not a mistake or an accident (like Sam and Josh), and you can be sure he seeks power, control, and domination. Through the bully's actions he is telling another child, "I'm stronger than you. I will hurt you."

Threat of Further Harm

When a bully trips a younger boy or stuffs him into a locker, it's not meant to be a one-time thing. A large portion of the power a bully has over another child is the constant threat that the bullying can, and will, happen again and again and again. The longer a child is bullied, the less likely it becomes that he will fight back or tell an adult.

Bullying Versus Normal Conflict

A certain level of conflict between kids is normal, even healthy, and teaching your child how to handle everyday difficulties will prepare her for life. The problem begins when it surpasses normal childhood conflict and meets the three above-mentioned common markers for bullying: an imbalance of power, intent to harm, and threat of future harm.

Once a conflict between one or more kids has escalated into a cycle of bullying, employing conflict resolution to solve the problem is no longer appropriate. The word "conflict" assumes that both kids are in part responsible for the current problem and need to work it out. In the process of working it out, both kids make compromises and the conflict is resolved.

But bullying is not conflict. It is aggressive victimization where one child is the perpetrator and the other is the victim. The victim is 100 percent innocent and the bully is 100 percent wrong. Forcing the victim to engage in conflict resolution or mediation with her bully is neither fair nor recommended. The responsibility for resolving the bullying lies squarely on the bully's shoulders. The bully should be told, "Your behavior is unacceptable and it will not be tolerated." The victim should be told, "No one deserves to be bullied. Every effort will be made to stop it." Making the victim feel safe should be top priority.

Remember, conflict is a part of life, and ordinary, everyday conflicts can make kids stronger. Bullying does the exact opposite; it systematically makes kids weaker by undermining their self-esteem.

Why Most People Underestimate the Impact of Bullying

The number one reason most people underestimate the impact of bullying is simple: most kids don't tell. Only 25–50 percent of kids who are bullied report it. There is a code of silence among children; they fear that telling an adult will make them vulnerable. They fear retaliation by the bully, they fear the adults won't take them seriously or will blame them, and they worry that the grownups—parents included—will inappropriately handle the situation.

Since the majority of bullying occurs in areas where there is little adult supervision, such as on the bus or playground, in hallways, stairwells, cafeterias, locker rooms, and in parking lots, it is rarely witnessed. And if someone tells, teachers are often faced with a he said/she said situation.

Adding insult to injury, many adults simply don't get it. Adults have become desensitized to all but the most egregious violence. A bump here, a shove there, most adults think, "What's the big deal?" Unless you have personally experienced long-term bullying, it may be hard to fully comprehend just how profoundly damaging even minor long-term bullying is to kids. Another concern is that most adults (parents included) have no idea how to stop bullying once they find out about it, and still others continue to think it's a normal part of growing up: "I dealt with it, and so can you."

The Triad: The Bully, the Bullied, and the Bystander

"The bully, the bullied, and the bystander are three characters in a tragic play performed daily in our homes, schools, playgrounds, and streets," writes Barbara Coloroso in her book *The Bully, the Bullied, and the Bystander*. And in order to gain a thorough understanding of the dynamics of bullying, you need to consider all of the three "actors" involved. According to Coloroso, they all play a significant role in the drama that unfolds day in and day out in children's lives.

The Bully

Simply put, a bully is someone who acts in an aggressive, hostile, or hurtful manner toward others. And contrary to popular belief, bullies are not big, dumb, ugly oafs (unless, of course, you happen to be watching Popeye). You can't tell if someone is a bully by what he or she looks like; the only way to identify a bully is by how he acts. It can be quite shocking when a parent gets a first glimpse of the bully who has been making their child miserable for weeks and he's three inches shorter and twenty pounds lighter than their child.

 Essential

If your child is the target of a bully, don't expect her to tell you outright, but she may drop hints—listen closely for them. She might ask, "Mom, did anyone ever tell a lie about you when you were a kid?" or make derogatory statements about herself like, "I'm such a loser." If your gut tells you something is wrong, it probably is.

Bullies are all shapes and sizes: they can be large or small, athletic or not, popular or not, boys or girls. A bully can be anyone, but there are a few things most of them have in common:

- Bullies only care about themselves.
- Bullies crave attention.
- Bullies have trouble empathizing.
- Bullies like to dominate.
- Bullies are arrogant.
- Bullies feel superior.
- Bullies blame their victims.
- Bullies feel strong feelings of contempt toward other children.

The Bullied

Just like bullies, kids who are bullied come in all shapes and sizes. Anyone can be the target of a bully, but there are a few things that might increase your child's chances of being picked on:

- If she is the new kid at school
- If she's the youngest or smallest in the class
- If she's extra sensitive, shy, or anxious to please
- If she's physically different (if she has a learning or physical disability)
- If she's socially different (poor or rich)
- If she's of a different race or ethnicity
- If she's simply in the wrong place at the wrong time

Bullies will often test the waters, trolling for victims at the beginning of a school year. Once your child has been targeted, how she responds to the initial bullying will determine whether she moves from one-time target to victim. You will learn how to practice bully proofing skills with your child in Chapter 13.

 ***Fact***

If your child has a physical or learning disability, he's at an increased risk for being involved in bullying situations. A 1991 study conducted by S. Ziegler and M. Rosenstein-Manner found that 38 percent of students identified as special education students were bullied compared to 18 percent of other students.

The Bystander

Bystanders are the kids exposed to the actions of the bully and the reactions of the bullied. Being a captive audience to the cruelty of other kids can be upsetting and can leave a child feeling guilty for not intervening, despite not knowing how at the time.

Not all kids who witness bullying react in the same way. Some kids ignore the bully and look away or pretend it isn't happening, some watch and laugh and even join in, and a brave few will try to stop it.

Children don't always fit neatly into bully, bullied, and bystander roles. Kids who are bullied can become bullies, bullies can become victims, and virtually every child bears witness to bullying at some point in their young lives.

CHAPTER 2

Types of Bullying

Merriam Webster's Collegiate Dictionary defines the term "bullying" as, "to treat abusively; to affect by means of force or coercion; or to use browbeating language or behavior." Note that the definition includes nonviolent actions such as coercion and browbeating language. Adults need to be aware that bullying is not always physical, obvious, or carried out in public. Shoves, punches, whacks, and smacks are only part of the problem. Bullying can also be verbal, social, emotional, relational, extortion, or it can be carried out via the Internet.

Verbal Bullying

The old adage "sticks and stones may break my bones, but names can never hurt me" is only half right—words can and do hurt. Words can be used as weapons, and the mouth can pack a powerful and lasting punch to the self-esteem. It doesn't matter if the verbal taunts or gossip is true; true or not, it's painful when someone says things about you that are spiteful or downright cruel.

Verbal bullying starts at a very young age and is popular with both boys and girls. Even in preschool classrooms, you can often hear teases and taunts such as, "You're a poopy head!" "No, you're a poopy head!" "You can't kick the ball! Nah-na-na-nah-na!" "You pick your nose!" "Do not!" "Do so . . . nose-picker!" Kids think these taunts are hilarious, and practically dance with excitement when they deliver such so-called funny lines. And granted, these kids aren't really trying to be cruel, they're just having a good time and seeking the attention and approval of their peers. When other kids laugh at the goofiness, a preschooler feels great.

Alert!

Kids bully as early as preschool. The most common way the pint-sized crowd puts down peers is with these three behaviors: verbal taunts—"You're such a crybaby! Boo-hoo-hoo"; exaggerated body gestures—the bully will rub his eyes and make a mock sad face; social exclusion—"Go away! Cry babies aren't allowed to play with us!"

Preschool is exactly where the intervention needs to begin. Too often adults see this behavior and think it's cute and funny. It's not cute and funny, it's a precursor to the more damaging teasing and taunting that older bullies employ. Today it's "You're a poopy head"; tomorrow it's, "You're a %@!#&." Virtually any behavior can become a habit, and even without the reinforcement of laughing peers and ineffective tsk-tsking of adults, kids can fall into a cycle of abuse. On the other hand, subtle encouragement or even the absence of discouragement can serve as powerful reinforcement to continue the behavior.

The difference between a four-year-old's taunt and a seven-year-old's taunt is the intent. Hopefully, a four-year-old learns by the time he's in first grade that taunting other children is not acceptable, and that it hurts other kid's feelings. So when this type of behavior continues in the later grades, you can be certain that the child who taunts is doing it with the specific intent to hurt the other child's feelings. It's no longer a version of the preschool goofy look-at-me antics that can, and should, be nipped in the bud. It's not one child entertaining others by making up silly and nonsensical names; it's a way to simultaneously one up and put down a classmate. And the older a child gets the worse it gets. Here are some of the ways bullies can use language and words to hurt:

- **Name calling**—"Crybaby," "Faggot," "Pizza face," "Fatso," "Butt face."
- **Taunting**—"Your butt is so big you need two chairs! Hahaha!" "Nobody likes you, not even the teacher!"
- **Swearing**—"You're a %@!#&*" "I'm gonna pound your %@!#&* face!"
- **Spreading rumors**—"Cameron doesn't shower and smells like a donkey's a**." "Jill slept with the entire basketball team and got herpes!"
- **Gossip**—"Beth hates Lexi, and says it's because Lexi is snobby and stuck up." "I heard Chandra slept with Emily's boyfriend behind her back."
- **Note writing**—"Dear freak, I hope you die!" "I'm out to get you. Watch your back!"
- **Whisper campaigns**—A group of girls pointedly stare at another girl while whispering in each other's ears. The intention is to make the lone girl feel like everyone is talking about her in a negative way.
- **Secret revealing**—One girl befriends another with the sole purpose to find out her secrets, which she then tells all of the other girls in an effort to embarrass and humiliate her.
- **Laughing at someone's mistakes**—Children with learning disabilities are frequent targets for ridicule.
- **Making up stories to get someone in trouble**—There is no limit on the string of lies a bully will tell to get his victim in trouble.
- **Insulting nicknames**—It can take an entire school career to shake a particularly nasty nickname given by a bully at a young age.
- **Hate speech**—These are racially or ethnically motivated insults or comments meant to demean.
- **Mocking or imitating**—This is often used to torture kids who stutter or have physical or verbal tics.

- **Sexual bullying**—This is often achieved through telling dirty jokes, writing graffiti on the bathroom wall, and uttering derogatory sexual slurs.
- **Threats**—When a bully uses fear to intimidate.
- **Prank phone calls**—It's mortifying for a child to have her parents hear what names and insults she's being called at school.

Verbal bullying can sometimes be more hurtful and damaging to a child's confidence and self-esteem than physical bullying. Verbal bullying attacks a child's personality, physical attributes, and social status. It slowly erodes his confidence and attacks his sense of self.

 Essential

Children of mothers who are prone to yell, scream, and verbally berate will often admit, "I wish she would just hit me and be done with it." Somehow, it's less painful to suffer a slap or a punch than to be forced to endure an ongoing verbal barrage. Some bullied kids feel the same way.

Kids can be taunted about anything and everything: height, weight, appearance, academic abilities, physical abilities, social skills, and home life. Virtually no topic is off limits. But it's important to remember that taunts are often exaggerated or even completely untrue. A girl who taunts another by calling her fat doesn't really care whether or not the victim is fat. The bully is trying to insult her, she'll stick with whatever taunt gets a reaction. Boys who are called "fags" aren't usually homosexual, but because the word gets the bullied kids so riled up, bullies continue to say it.

Physical Bullying

Physical aggression is the most widely recognized and publicized form of bully behavior. This is the type of behavior that gets adult attention, garners school suspensions, and occasionally makes headlines and the six o'clock news. Typically, the behavior is action oriented, involving such behaviors as hair pulling, pinching, pushing, shoving, slapping, kicking, tripping, poking, stabbing, spitting, hitting, punching, head butting, choking, imitating wrestling holds, throwing an object at someone, pushing books out of one's hands, and hiding or destroying of property. Girls are more apt to use mild physical aggression such as pulling hair, slapping, and scratching; boys are more likely to punch, shove, and throw objects. Here are some examples of physical bullying:

- When lining up for recess, Henk repeatedly pushes Matthew forward so he stumbles into all the girls.
- In the cafeteria, Carla sticks out her leg to trip Ellen. Ellen's tray of food goes flying and lands next to her on the floor.
- Every day when Billy reaches for a blank piece of paper, Joao (who sits next to the supply cabinet) smacks a ruler across Billy's knuckles.
- Each Friday, Paul takes great pleasure in stuffing Conner into his locker and slamming the door shut. Conner can't get out and usually misses the bus by the time a teacher finally hears him banging and lets him out.
- When the lights are dimmed in the classroom to watch a film, Shawna always feels the sting of spitballs hitting her neck.
- Tony is often held down by three boys on the playground and forced to eat dirt.
- Ned punches Jose in the shoulder during the entire bus ride home. This happens every day without fail.
- Sophie uses a different color permanent marker to draw all over Amanda's clothing each day. Monday is red, Tuesday is orange, Wednesday is purple, and so on.

Physical bullying can occur even when there is no actual physical contact. The bully can shake his fist in your face, slam a book down on your desk, or invade your personal space. This is referred to as posturing. Posturing is a common scare tactic bullies use to intimidate and frighten their victims. Once a bully gets a reputation for being violent and cruel, a simple threatening move like a fisted hand or a mock air punch can strike fear into a bullied child's heart. The threat of physical violence is sometimes just as effective as actual physical violence.

Another form of physical bullying involves actions that are meant to sexually intimidate or harass. A sexual bully might lift up a girl's skirt, "pants" a boy, push the bodies of two kids together, pinch someone's bottom, grab a girl's breasts or snap her bra, make unwanted sexual advances, or pressure someone into unwanted sexual activity.

One of the biggest problems with the continuation of physical bullying is the potential progression and escalation of violence. If the bully trips or shoves you today, what will he do to top it tomorrow? The danger for ever-increasing levels of violence exists.

Social, Relational, and Emotional Bullying

Social bullying happens when a child is humiliated or demeaned in front of her peers. This happens more frequently among girls, and can be devastating to a child's self-esteem due to the public nature of the torments. A target of social bullying may hear giggling as she walks by or everyone might get up and leave as she sits down. These actions are hurtful because the single biggest fear for a tween or teen is to not be liked, to not fit in.

Here are a few common ways girls carry out social bullying:

- Pinning a note on a girl's back that says "I'm a loser" to publicly embarrass her.
- The popular girls will call an unpopular girl over to their lunch table just to tell her (loudly) that she should go on a diet because she's too fat.

- Passing a note around class that says "Molly has cooties—stay away from her!"
- Telling a quiet, shy girl that the school jock wants to go out with her—when he doesn't.

All of these actions are meant to humiliate the girl in front of her peers, in a public forum. Being publicly embarrassed and ostracized is one of the worst types of bullying—simply because everyone is there to witness it. And when no one sticks up for the bullied girl or defends her, she feels utterly and completely alone. Over time, she may begin to believe that she is a loser, that she is fat, that she is unclean, or that she is unlovable.

There are two kinds of social bullying: nonverbal and psychological. Nonverbal social bullying is when kids point, stare, laugh, make faces, roll their eyes, make the loser sign with their hand, or stick up their middle finger. A child can be singled out and ridiculed without a single word being spoken. Psychological social bullying is when kids exclude, isolate, shun, ostracize, ignore, or turn their back on someone. To spend the majority of your day in a classroom with twenty kids who pretend you don't exist can be torture to a young person. Think of this type of abuse as the silent treatment on steroids.

 **Fact**

A recent Families and Work Institute study reports that two-thirds of young people reported having been the victim of mean-spirited teasing or gossiping at least once in the past month, and one-quarter have had it happen five or more times.

Relational Bullying
Relational bullying entails intentionally damaging the social status of the victim. All kids, especially girls, want and need to have friends;

a relational bully will do everything in her power to undermine this. Here are a few examples of what a relational bully will do to bully her victim:

- Tell other kids to stop being friends with her
- Give her the silent treatment and encourage others to do the same
- Spread untrue rumors about her with the intent of getting others to reject her
- Invite all the girls from the class to a party—except her
- Allow only "the chosen" girls to sit at the popular lunch table

Studies have consistently shown that girls place great value and significance on their relationships. Having friends and being able to share the ups and downs of the tumultuous preteen and teen years is vital to a young female's healthy emotional development. Girls yearn to have positive and close relationships with other girls their own age. A girl wants to giggle and dream and dissect every fascinating thing that happened to her during the school day. She wants to have someone to sit with, to play at recess with, to sit on the bus with, to have sleepovers with, and she wants someone who "gets" her; someone who understands everything she's going through because she's going through it, too! Girls want friends. One friend is good, several friends are even better.

Alert!

Researchers at the Families and Work Institute asked a nationally representative group of 1,001 fifth through twelfth graders what one change they thought would help stop the violence young people experience today. The majority of kids reported that emotional violence was very real to them, and that it seemed to trigger more extreme types of violence.

A relational bully often has the sophistication and interpersonal skills needed to fracture another girl's relationships and turn her, over time, into a social outcast. The bully will convince her peers (through any means she can) to exclude or reject a particular girl. This can have a devastating effect because the rejection comes at a crucial time, when making and strengthening social connections is an important developmental task.

Relational bullying is hard to detect because it's not as obvious as some of the other types of bullying. It's subtle and sophisticated, and it's often done out of earshot of the adults. It can be hard for the victim to prove she's being mistreated. The bully (who is often popular and in high social standing) will simply feign innocence and say, "She must have misunderstood. I would never do such a thing!" If the bully has successfully concealed her vicious and hateful behavior, most teachers and parents will have a hard time believing that such a sweet girl would do such a mean thing.

The Emotional Bully

The emotional bully uses manipulation to get what she wants. Here's how:

- "You can't be my friend if you're friends with so and so."
- "If you want to be my friend, you will invite me, not Amy, to sleep over."
- "If you were my friend, you would do it."
- "I'll tell everyone all your secrets if you don't stay friends with me."

The emotional bully demands exclusivity and isolates her victim from her entire peer group. She gets jealous when the victim pays attention to anyone else, and will use emotional blackmail to continue to control her.

Extortion

If your child comes home ravenously hungry every day or missing his jacket, hat, sneakers, or iPod, he may be the victim of an extortion bully. Opportunistic bullies will use force or the threat of force to obtain money, food, or personal belongings from other students. Young children are particularly vulnerable to this type of extortion by older and bigger children. Most second graders would find it virtually impossible to stand up to a fourth or fifth grader who demanded their money or possessions.

The extortion bully might actually want what another child has, such as a cool hat, a neat toy, money, or an expensive gadget like an MP3 player or iPod. Or he may just want to destroy what the other child has. This bully will take a child's model plane that he brought in for show-and-tell and hurl it onto the pavement. He'll grab the victim's cell phone and stomp on it until it is smashed into little pieces. He'll take the victim's shoes and throw them out the bus window.

This type of bully victimizes the child twice. First, he robs the child of his possessions; then the child has to face his parents (or teacher) and explain what happened to his belongings. If your child isn't forgetful or the type of kid who often loses his possessions but he suddenly starts to "lose" or "misplace" things, be aware that an extortion bully might be targeting your child.

It's also possible for this type of bully to make the victim steal for the bully. The bully may make him take money or possessions from another child or from younger kids or steal from the classroom supply closet. This leaves the victim open to blackmail in the future. At any time, the bully can threaten to turn him in and get him into trouble. The victim becomes an unwilling accomplice and is forced to continue to steal for the bully to avoid getting into trouble.

Direct Bullying Versus Indirect Bullying

Bullying can also be labeled as direct or indirect. Direct bullying is when the bully confronts the victim face to face. Examples of direct bullying would include relatively open attacks on the victim. A child who is punched, kicked, slapped, called nasty names in the lunch line, refused a seat on the bus, or threatened in the bathroom is the victim of direct bullying.

In the case of indirect bullying, the bully systematically undermines the victim's reputation by spreading rumors and malicious gossip with the intent of ruining the victim's social standing. This type of bullying can be difficult to stop because the identity of the person responsible for the bullying may never be discovered. Girls are more apt to utilize these more subtle indirect strategies, whereas boys are more likely to engage in direct bullying.

 Essential

Never blame your child for being bullied. Don't tell her she's too sensitive or too emotional or that she's overreacting. To say those things is to place the blame for the bullying on her. No one deserves to be bullied, no matter how sensitive or emotional she may be.

There is some evidence that suggests that as kids move their way through the school system, there is a gradual shift from direct to indirect bullying. Boys are still more likely than girls to engage in physical bullying, but overall, the level and frequency of indirect bullying generally increases as the level of direct bullying decreases. And because indirect bullying (i.e., social isolation and hurtful gossip) is harder to detect, schools may seriously underestimate the extent of this ongoing problem. It's important for adults to remember that regardless of whether the bullying is direct or indirect, if it meets the three criteria of bullying (imbalance of power, intent to cause harm, threat of future harm), it's bullying—plain and simple.

Cyber Bullying

The Internet has opened up a whole new fascinating and fun world of communication for kids. E-mail, instant messaging, online journals and blogs, and text messaging allow kids never-ending access to their budding social lives. Online, they continue conversations started during the school day. They do homework together, discuss their latest crushes, talk about friends and family, and make weekend plans. They talk about everything and they talk about nothing. And they gossip. And gossip. And gossip. The wrong thing gets back to the wrong person and—BAM!—the bullying begins.

 **Alert!**

According to the Pew Internet and American Life Project, about one-third of all teenage Internet users say they have experienced one or more of the following: received threatening messages, had their private e-mails or text messages forwarded without consent, had rumors about them spread online, or had an embarrassing picture posted without permission.

When your kids are online, you likely worry about the things all parents worry about: pornography, sexual predators, and identity thieves. While it's good to talk with your kids about inappropriate website content, sexual predators masquerading as teenagers, and identity thieves, you must also be aware that one of the most likely dangers lurking online is kids bullying kids.

It's a well-known fact that bullies thrive in places where there is little or no adult supervision. Therefore, with no adult supervision, and with a relatively high degree of anonymity, bullies roam free in cyberspace, writing insults and ridicule on the proverbial bathroom walls. They hide behind technology and use the Internet as their own personal weapon to anonymously intimidate and humiliate.

In the good old days, if someone was bullying you, you ran home, slammed the front door, and you were safe. Home was a refuge—a place to get away from it all. Today, a bully can find you everywhere. He can continue to harass you at all hours on your cell phone, and he can enter your home through your computer. Here are some common technology tools that cyber bullies use to harass your kids.

Chat Rooms

Peer abuse often occurs in chat rooms. A chat room is a place online where kids gather together to "chat." A common way to victimize another chat-room child is for a bully to lure that child into a conversation, befriend her, and learn all kinds of private information. The bully will then post or print out this private information for all to see.

E-mail

A bully will send harassing and threatening e-mails to another child. In the e-mail, he will likely say obnoxious and derogatory things he wouldn't say in person. For instance:

- "You have no friends. Everyone hates you! You are a big, ugly loser!"
- "Everyone wishes you were dead!"
- "You better not come to school tomorrow! I will beat you to a pulp!"
- "I know where you live. If you rat me out, I will find you and kill you!"

Can you envision finding one or more (or even hundreds) of these messages on your child's computer screen? If you think they frighten you, imagine what your child might be feeling. With over 90 percent of today's teens going online to use the Internet or access e-mail, it should be a concern for every parent.

E-mail bullies can take the online harassment a step further. The bully can hack into your child's e-mail account and send messages to other children that appear to be from your child. This can create a great deal of hostility and resentment from other students, and your child may suffer even more torment from the students who received his supposed e-mails.

Websites

Some students create elaborate "bash boards." Bash boards are a type of online bulletin board where people can post their thoughts and opinions. These are often intentionally set up to contain malicious and hateful statements. The bully wants your child to see the website and be humiliated. The website might also contain doctored photographs of your child designed to denigrate her further.

 **Fact**

MySpace is currently one of the largest online social networking sites where anyone over the age fourteen can create an account free of charge. Your child can create a profile page where she lists her hobbies and interests; she can upload photos, create a blog, keep in touch with old friends, and make new ones. Word to the wise: supervise carefully.

Online Exclusion

Blocking someone from an IM group or buddy list is a deliberate way to exclude and socially isolate. Social networking websites like Facebook and MySpace are set up to allow the creator of a page to restrict acceptance to these online communities to a select few. This is a prime example of online social bullying. Not only is your child snubbed and ignored in the real world, she's snubbed and ignored in the cyberworld, too. And if your child isn't being bullied in the real world, snubbing online can often mean the start of exclusion and isolation in the real world. It can be a slippery slope and a rapid descent into a cycle of abuse for students not capable of handling the first few instances of cyber bullying.

Cell Phone

If your child has a cell phone, he's vulnerable to receive harassing phone calls. In the past, prank phone calls were limited to the home and usually adults dealt with them. Today, a bully can repeatedly call and harass your child on his own personal phone. He can post your child's cell phone number online with a message like, "For a good time, call . . ." or worse. An intentional invasion of privacy like that can be dangerous to your child's physical safety. Many victims of bullying are forced to repeatedly change their cell phone number after their number is posted online.

Text Messages

It's a simple task for a bully to send a cruel or threatening message every five minutes throughout an entire day. These nasty messages can be sent either from online or from one cell phone to another in a matter of seconds. All a bully needs is your child's cell phone number and he can instantly launch an immediate and unrelenting text message assault.

Digital Photos

The proliferation of cell phones that can take digital pictures have made kids vulnerable in ways never imagined before. Bullies can sneak these phones into bathrooms and locker rooms where they can take secret snapshots of kids in less-than-flattering or compromising positions. A revealing or embarrassing photo can be shared immediately with others by sending it to other cell phones, e-mail accounts, or posting it online. It's humiliating enough to have your head jammed into a dirty toilet and flushed, but when your child knows a close up of his "flushing" was e-mailed to everyone at school it ups the humiliation quotient.

The photos circulated among peers don't even have to be real. A bully can simply take a seemingly innocent picture of your child, superimpose her head onto a pornographic image, and make it look like she's doing something illegal or immoral. Voila; instant mortification.

The Videotaped Assault

In Lakeland, Florida, a group of six teenage girls videotaped the beating of a sixteen-year-old classmate. The attackers planned to post the half-hour long video on MySpace and YouTube. After the crime was reported, the tape was turned into police; the teens were arrested, and face charges ranging from felony battery to kidnapping. Obviously, the Lakeland, Florida, case is extreme. But the potential does exist for a bully to record abuse and use it to victimize her target over and over again. But the idea of filming a bullying episode or physical assault and posting it online for other kids to watch is not new, it has been happening for years. And even before the world wide web and YouTube and MySpace, teens found other ways to publicize and spread the word about these types of premeditated fights and beat downs.

Alert!

Don't be surprised if your child hides cyber bullying from you. Worries that you will overreact and ban her from the Internet, take away her cell phone, or disable her text message function keeps her silent. Kids are so tied into technology by the time they hit puberty that they can't imagine life without it.

Be Vigilant

Technology has great advantages, such as extraordinary access to up-to-date news, information, and research; the capacity to communicate in real time with people around the globe; and the ability to keep in touch with your loved ones any time from any place. But, it also has great dangers. The methods that can be used by online bullies to torture and harass are unlimited. It seems like every day new and alarming ways for kids to victimize each other appear. And the cyber bullies seem to have an unlimited supply of appalling and creative ways to apply their particular brand of cruelty. Add to this the new and constantly evolving nature of technology, and the danger it poses can seem overwhelming.

Your first parental instinct may be to unplug the computer and never let your child near it again. And sure, in theory unplugging her computer, canceling your Internet account, and taking away her phone would protect her. But in practice, she could still be cyber bullied. There may be online content that her peers may tell her about or print out and show her.

Most schools already have policies and safeguards in place that make it risky for students to send threatening or harassing messages from a school computer—chances are they will get caught. These policies are meant to lessen cyber bullying at school, but at home, all bets are off. Many parents are just too busy and too preoccupied to police their child's every move in cyberspace. Parents trust their kids, but the anonymous nature of the Internet gives kids the courage to say things—cruel and crude things, sometimes criminal things—they would never say to someone in person. And the bullies always seem to be one step ahead of parents, the schools, and the law. Unfortunately, the problem continues to grow, and no one knows exactly what the future may hold.

The real key to staying safe online is to educate and teach your child about all the potential Internet-related dangers: identity thieves, online predators, inappropriate mature content, and peer harassment and bullying. With advance planning and a few basic safeguards, you can protect your tech-savvy child. Chapter 16 will explain how it can be done.

CHAPTER 3

Types of Bullies

Not all bullies are the same. Let's look at three fictitious bullies: Bluto (Popeye the Sailor Man's bully) uses brute force to get what he wants. He's big, he's strong, and he's determined to get what he wants through sheer physical domination. Butch (Alfalfa's bully) threatens and invades the personal space of the Little Rascals characters. And Angelica Pickles (the Rugrats bully) is a mean-spirited and vindictive little girl who carries out her pint-sized dictatorship right under the noses of the cartoon grownups. All three are different; all three are bullies. Here is a roundup of the most common types of bullies.

Confident

Clearly this is the Bluto type of bully. He's confident, he's aggressive, and he feels a sense of superiority over his peers. He owns the school—or at least he acts like he does. Most of his friends are his friends not because they like him, but because they would rather be on his good side than on his bad. This type of bully has a big ego; he feels entitled to bully whomever he pleases whenever he pleases. He might be the fourth grader who stands a head taller than the rest of the class, the captain of the high school football team, or the popular boy who has a reputation for being the class leader. He likes the physical power he has over his victims and he often boasts about his alpha-dog position.

Kyle is a popular athlete with lots of friends and good grades. He seems to have it all. So why does Kyle shove Brian against the lockers, pour Coke on Sean, and draw the word "loser" in permanent marker on Brett's forehead? Why does Kyle constantly pick on these three boys? It's because Kyle needs to feel like he's the one in control of the other boys. His goal is to be the only dominant male in the classroom, and he wants everyone to know he's willing to get rough if he has to in order to remain top dog.

 Fact

The 1998 book *Bully: A True Story of High School Revenge*, written by Jim Schutze, and the 2001 movie *Bully* are both based on the chilling true story of the 1993 murder of Bobby Kent. Seven Florida teenagers joined together to enact revenge on Bobby, a boy who harassed, abused, and bullied them all. Be warned: This is a difficult movie to watch.

Social

This is the mean girl type of bully. She's socially dangerous because she wields her power through rumor, gossip, and exclusion. She takes pleasure in systematically isolating one or more of her peers. She may target a girl she's jealous of or a girl she deems socially inappropriate, or she may snub another girl just out of spite. She enjoys her popular status and will do just about anything to make sure she remains on the top of the social ladder. The social bully is usually devious and manipulative. She does her dirty work under a veil of sweetness, and will operate behind the scenes in order to protect her so-called good girl reputation.

Samantha is a social bully. She circulates a "slam book" amongst the popular girls in her fourth-grade class. Samantha and her friends giggle and point out certain girls and then make it obvious that they are writing their names down in the book. Most of the targeted girls have never seen the book, but Samantha makes sure everyone in the class knows what it contains. The slam book contains lists: the ugliest girls, the dumbest girls, the fattest girls. No one wants their name to be written in the book. Samantha's favorite activity is to bring the book over to an unpopular girl, pretend to let her take a peek, and then slam the book closed seconds before she can read the list. For the unpopular, not knowing what is written about them in the book is torture. The cover of the slam book says "Samantha's Private Journal," and is decorated with purple hearts and yellow flowers. No adult would guess that harassment and hate filled the pages of that innocent-looking notebook.

 Essential

For a sneak peek inside how female teenage social cliques operate, watch the movie *Heathers,* a 1989 black comedy starring Winona Ryder about a group of vicious but popular high school girls who pay a high price for their behavior. Or the 2004 sleeper hit starring Lindsay Lohan, *Mean Girls,* which is based on the nonfiction book *Queen Bees and Wannabes* by Rosalind Wiseman.

Detached

This bully seems to have little recognition of and no remorse for his bullying behavior. Cold and unfeeling, the bullying isn't retaliation for perceived hurts, it isn't to preserve his position on the social ladder, and it isn't meant to gain the respect or adoration of his peers. He bullies simply because he can. This bully isn't likely to stop; he's vicious and will bully when no one is around to stop him or see what he's doing (which is unlike most other bullies). The bullying may become habitual, and even when the bully doesn't seem to be getting anything out of it, he'll continue to do it. This bully often has underlying psychological problems and could benefit from counseling.

Nate hates his life. He hates school. And he hates his classmates. Nate will pick on anyone who gets in his way, annoys him, or crosses his path when he's in a foul mood. But Nate doesn't troll for regular victims; he finds them through happenstance. Any one of his classmates or peers could be his next victim. Any many fall victim to Nate's abuse over and over during the school year. Nate is an equal opportunity bully—he'll bully boys and he'll bully girls. He'll bully big kids and little kids. He'll bully anyone and everyone. Nate's classmates steer clear of him because they know he's slightly "off." Rarely does anyone tell on Nate because they fear the severity of his retaliation.

Alert!

When bullying is first reported, parents and schools often play the blame game. The victim's parents blame the school for failing to protect their child, the bully's parents blame the school for overreacting and being too strict, and the school blames both sets of parents for bad parenting. Reacting in this manner can lead to a lose-lose situation.

Hyperactive

The hyperactive bully is like a firecracker—he can go off at any second. This type of bully is usually a high-strung child who struggles both academically and socially. He may have a learning disability or attention deficit hyperactivity disorder that makes it difficult for him to exercise proper impulse control. This type of bully doesn't have many friends and will act aggressively at any perceived hostile act of a classmate, regardless of the actual intent.

Carl is uptight, unpredictable, and is considered to be a high-maintenance kid. Some days Carl manages to behave just like a regular kid—one of the gang. On other days, Carl is like a volcano ready to erupt. On those days, the other kids in the class walk on eggshells around Carl. But things are lively and active in a fifth-grade classroom, and on one of Carl's off days, all it takes is for one of the boys to bump into Carl and—Pop!—he explodes. Carl will holler insults, push the offending boy away, and be primed for a knock-down, drag-out fight. His overreaction frightens some of his classmates. And once someone "crosses" Carl, he's quick to react in a dramatic and negative way in the future. Carl doesn't intend to be a bully, but his excess energy, his lack of proper impulse control, and his frustrations over his learning difficulties often exacerbate his volatile nature.

 Fact

A 2007 Swedish study conducted by Holmberg and Hjern that followed 577 fourth graders for one year found that children with attention deficit hyperactivity disorder are almost four times as likely as non-ADHD kids to be bullies. And those same kids are almost ten times more likely than non-ADHD kids to have been bullied before the onset of their ADHD symptoms.

Bullied Bully

This bully is the one who has been there, done that. This child has been on the receiving end of bullying behavior on more than one occasion in her young life. And according to a University of Washington and University of Indiana study, being bullied at home happens to a lot of kids. To be specific, 97 percent of the children in the study who bullied others had been bullied themselves. Not surprising, since it's widely agreed that witnessing violence at home makes a child more prone to aggressive behavior.

A bullied bully may have an abusive parent or a parent who batters the other; she might have been threatened and pushed around by an older sibling or bullied by a peer. This bully bullies other kids to right the scales of justice. She feels powerless and angry at being a victim and she lashes out at other children to get revenge and gain a sense of power and control. This child is often not popular with her peers because of her seemingly remorseless and hostile attacks.

 **Alert!**

> The Southern California Center of Excellence on Youth Violence Prevention reports that children who are generally considered to be bullies by age eight are six times more likely to commit a crime by age twenty-four. These same kids are five times more likely to have a serious criminal record by age thirty.

Susan is the six-year-old tiny terror of the first grade. She's mean, she's spiteful, and shockingly, she has the vocabulary of an irate truck driver. Susan usually spends half the day in the principal's office for harassing, insulting, and attacking her peers. When she's sent back to the classroom, she mopes around introverted and depressed. Susan wants other kids to like her, but is unable to interact in a normal first-grade fashion. Susan has learned that the only way you get what you want is by force. So naturally, Susan tries to force other kids to play with her, to give her things, and to be her friend. When forcing a kid to be her friend doesn't work, Susan blows up and wants to inflict pain on the other child. So Susan bullies them. When Susan makes other kids feel the anger and powerlessness she feels when she's being bullied, it makes her feel better—at least for a little while.

Bunch of Bullies

This type of bullying involves a group of children who do and say things they probably wouldn't do or say if they were alone with the bullied child. A pack mentality takes over when these kids are together and they all blindly follow the dominant or alpha-dog kid in the group. This type of bullying is dangerous because kids' inhibitions are lowered when in a group. When the level of personal responsibility is low as the result of being in a group, it lowers the ability to judge right from wrong.

Jesse, a known bully, sees Hanna walking home from school. Jesse gathers her friends and starts after her. When Hanna stops at the curb of an intersection, Jesse unzips her book bag and dumps out the contents. As Hanna crouches down to pick up her books, Jesse kicks one into the road and says, "Oops! My bad!" Jesse kicks another and another and encourages her friends to join in the fun. They do and soon there are books, notebooks, and papers strewn all over the busy intersection. Jesse and the girls laugh and joke about how Miss Perfect Little Hanna might have to turn in her homework with skid marks all over it.

It's likely that some of Jesse's friends would never have participated in such an unkind act in the absence of peer pressure. The ability to say, "But everyone was doing it" seems to give some kids the opportunity to rationalize their actions as excusable. Some of the girls may have been uncomfortable kicking the books, but did it anyway because it was easier to go along with the crowd than outright refuse. And others were probably happy to participate in the harassment once it started, but wouldn't have initiated it on their own. The problem with group bullying is that it can escalate and easily get out of control. If Jesse had been kicking Hanna instead of kicking her books, the pack mentality could have caused her serious physical injury.

Gang of Bullies

When kids come together for the express purpose of gaining power and dominance, it becomes a gang of sorts. Different from a bunch of bullies where there is one alpha bully who has a group of henchmen to help him bully, the gang of bullies are all alpha dogs. These kids will often try to one up each other with an escalating level of bullying and violence.

Thankfully, this type of bullying isn't common (unless your child attends a school that has gang-related problems). Bullies that bully in gangs can be extremely dangerous, even deadly. The cruelty of a single bully can be bad, add to it any number of bullies who are equally cruel, and you get one scary situation.

 **Question?**

Have you heard the term "happy slapping"?
This is a fad that originated overseas, in which a teenager or young adult attacks an unsuspecting stranger while an accomplice records the assault. These assaults are then posted online for others to watch. Some of these incidents have been brutally violent, and people have been killed.

Keep in mind that these are just archetypes of the most common types of bullying. Not all bullies will fit into one of these categories and even the ones that do may not fit the stereotype perfectly. But being aware that there are some common types may help you and your child devise more successful strategies for handling the situation.

CHAPTER 4

The Bully

What makes a child become a bully? It's a question researchers have been diligently trying to answer for years. Are bullies born with a bullying gene? Do children learn to be bullies through their environment and social conditioning? Is a certain type of parenting to blame? Is exposure to violent television or video games the problem? The answers to these questions aren't always clear. But it is known that bullying behavior often has its origin in early childhood, and that a variety of environmental and social factors combine to create a child capable of bullying.

Characteristics of a Bully

Let's start by debunking the biggest myth of them all: Bullies bully others to cover up their own sense of inadequacy or poor self-esteem. Research has consistently shown that bullies actually possess normal, if not higher, levels of self-esteem than those of their non-bully peers. The popular theory that bullies are just miserable kids who lash out in a misguided attempt to raise their level of self-esteem has been proven untrue. That's not to say that some kids don't fit that profile; no doubt some do. But the majority of kids who bully do it for reasons that are less underdog and more alpha dog. Recent research has compiled some common characteristics that most bullies share:

- A bully has the need to feel powerful and in control.
- A bully has the need for attention.
- A bully has the need to feel superior.
- A bully feels that he does no wrong.
- A bully has no empathy.
- A bully is quick to feel anger and aggression.
- A bully enjoys inflicting pain and suffering.

Surprisingly, most bullies see themselves in a positive light. This is directly correlated with the fact that they have very little awareness of what others think of them. No kid wants to suffer a bully's wrath by telling him the truth, so no one does. The bully's confidence survives, and even thrives, simply because he lacks the feedback to perceive his reputation correctly in social situations.

Think of the Queen, Snow White's wicked stepmother, in the childhood fairytale *Snow White and the Seven Dwarfs* by the Brothers Grimm. Every morning the Queen looks in the mirror and asks, "Mirror, mirror on the wall, who is the fairest of us all?" to which the mirror always replies, "Tis you." One day the Queen asks her mirror the usual question, and it responds, "Queen, you are full fair, 'tis true, but Snow White is fairer than you." The Queen reacts with rage and jealousy and orders a huntsman to take Snow White into the woods, kill her, and return with her heart as proof that she's dead. A chilling story to say the least.

Now imagine the typical bully who sees and judges himself through the eyes of his peers (his magic mirror). When he looks in the mirror, what he sees is that the vast majority of kids either approve (the kids who laugh at or join in the bullying) or don't actively disapprove of his actions (the kids who ignore it). When classmates join him in his bullying efforts, he feels like the Wicked Queen when she looks in the mirror, asks "Who is the fairest of us all?" and it says, "Tis you." This reflection of approval and acceptance (even if it is false) reinforces his desire to remain "the fairest in the land."

Kids intuitively know that if they shatter the bully's self-serving image, they risk the wrath of the "Queen." The Queen might come after them for revenge as the Queen does to Snow White. So day after day, they stay silently approving. They tell the bully, "Tis you." And kids aren't the only ones who are unwilling to reflect the truth back at the Queen-type bullies. Adults often won't stand up to a boss who is overbearing or verbally abusive. After all, who wants to risk their job by telling the boss that he's a bullying jerk? Battered spouses don't tell the truth for fear of repeated abuse, and victims of hazing rarely speak out against the monsters who hazed them. Because of this, bullies young and old continue to have an inaccurate and distorted view of what others think of them.

Alert!

Many parents will admit that they would rather have a child who bullies than one who is bullied. The reason is simple: Society rewards the tough, the strong, and the powerful and shows nothing but contempt for those who show weakness (i.e., those who are physically, emotionally, or mentally fragile).

One important facet of bully prevention and intervention programs teaches children how to reflect correct and accurate information back to bullies. All kids (and adults, too) must learn to project the attitude that bullying is wrong and that it will not be tolerated. When bullies stop getting active or tacit approval for their actions, when they stop getting socially rewarded for abusing other kids, they'll start to see themselves in a more accurate light.

The objective is to get bullies to see that over the long term, bullying erodes their social standing and undermines their ability to have authentic relationships with their peers. Studies have shown that kids who bully are at serious risk for depression and social isolation, that they tend to lead adult lives filled with aggression and abuse, and that they are more likely to get into trouble with the law. Not surprisingly, bullying can be as harmful to the bully as it is to the bullied. Here are a few of the characteristics that may make a child more likely to bully:

- He has a low tolerance for frustration
- He has difficulty conforming to rules
- He has little respect for authority
- He is impulsive
- He exhibits other antisocial behavior (vandalism, stealing, truancy, substance abuse)
- He is cruel to animals

Why Do Some Kids Bully?

There are many reasons why kids bully, but the most common and widely accepted one is social conditioning. Social conditioning is when a child learns to conform to his environing culture. Simply put: a child learns how to behave by modeling the behaviors of those around him. For instance, if Dad is a grown-up bully and berates, puts down, and pushes around Mom, the child learns that it's okay to threaten, berate, and overpower in order to get what you want. This partly explains why bullies need, and should receive, as much intervention and assistance as victims do. And it explains why intervention should happen quickly and at a young age. Changing a child's behavior patterns early on is usually more successful than at later ages.

In the early developmental years, the average child experiences an increase in her level of frustration and aggression until around age two. This is predominantly because a toddler's language and communication skills are unable to keep up with her ever-increasing wants and needs. She knows what she wants, but often can't express it properly; this leads to the classic temper tantrum—a child's first attempt at bullying her parents.

It looks something like this:

A mom is at the park with her two-year-old daughter. The daughter is playing happily in the sandbox. A little while later, the mom tells her daughter that it's time to leave. The child ignores the mother's attempts to get her to leave and continues to play in the sandbox. When the mother runs out of patience, she approaches her daughter, gently takes away the shovel, and tries to pick her up. The daughter shrieks in protest, flails her arms (hitting her mother in face), and bursts into tears. The daughter won't allow the mother to pick her up, and she throws sand in the mother's face. The harder the mother tries to pick her daughter up, the harder she screams and fights. The daughter believes that if she keeps fighting her mother, her mother will eventually give in and let her stay at the park.

A wise mother knows that giving in would be the worst possible solution. The best solution would be to give the daughter a chance to calm down and as soon as she's calm, leave the playground. Option number two would be to pick her up (if possible), carry her to the car, and put her in the car seat once she's calmed down. To give in to a child's first attempts at bullying would be a mistake. She will learn that bullying people (her parents included) is a way to get what she wants.

Most parents spend a significant amount of time and effort teaching their two-year-olds how to control aggressive impulses and to delay gratification. This is an extremely important developmental task for a child to master. When parents fail to teach their two- or three-year-olds how to handle anger and aggression in a socially acceptable manner, they set the stage for bullying in the later years. If you think it's hard to teach a toddler impulse control, try teaching it to an out-of-control eight- or ten-year-old for whom it's become a habit. Researchers have studied two types of parenting styles that can be harmful to the developing child and may add to the type of social aggression that most bullies display: permissive and authoritarian.

Permissive Parenting Style

A permissive parent will allow a two-year-old's temper tantrum to go on and on and on. That same parent will attempt to bribe the child. When you allow a tantrum to go on and on, and make no attempt to comfort the child, it only serves to make her feel more out of control. And bribing teaches her that if you behave badly enough, you can always get what you want. When this child is ten, she'll believe that she can do whatever she pleases, whenever she pleases. She'll constantly push the envelope of proper behavior in an attempt to find a boundary—any boundary. And when she crosses the line, she won't be willing to change her behavior until she receives a bribe or reward. She'll think nothing of using threats and strong-arm techniques to bully her parents as well as her peers.

Extremely permissive or uninvolved parents take a hands-off approach to parenting. Their main goal is to avoid conflict and keep the peace. Discipline and limits are few and far between and can be virtually nonexistent. The children do what they want when they want, and when there are behavioral problems, the parents will often blame other people's kids or stick their head in the sand and ignore the problem, hoping it will go away. But kids need limits and guidance. They need age-appropriate discipline that teaches them how to behave appropriately in myriad social situations. And they need their parents to be responsible and in charge. Instead, with permissive parenting, they get very little guidance and wind up with no sense of family connectedness. Without a sense of connectedness and belonging, these kids have nothing to anchor them and no one to keep them in line. This self-parenting puts kids at a distinct social disadvantage and leaves them feeling that no one loves, values, or cares for them.

Authoritarian Parenting Style

The other potentially harmful parenting style is labeled authoritarian— the parent rules with an iron hand. An authoritarian parent can be so focused on maintaining control and proper discipline that the relationship between parent and child suffers from insufficient levels of love, affection, and attention. This doesn't mean that an authoritarian parent doesn't love her child; it simply means that the love is often portrayed as being conditional on the child's ability to obey.

The child of an authoritarian parent will often receive harsh punishment for relatively mild childhood crimes, and it's not uncommon for authoritarian parents to use spanking as the primary means of discipline. When the spanking eventually fails to curb misbehavior (as is often the case), the punishment escalates and can become physically or emotionally abusive, or both. The danger of this type of parenting is that children become very good at obeying authority, but fail to develop a strong sense of inner discipline. Without inner discipline, and with the experience that "might is right," a child will naturally see bullying as an acceptable means to an end.

Alert!

Some bullies don't stop bullying just because they grow up; they just become grown-up bullies. Bullies are everywhere—on college campuses, in dating relationships, in the workplace, in marriages, in the military, in politics. This is proof positive that not enough intervention is being done at early ages.

An authoritarian parent will attempt to stop a two-year-old's temper tantrum by giving the child a spanking. Here's the rub: When kids receive harsh punishment from their parents for aggressive behaviors, it only teaches them to be more aggressive. By the time that same child reaches the age of ten, her temper tantrums resemble full-blown rampages. She'll act out physically, destroy property, and project her frustrations onto innocent victims by bullying them.

Some bullies come from relatively normal families and are merely seeking attention. Others may think bullying is a way to be popular amongst their peers or that it will make it easier to get what they want. And some kids try out bullying temporarily because they've seen someone else do it. Some bullies want to hurt other kids and set out intentionally to do so, and some just don't fully comprehend how hurtful their actions can be. Some bullies pick on a particular type of child and some will pick on a random kid for no specific reason.

The reasons girls bully can be somewhat different. A girl will bully another girl because she's jealous. She may be a bit insecure and realizes she can become popular by social dominance, even though she may not be well liked. She may adhere to the survival of the fittest mentality and bully because a good offense is the best defense. In other words, to prevent being bullied, she becomes one. She may not fit in with typical gender stereotypes and choose to model her behavior after the male bullies. Or she may simply do it for sport and find it highly entertaining to watch her peers squirm and be miserable.

 Fact

According to studies conducted by Swedish researcher Dan Olweus, many bullies are raised in environments where physical punishment is routine, where physical aggression is an acceptable way to handle problems, and where the parents are emotionally distant and uninvolved.

The Bully's Role in the Triad

As mentioned in Chapter 1, in order to understand of the dynamics of bullying, you need to consider all the actors involved: bully, bullied, and bystanders. These three types of actors make up what is called the bullying triad, and according to Barbara Coloroso, all three of these actors play a significant role in the drama that unfolds day in and day out in children's lives. The bully's main role in the triad is to "get the party started." The bully is the one who starts the show. He decides the when, the where, the how . . . and, to many parents' dismay, who will serve as the star of the bullying show.

The Stereotypical Bully

Bluto is the most well-known stereotypical bully. He's big. He's dumb. He's violent. And he picks on Popeye, who is weaker and smaller. That is until Popeye downs some spinach and grows enough muscle to defeat the big brute. If it were actually that easy, kids could identify bullies simply by what they looked like and steer clear in the middle school hallways. Or they could down a leafy green vegetable and do a bit of pounding back themselves. If only it were that easy. Trouble is; most bullies don't look a bit like Bluto, they look exactly like any other regular boy or girl. And there's no magic green vegetable powerful enough to give a nonagressive kid the strength to face up to the big, bad bully.

Alert!

Young children who have aggressive or hot-tempered personalities are more likely to grow into aggressive tweens and teens than those with calmer and more laid-back personalities. Fortunately, you can teach your child the skills she needs to remain in control of her shorter fuse.

Today, thanks to a number of studies and books published on the topic of female aggression, the stereotypical bully myth has been officially debunked. The world now understands that bullies come in all shapes, sizes, and genders, and that girls can be as vicious and violent as boys; sometimes even more so. The intricacies of gender-specific bullying will be discussed in later chapters.

Common Places Bullying Occurs

As stated previously, most bullying occurs out of the sight of adults. This doesn't necessarily mean that an adult isn't present. For example, a large portion of bullying occurs in the classroom, right under the teacher's nose. This happens because the teacher can't be watching all the students all of the time—that's impossible. And children are very good at figuring out exactly what they can get away with and when.

Obviously, the most common place for your child to be bullied is at school. After all, the majority of your child's waking hours are spent in school. School is also where your child is exposed to hundreds of other kids; some older, some younger, and many more of the same age. But bullying also happens outside of school, at after-school activities, weekend sporting events, in neighborhoods, and in your own back-yard. It can happen anywhere, anytime, to anyone. Parents and school officials used to believe that most bullying happened on the way to or from school. Perhaps this was true when groups of kids walked, unsu-pervised, to the neighborhood school. But now the majority of tradi-tional bullying events occur during regular school hours. And, to add to the unpleasantness, outside of school hours, a growing number of kids are being cyber bullied in their own homes.

The Mean Bully

The youngest of the bullies is the mean bully. He hasn't been bullying long, but he likes the feeling he gets when he makes another kid cry. He likes it when other kids laugh at his actions and he craves the attention. When he gets attention, it just reinforces his bullying behavior. This bully can be found in preschool through about the first or second grade. He's learning the ropes, and will try out different ways to bully. He may inten-tionally exclude another child from a playground game or not allow him to play on a certain piece of equipment. He might call a child a name (with young kids it might be something as unimaginative as stinky butt or booger face), and if it makes other kids laugh, he'll continue to do it.

Tony is a kindergarten bully. Recess is his favorite time of day. At recess he makes fun of Marc; Tony loves to make fun of Marc. Just the other day, Tony made all the boys laugh (and some of the girls, too!) when he called Marc a midget. Tony thought it was great! Marc got really mad and started to cry. When Tony taunted, "Marc is a midget. Marc is a midget . . . ," Marc threw sand at Tony. The teacher saw Marc throw the sand and

Marc had to sit in time-out. Tony couldn't have planned it any better. Tony made sure to give Marc the evil eye so he wouldn't tell on him.

Is Tony a bully? Absolutely. All three characteristics of bullying behavior are present (imbalance of power, intent to harm, threat of further harm), despite the young age and relative immaturity of the children involved. Should parents and teachers take this little incident seriously? No doubt about it. If nothing is done to intervene on behalf of both boys, this scenario will likely continue to occur and worsen over time. By the end of the school year, Tony will be viewed by his peers as a bully, and Marc will be viewed as a victim. Tony will assume that bullying other kids is what he needs to do to be liked and accepted, and Marc will have suffered a blow to his self-esteem that could make him more susceptible to bullying in the future.

 Essential

It can be extremely difficult to hear that your child is a bully, but there's no need to overreact. Consider it a fortuitous thing that you found out when you did. Early intervention is the key to getting your child the help he needs to avoid engaging in bullying behavior in the future.

Simple early intervention strategies could prevent this bully/victim scenario from becoming entrenched in the developing personalities of both boys. But in order to do that, the bullying must be seen by the teacher (or reported to the teacher by another child), recognized as bullying (which can sometimes be difficult when old entrenched myths prevail—bullying is a push, shove, smack, or whack), and dealt with properly (which must include effective input from the teacher, the school, and the parents).

The Meaner Bully

This bully has been practicing her craft for many years and is now ready to exercise her bullying muscles. She's older. She's wiser—she knows how to avoid getting caught. She's meaner. And she'll choose her target carefully. She'll choose someone she knows won't fight back or tell because she can't risk losing her status as a top dog.

Molly rules the middle school. She decides what is cool and what is not. And she decides who is cool and who is not. Molly likes to pick on Gretchen. One day when the teacher was out in the hallway, Molly lifted up the bottom of Gretchen's skirt and said, "Ewwww . . . how gross! Hairy gorilla legs!" After that day, everyone called Gretchen gorilla legs. Gretchen shaved her legs, but it didn't stop the taunting. Molly was thrilled to discover how easy it was to bestow a nasty nickname. Molly now gives all the undesirable girls unflattering nicknames. When one of Molly's victims tells on her, Molly feigns innocence and says, "I would never say such a thing! Poor girl! I'll see what I can do to help." All of the other girls are terrified Molly will give them a hideous nickname, so they are all super nice to her—and Molly likes it that way.

Middle school may be rife with bullies, but kids don't seem to understand that it doesn't have to be that way. Middle school is when adolescents get secretive and they want to keep the life they have outside of the one they share with their parents private. An adolescent's main developmental task is to separate from her parents and become independent. Add to this the overwhelming need to fit in with her peers and be one of the gang, and you have a situation fraught with conflict. Unfortunately, this developmental stage coincides with the peak of bullying, at eleven to twelve years of age. This means that bullies like Molly often get a free pass because no one is willing to tell on them for fear of being ostracized. The tragedy is that when no one tells, Molly is emboldened to keep bullying her peers, and sadly, Molly also won't get any help.

The Meanest Bully

Well versed in the art of bullying, this bully is extremely difficult to stop. His bullying is an entrenched part of his personality. His identity is defined by his aggressive and abusive behavior, and he has no intention to stop.

Chad is feared by all. He's bullied dozens of the students on his sports teams and in his school. He sees himself as a strong, masculine young man who knows what he wants and is willing to stop at nothing in order to get it. Chad doesn't know it, but it's too late for him. He's been bullying others for so long that he doesn't even realize he's doing it. It's a part of who he is, and he's blind to the difficulties his bullying behavior has caused—both for him and for others. Chad will be attending college in the fall and plans to be big man on campus there, too. And while he probably won't be big man on campus, there's no doubt he'll be big bully on campus. And when Chad enters the workforce he'll be a bully boss, and when he marries he'll bully his wife—and kids. And the bullying cycle will continue because his child will learn to be a bully, just like his old man. Depressing, isn't it? But that's what happens when the cycle of violence isn't broken.

CHAPTER 5

The Bullied

Some kids walk around feeling like a constant target—like they have a big red bulls-eye on their back, or at least a sign that says "Bully me." Those students who get bullied spend their days at school in constant fear of when and how they will be bullied again. For them, school is a hostile and dangerous place. They may withdraw from school activities, sports, and peer-related social situations. And in extreme cases, they may try to avoid school altogether.

Characteristics of a Bullied Child

There is no single definitive characteristic or set of characteristics that will positively identify which children will be singled out and targeted by bullies. You can't line them up on the first day of kindergarten and identify which kids will be targeted by bullies. But over the years, researchers have been able to pinpoint a few indicators that may increase a child's vulnerability.

Swedish researcher, Dan Olweus, a widely recognized expert on bullying, reports that children who are victims of bullying typically have a few traits in common. These traits include being anxious, insecure, cautious, having low self-esteem, being younger than the attacker, and being reluctant to defend themselves or retaliate when confronted by students who bully them. In addition, bullied kids tend to have very few friends and may lack age-appropriate social skills. When kids don't have friends, there is no friendship network to back them up and support them against a bully's attacks, which makes them easy targets.

 **Fact**

According to the National Mental Health Information Center, 40–75 percent of bullying takes place during breaks in places such as hallways, bathrooms, and during recess. In places where the amount of adult supervision is inconsistent and unreliable, bullying is easy to carry out undetected.

In addition, Olweus notes that bullying victims tend to have overly close relationships with their parents, and their parents can often be described as overprotective. Not being as independent as other kids can cause a child to doubt his own abilities, which undermines his confidence. Surprisingly, physical characteristics such as weight, height, appearance, dress, having braces, or wearing glasses don't appear to be strongly correlated with victimization. But if a child is physically weaker than his peers, his chances of being bullied increase.

 **Alert!**

If you notice sudden changes in your child's personality, such as unexplained mood swings, crying jags, excessive and uncharacteristic anger, social withdrawal, acting out in school, or refusing to talk to you, she may be the victim of bullying. Don't just ignore it and hope it will go away; chances are it won't.

Passive and Provocative Victims

Passive victims are the children with the above-mentioned traits: nonaggressive, anxious, physically weaker, and not having friends to protect them from being bullied or support them after it happens. Provocative victims are children who are both anxious and aggressive. These kids have poor social skills, limited impulse control, and can inadvertently irritate and alienate their peers. A bully will exploit this to his advantage by pushing the buttons of the victim and provoking an outburst. The bully then gets a good laugh when the teacher punishes the victim for disrupting the class.

In Chapter 13, you will learn ways to increase your child's self-esteem, improve his confidence, and strengthen his friendship bonds. The simple strategies outlined will help keep your child safe from bullies.

The Bullied Child's Role in the Triad

Again, to understand the dynamics of bullying, you need to consider all three actors involved—bully, bullied, and bystanders. These three make up the bullying triad and all play a significant role in the drama. The bullied child's main role in the triad is to serve as the "star" of the show. The victim, and how he reacts to the bullying, is the focal point of the action, and all eyes are upon him.

 Essential

If you suspect your child is being bullied, ask open-ended questions like: What is the best thing that happened to you today? What is the worst? What was the funniest thing that happened today? What was the craziest thing that happened today? What was the cruelest? What was the nicest?

The Making of a Victim: F-E-A-R

Your child's first reaction to a bullying incident will determine if she will be approached by the bully again. A bully is not looking for a confrontation. The bully is seeking a fear reaction, and if she does not get one or she gets an unexpected or undesirable reaction (such as being ignored, laughed at, or stood up to), she probably won't try again. Bullies don't want their power to be challenged or undermined, but if the bully senses fear, she will exploit it.

 Fact

> Ask any child in elementary, middle, or high school who is being bullied by whom and they will tell you. The teachers don't know, the principal doesn't know, the bus driver doesn't know, the parents may not even know—but the kids, they know.

Shaina is a normal, if somewhat shy, nine-year-old. On the second day of school, Shaina is at her locker when she is approached by a girl named Teesha. "This is my locker now!" Teesha announces and grabs Shaina's belongings out of the locker. She tosses them on the floor. "If you tell the teacher, you'll be sorry!" Teesha glares at Shaina and shoves her backward. Shaina is so frightened she hurries away and disappears into her classroom without picking up her stuff. For the rest of the year, Teesha continues to terrorize Shaina every chance she gets. Every day, Shaina feels the weight of her victimization, both psychologically and physically, as she lugs every one of her books around in her backpack (Shaina never asked the teacher for a new locker).

If Shaina had reacted differently to her first interaction with Teesha, she may have been able to avoid becoming Teesha's own personal punching bag for the year. Researchers have studied exactly how bullies stake out their victims. Here's how it usually goes:

- The bully will scan the playground (or classroom, or lunch room, or school bus, etc.) looking for a child who is alone and who has the hangdog "please don't notice me" look of a victim.
- Once he singles out a child who fits his requirements, he moves closer and looks around to see if anyone is watching—particularly the teachers.
- Once the bully determines that he won't be seen, he brushes by the victim and "accidentally" bumps him (or knocks the ball out of his hands, or dumps over his sand bucket).
- When the child shrinks away and looks fearful, and doesn't react with anger or indignation, the bully knows he has found a possible victim.
- Over the next few days, the bully will increase his "accidental" aggressive interaction with the victim to continue to gauge his reaction (and the reaction of others on the playground). He's making sure that there is no group of friends or buddies to come to the victim's aid.

When the bully finally realizes that he's found a kid who won't fight back or tell and who doesn't have a network of friends to support him, the bully will escalate the bullying as much as he can without risking getting caught. And the bullying cycle begins.

Alert!

In her book *The Bully, the Bullied, and the Bystander,* Barbara Coloroso notes that when bullying escalates into regular, systematic violence against a child, terror is added to the situation. Coloroso says that once terror is struck in the heart of the victim, the bully is free to declare open season on the victim without fear of recrimination or retaliation.

Many bullied kids experience learning difficulties because they become so anxious and stressed out trying to avoid the bully that they are unable to concentrate on what goes on in the classroom. If the bullying intensifies, the victim will become completely preoccupied with devising specific strategies to evade the bully. She may repeatedly "miss" the bus, fake an injury to avoid gym class, or feign an illness to be allowed to stay home.

More and more parents are turning to home schooling as a way to protect their kids from systematic bullying. The National Center for Education Statistics reports that in 2003, approximately 1.1 million children were home schooled. And statistics show that bullying and school violence is high on the list of reasons parents and students choose to home school. Parents are no longer buying into the myth that their kids need to learn to live with bullies and bullying. And researchers will admit that it's now known that dealing with bullying and "toughing it out" does not help children cope better when they become adults. In fact, the exact opposite is true. Bullied kids have a higher risk of depression and low self-esteem in adulthood.

 Essential

One of the best ways to keep informed about what is happening in your child's school is to become a volunteer. When you volunteer, you establish relationships with teachers and school personnel, and these relationships can turn out to be beneficial if and when your child encounters a school-related problem.

Once a child is singled out and chronically bullied, other kids may label her an easy target and start bullying her, too. In time, the bullied child's self esteem is so compromised that she may come to believe that she's responsible for the bullying—that somehow she deserves to be bullied. This is, of course, completely and utterly false. But the immature cognitive thought process of a young child can make her current bullying situation seem like a never-ending and inescapable nightmare. In cases of extreme bullying, the victims can become depressed and even suicidal. Or they may turn the anger and frustration outward and fight back, with devastating consequences.

Sometimes kids get bullied as the result of a single unfortunate event. It's usually an embarrassing moment that took place in front of other kids. Crying, wetting your pants, throwing up, or falling down can all prompt teasing and taunts that can escalate into bullying. And some kids can be on the receiving end of a vicious bullying event that happens just once. If it happens just once, it's not considered bullying. You can call it an attack or an assault, but you can't call it bullying. Bullying has to meet the three markers: imbalance of power between the bully and the child being bullied, intent to harm, and the threat of future harm. A one-time fight or traumatic incident is not considered to be bullying behavior.

Why Me?

Child psychologist David Schwartz conducted a study of children from eleven different schools. None of the children in the study knew each other before being chosen for the study. The children were sorted into thirty playgroups, each consisting of one popular, one neglected, two average, and two socially rejected boys. Over a period of five days, the children's play sessions were monitored and videotaped. Schwartz found that the socially rejected boys behaved in a submissive manner right from the start, even before bully/victim situations developed. The "victim" kids didn't initiate conversations, made no suggestions, requests, or demands about what they all should play, and they spent their time playing passively away from their peers instead of playing with them. The victim kids clearly didn't have the social skills necessary to blend in and get along with their peers.

Alert!

Many kids who were bullied go on to lead normal, productive adult lives. Mel Gibson, Kate Winslet, Tom Cruise, Kevin Costner, and Tyra Banks are just a few of the many celebrities who openly admit they were bullied as kids. Take heart; bullying doesn't always have lasting negative effects.

So what is a parent to do when your child comes home from school crying and asks, "Why me? Why is that bully picking on me?" It can be hard to look him in the eye and explain that the main reason he's being bullied is because he's vulnerable, and that his vulnerability is being exploited by a peer who has been socialized to believe it's acceptable to hurt and humiliate someone who is weaker than he is. The concept is hard enough for an adult to understand; but there are antidotes to bullying, things you and your child can do to develop his individual strengths and build a support system. It can be a daunting task, but one that can ultimately be successful. Chapters 13 and 14 will give you the strategies and skills you need to help your child break the bullying cycle.

Passive and Provocative Victims

There are two basic kinds of victims: passive and provocative. A passive victim is quiet, shy, and introverted. He is the child on the playground who plays alone and refuses to make eye contact with the other children. This child is often the target of verbal and relational bullying. When bullied, he easily gives in to the bully and passively accepts his fate. This reaction serves to continue the bullying cycle and leads to the victim becoming more and more socially withdrawn.

Provocative victims are usually active and disruptive kids. A provocative child will act out in socially unacceptable ways that his peers find distasteful, and over time he becomes a social misfit. Once he is labeled a social misfit, the other kids believe that he deserves to be bullied, that he brings it on himself somehow. This isn't true, of course, but that's the way children will respond.

 Essential

Talk about school often with your child, and pay attention to what he says. Ask specific questions about your child's activities and friendships. Explain what bullying is to your child and provide examples of bully behavior. Encourage your child to tell you when bullying happens at school.

Why Victims Don't Tell

Children don't tell parents they're being bullied for myriad reasons. Bullying is scary, humiliating, and confusing, and when it first happens, most kids aren't sure what to make of it. Here are a few of the reasons kids might be hesitant to admit the abuse to their parents:

- Embarrassed at being a victim
- Scared that the bully will retaliate
- Thinks he must remain silent in order to belong
- Feels like she did something to deserve it
- Afraid you won't believe him
- Worried other kids will call her a tattletale
- Assumes you would expect him to tough it out

But even if your child doesn't come right out and say, "Mom, I'm being bullied," chances are she's trying to tell you in other, less obvious ways:

- She doesn't want to go to school
- He "accidentally" misses the bus every day for a week

- She complains of stomachaches in the morning
- His grades drop suddenly and without explanation
- She is "losing" belongings or they are coming home broken
- He asks for more and more lunch money
- She has nightmares or is becoming withdrawn
- He comes home with mysterious cuts and bruises
- She wants to drop out of after-school activities or sports
- He skips school
- She talks about or attempts suicide

Alert!

If you suspect your child is being bullied, don't beat around the bush—ask direct questions like: "Are there any bullies in your class?" "What kinds of things do they do or say?" "What kinds of kids do the bullies pick on?" "Do you feel unsafe around the kids who bully?" "Do they ever bully you?"

If your child comes right out and tells you she's being bullied, tell her that you're proud of her for telling you. This reinforces that you value having an open line of communication with her. Believe what she says, and express your gratitude that she is allowing you to help her sort through her problem. Assure her you will try to find solutions. Don't overreact by getting upset, angry, and stressed out. If you act as if it's the end of the world, your child will sense your panic and become even more distraught. Tell her you will do everything you can to help and reassure her that you will make a plan of action together. Then quickly read Chapters 13 and 14 for a primer on how to help kids who are being bullied!

The Victim Who also Becomes a Bully

Some kids who suffer at the hands of peer bullies turn their pain inward and become silent, downtrodden, and depressed. But other kids handle it differently. These victims will turn the tables and find a victim of their own. Ever hear the idiom "turnabout is fair play"? Well, the bullied bully does just that; she evens the scales of justice by forcing other kids to suffer the same pain and torment that she does. If mom verbally abuses her, chances are she'll verbally abuse her peers. If her dad physically abuses her, she may physically abuse her younger brother. If she was the victim of rumors and gossip throughout third grade, she will be the one to start the rumor mill churning about the transfer student on the first day of fourth grade. But not all kids who are bullied lash back. In fact, the majority don't. The majority of kids who are bullied are non-aggressive, nonviolent, and quietly absorb and internalize the abuse.

CHAPTER 6

The Bystander

According to the dictionary, the term "bystander" is defined as "one present but not taking part in the situation or event; a chance spectator." That definition suggests that the onlooker is passive and uninvolved, and in some cases that may be true. In others, the bystanders play a very significant and destructive role in the drama between a bully and his victim. The bystanders are the built-in audience that a bully needs in order to show off his bullying prowess.

Characteristics of a Bystander

Most kids don't want to witness bullying. They report that it makes them nervous and uncomfortable, and they would prefer it didn't happen at all. Studies indicate that about 70 percent of kids are bystanders to the regular bullying that goes on in their schools, and in most instances the bullying events are witnessed by more than one bystander.

The term "bystander" suggests that the onlookers are neutral, uninvolved, and emotionally detached from what they are observing. But in the case of classmate-on-classmate bullying, this couldn't be further from the truth. Bystander kids are profoundly affected by the bully/victim drama that can stir up feelings of confusion, uncertainty, excitement, and fear.

The Bystander's Role in the Triad

The bystander is the last of the three actors involved in the complicated dynamics of bully, bullied, and bystanders. Of those three actors, the bystander role may very well be the most powerful role of all.

The bully starts the action-oriented drama, the bullied child stars in the show, but as they say in showbiz, "Without an audience, there is no show." In other words, if there are no kids around or if no one is paying attention, who will the bully show off to? Who will watch his display of power and dominance, his one-upmanship, his demonstration of superiority? No one—that's who. Most bullying would not take place if it weren't for the bully's need to show off and get validation of his strength from his peers.

Bystander Roles

Every child who bears witness to bullying has to make a difficult decision, and each child wrestles internally with his conscience and his level of courage to arrive at that decision. Will he take part in the bullying to ensure that he doesn't become the next target? Will he hang back, unwilling to actively participate, but willing to encourage the bully nonetheless by laughing at the actions unfolding before him? Is he uncomfortable enough with the bullying that he looks away and tries to pretend it's not happening? Or will he listen to his strong, internal moral code and somehow find the courage to tell the bully to knock it off?

The Assistant

Many bullies have a sidekick, and some will have multiple sidekicks who serve as the bully's henchmen. Bullies like to have the safety of backup bullies, just in case one of his victims has the nerve to stand up to him. And the assistants are more than happy to provide backup to the bully because the assistant can engage in bullying behavior without having to be the ringleader. This allows him to excuse his behavior by saying, "I wasn't the one who started it." He can live vicariously through the bully without having to be mean enough or cruel enough to do the worst of the bullying. This type of assistant can be called a bully-lite.

 **Fact**

> Do you remember Woim? He was Butch, the bully's sidekick in the *Little Rascals* Our Gang series. Woim was the typical bully assistant. He would never instigate the bullying, but would join right in once Butch started in on Alfalfa.

Ben, the neighborhood bully, roams the neighborhood with five of his buddies. Some nights they get lucky and stumble upon the younger boys playing kick ball in the courtyard. Ben loves to torment the younger boys. Ben grabs their ball and points to one of the boys. Ben's henchmen surround the chosen boy and make it impossible for him to escape. Ben then beats down the boy with the ball until he lies huddled on the ground crying.

Are Ben's henchmen bullies or bystanders? They are both. They don't start the action, but they assist Ben in carrying it out. It's bad enough to be bullied by one boy; imagine how helpless and scared kids are when there are multiple assistant bullies to contend with?

The Encourager

Many children fit into this category. They don't actively bully the victim like the assistants do, but they are still a part of the action. They watch what is happening and are engaged in the situation. They may think what the bully is doing is funny, or they might laugh because they feel it is what is expected. Encouragers know that the bully wants an audience for his display of power and dominance, and most kids will oblige. Peer pressure is a powerful thing. So powerful that even "good" kids will behave badly under certain circumstances.

A second-grade girl named Kayla was being bullied by a classmate. The bully, named Emma, delighted in tormenting and embarrassing Kayla. One day at lunch, Emma intentionally poured a container of milk in Kayla's lap. When Kayla stood up, Emma pointed to Kayla's lap and loudly announced, "Look everyone! Kayla wet her pants!" All the kids at surrounding tables laughed. Kayla was devastated.

In this case, Emma pouring milk on Kayla was less embarrassing than the public humiliation that followed when all the kids saw the large wet spot, assumed she'd actually peed her pants, and laughed at her.

The Avoider

This is the child who is most affected by the bullying he witnesses. He feels badly for the victim, strongly dislikes what the bully is doing, but yet he's unable to engage. He wants to do something to help, but can't. He might be afraid he'll be the next target, he might be worried that other kids will make fun of him for trying to help, or he may not have enough confidence in his abilities to believe that he really can help. The feelings of guilt and helplessness that this type of bystander feels can have a lasting negative effect on his self-esteem.

Henry is the feared one on the school bus. He's a fifth grader who regularly trips kids, smacks their heads together, and squirts ketchup packets on them, saying, "Bang! You're dead." This harassment happens every day on the trip to and from school. Tevon wishes he could stand up to Henry to tell him to stop, but he can't seem to do it. Every day in his head he rehearses what he would say, what he would do, and what the outcome would be if he just stood up to Henry. Every day Tevon watches Henry harass and bully the kids on the bus, and every day that he does nothing to stop it he feels lousy.

Why don't any of the kids tell the bus driver, a teacher, or their parents? Henry is just one boy. A bully maybe, but still just one boy. There are probably seventy other students on the bus; why won't anyone stand up to Henry? It's hard to understand how a single boy can cause such terror and abuse when he's so utterly outnumbered. But it happens. It happens on buses and in classroom, and until we empower kids to step forward to support the minority of kids being bullied, it will continue to happen.

The Hero

This bystander is a true hero. She will step in and confront the bully and tell her, "Stop it!" She sees the injustice of one child picking on another and isn't willing to ignore it. She understands that the victim of bullying needs help, not more abuse, and she's willing to give it. This child usually has high levels of confidence and self-esteem. She gets along well with others and isn't afraid that her friendships or social standing will be negatively affected if she stands up to the bully.

Studies show that in 50 percent of bullying events, if just one person who witnesses the bullying said, "Stop it!" it will stop. That means if a single child intervenes on behalf of your child when she's being bullied, half of the time it will stop. That's an amazing statistic. And probably true. Think about it: A bully doesn't want his authority challenged or undermined. So when a bystander challenges his authority to bully, the bully has two choices—to continue to bully or to stop.

Why Bystanders Don't Tell

It's simple: they don't want to become a target themselves. Well, it's actually more complicated than that, but that is usually the number one reason kids don't intervene. Think about it. If you're eight- or ten- or twelve-years-old and the mean girl in class is telling cruel lies about the new girl and socially snubbing her, what are you going to do? If you intervene, you risk drawing the attention and ire of the mean girl, and she may bully you instead. Most kids will admit that when another child is being targeted, they are secretly relieved it's not happening to them and they stay silent in order to keep it that way.

Another reason a bystander won't tell is if he somehow found himself caught up in the excitement and intensity of the bullying, "lost his head," and joined in. He may feel lousy that he joined in to prove that he was also tough and strong. He may realize that what he did was wrong but fears getting in trouble, so he stays mum. Some kids stay quiet in order to remain part of the gang—one of the boys. To tell would be to isolate himself from his peers.

Many kids don't tell because they don't think it would do any good. They don't tell their teacher because they think the teacher won't believe them or won't want to deal with the complications of the situation. And they don't tell their parents because they think their parents will say, "It's no big deal. It's just part of growing up. He'll be fine."

Alert!

Ask kids why it's hard to defend someone who is being teased, and they will give these responses: "The bully is someone I would like to be friends with." "Siding with the bully makes me feel stronger." "I think it's funny." "Telling someone wouldn't help anyway." "The bully might pick on me next!"

Why Bystanders Aren't Innocent

Silence encourages bullying. To remain silent is to give tacit approval for what is happening. But kids don't realize the power their silence gives to a bully. They don't understand that by doing nothing, they are doing the most harmful thing possible. Bystanders who don't tell are part of the problem—they are a big part of the problem. And the only way to break the silence is to empower kids to feel safe and supported when they stand up to the bullies on behalf of other kids or tell an adult about the bullying. If all bystanders were unified in their disapproval and condemnation of bullying behavior, it would have to stop.

Mara is being taunted by Leah. Mara is crying and hugging herself while Leah hurls ugly insult after ugly insult at her. A group of girls sitting close by notices the bullying and one girl says, "Hey! Knock it off! Leave Mara alone!" Leah stops for a minute, then lets another insult fly. This time, all of the other girls speak simultaneously, "Go away!" "Stop it!" "What's your problem?" "Can't you see you hurt her feelings?" Leah, outnumbered, backs away.

 **Fact**

> The term "innocent" is defined in the *Merriam Webster's Collegiate Dictionary* as "free from guilt or sin especially through lack of knowledge of evil." Given this definition, there would be no such thing as an "innocent bystander" to bullying.

If all kids came to the aid of victimized kids (as this group of girls did for Mara), the world would be a much happier place. The bullies wouldn't be allowed to get away with bad behavior, and perhaps they would realize that their behavior is not funny or entertaining; it's hurtful and degrading, and it's high time it stopped.

How Bystanders Can Stop Bullying

Bystanders have the power to stop bullies. But most bystanders are children, and often children don't realize the power they hold. In most instances of bullying, there is one bully, one victim, and many bystanders. Anti-bullying intervention and education programs teach children to recognize that there is strength in numbers, that all it takes to stop the bullying is for a few students to stand up and confront the bully. A bully wants to impress the bystanders with his aggressive and abusive actions. If enough bystanders express disapproval, he'll stop.

Kids need to know that other kids feel the same way that they do about bullying. And parents can encourage children to be part of the solution, instead of part of the problem. If you want your child to take action when he witnesses bullying, here are a few things you should discuss beforehand.

Empathy and Compassion

Talk with your child about how the victim of bullying must feel. Ask your child how she would feel if it were happening to her. Would she want and need others to intervene on her behalf? If your child knows someone who has been bullied, she can offer a helping hand. She could extend an invitation to help her report it, invite her to participate in a group activity, or she can privately express that what happened was not fair or deserved. Just reaching out to a bullied child is a great first step. Be sure to set a good example for your child and reach out to the parents of kids who don't quite fit in.

Show Support

Tell your child that you are there for her whenever she needs to talk about the situation. Listen to her concerns and take them seriously. If your child isn't comfortable standing up for a bullied child, do not force it. Encourage her instead to talk with other bystanders to see if anyone else is willing to join her in standing up for the bullied child. Point out that if enough kids stand up to the bully, the bully will have to stop.

Explain the Need to Tell

Encourage your child to report bullying to an adult. Most kids don't want to be labeled a tattletale; explain to her that there is a big difference between tattling in order to get someone in trouble and reporting to prevent another child from being hurt or humiliated. If the bullied child won't get help because she's scared, you and your child can still try to get help for her.

Find an Alternate Solution

Think of some concrete ways your child might stop someone from bullying. Can your child get the attention of an adult? Perhaps your child could create a diversion or distraction.

Know When to Get Help

Let your child know that there are certain instances where she should never try to intervene, as it might be too dangerous. If the bully is mentally unstable, if there is a weapon involved, if there are multiple bullies, or if the bully is violent, instruct your child to go get adult help immediately.

 Fact

> The outcry from the murder of Kitty Genovese in 1964 (in which dozens of witnesses heard the attack, but no one helped the dying woman or called the police) uncovered a psychological phenomenon called the Genovese Syndrome or Bystander Effect. Simply put, as the number of witnesses to a misdeed or crime increases, the chance that anyone will intervene goes down. Most people assume that someone else will help, and tragically, as in Kitty's case, no one does.

There can be ongoing discussions on how to prevent kids from being inadvertently socialized into bullies, instructions on how to bully-proof and raise the self-esteem and confidence of your children, and warnings about the potentially destructive nature or untapped positive potential of bystanders. But ultimately, there is only one permanent way to stop the phenomenon of children hurting other children, and that is to establish a social climate where aggressive and abusive behavior is not tolerated.

CHAPTER 7

Factors That Lead to Bullying Behavior

Are bullies born or raised? The age-old nature versus nurture debate is alive and well in those who study aggressive behavior. On one side of the debate, nature researchers believe that heredity and hormone levels in the human body can cause increases in aggressive behavior. The nurture crew believes in the blank-slate theory—a child's understanding of and reaction to the world come entirely from his experiences and observations. Many researchers now believe that while biology can cause certain predispositions, environment plays a significant role in the development of aggressive behavior.

Violence in the Family

Parents are a child's first and most powerful role models. From a very early age children mimic what they see their parents say and do. A young girl will want to brush her hair—just like mom. She will want to talk on her pretend phone, play with her pretend baby, and cook with her plastic food—just like mom. A young boy will want to shave his face—just like dad. He will want to help shovel the snow, fix the car, and mow the lawn—just like dad. Most parents think this behavior is cute and will reinforce it with comments like, "Look at you taking care of your baby doll! You're such a good mommy!" and "What a big, strong boy you are! You will be a great dad someday!"

But what if what the little girl sees is mommy yelling at the bank teller, insulting the grocery clerk, and badmouthing the other moms in the playgroup? And what if the young boy sees his father berating his mother, insulting the dinner she's made, and tossing his fork across the room after he pronounces the evening meal disgusting and inedible? What if these kids witness more severe forms of domestic violence? What then? Can you really be surprised or shocked when the little girl becomes a playground terror, bossing around other kids and pushing them down when they don't cooperate? Or when the boy insults the artwork of a classmate, rips it into tiny pieces, and tosses it in the air, saying, "The only thing this is good for is confetti." These kids have learned, by watching their parents, that violence is normal and it's acceptable to use it on others, including their peers.

Researchers in the United States are finding connections between violence at home and aggressive bullying behavior in school. One of the first studies to specifically examine the link between exposure to domestic violence and involvement in bullying was conducted by the University of Washington and Indiana University. Researchers there found that children who were exposed to violence in the home engaged in higher levels of physical bullying than children reared in nonviolent homes.

Social Learning Theory

One possible explanation for this link between witnessing and repeating certain behaviors is called social learning theory, which was originally proposed by Albert Bandura, renowned researcher on human behavior. Bandura conducted hundreds of studies, but one study stands out—the Bobo doll experiment. Bandura made a film of a woman beating up a Bobo doll (a Bobo doll is an inflatable, oval, blow-up clown doll with a weighted bottom that allows it to bob back up after you knock it down). Bandura showed the film to a group of kindergartners, who saw the woman punch, hit, and smack the Bobo doll with a plastic hammer. Bandura then placed a Bobo doll in the kindergarteners' normal play area and they were then let out to play. The observers saw the kids beating up the Bobo doll. They punched, kicked, and hit the Bobo with little hammers. They yelled, "Sockeroo!"

just like the woman in the film did while she was attacking the Bobo doll. Essentially, the kindergartners imitated exactly what the woman had done in the film.

 Essential

In a follow-up study, Bandura found that when children observed the woman in the film being punished for her aggressive behavior toward the Bobo doll, they were less likely to act aggressively toward the Bobo doll. Bandura also found that there was no difference in children who saw the woman rewarded for acting aggressively or receiving no reward.

This experiment was repeated with many variations, yet always yielded similar results. Bandura eventually called the Bobo doll phenomenon observational learning or modeling, and he labeled the theory social learning. Social learning theory simply means people learn new information and behaviors by watching other people. The girl who is in the car when her mother spews mean-spirited gossip about a neighbor will learn that it's okay to trash talk her friends. And the boy who sees his father shove and slap his mother will see nothing wrong with shoving and slapping the annoying boy who rides the bus with him. In simplest terms, it's a monkey see, monkey do situation.

Domestic Violence

Domestic violence is defined as physical, sexual, psychological, or financial abuse that occurs between adults involved in an intimate relationship, and is usually characterized by long-term patterns of abusive behavior and control. Each year the millions of children who bear witness to the domestic abuse of one or more of their parents are left with deep emotional and psychological scars. They may suffer from:

- Depression
- Anxiety
- Aggressive behavior
- Conduct problems
- Impaired concentration and school performance
- Physical ailments (headaches, stomach aches, sleep disturbances)
- Post-traumatic stress disorder

Child abuse experts have long been lobbying to include exposure to domestic violence as a form of child abuse in and of itself, mainly because of the negative effects on a child's emotional, social, and cognitive development. Adding to the violence is the fact that approximately half of the men who batter their wives also abuse their children.

Alert!

According to a federal study done in 2000, it is estimated that between 3.3 and 10 million children witness domestic violence annually. Domestic violence is the most common unreported crime in America today and it occurs in families from all social, cultural, religious, educational, and economic backgrounds.

Child Abuse

Each year, there are 3 million reports of child abuse and neglect made in the United States, and hundreds of children die every year as the direct result of being abused. Children are abused by their parents for a number of reasons. The most prevalent are:

- **Unrealistic expectations:** If the parent lacks sufficient knowledge of child behavior and development, she will set unrealistic and unattainable goals for her child.

- **Prior abuse:** If the parent was abused as a child, he may now lack the appropriate skills for successful nonviolent parenting.
- **Alcohol or substance abuse:** If the parent engages in substance abuse to such a degree that it contributes to violent behavior, it often leads to child abuse.
- **Financial pressures:** If the family lives in chronic poverty or experiences a sudden loss of financial stability, it can lead to domestic violence and child abuse.

Abuse impairs a child's ability to develop healthy and trusting relationships with family members. Families are supposed to provide children with warmth and nurturing, emotional support, unconditional love, and a sense of belonging. Families are supposed to guide and teach children proper social behavior and help them develop an internal code of conduct that will serve them well in later life. And families are supposed to protect their young and shield them from harm.

Unfortunately, some families beat and berate, slap and scold, injure and insult their children. And those children learn that physical and verbal abuse are the right way to do things. They think, "If this is how Dad gets his way, then it should be how I get my way, too." Remember the study of kids who were bullies? Ninety-seven percent reported having been prior victims of abuse. That's an overwhelming statistic; but, in all fairness, not all kids who are abused act aggressively or become bullies.

 Fact

Child abuse and neglect includes the physical or mental injury, sexual abuse, negligent treatment, or maltreatment of any child under the age of eighteen by a person who is responsible for the child's welfare under circumstances that indicate the child's health or welfare is harmed or threatened.

In normal families there are conflicts and disagreements, arguments and spats, misunderstandings and hurt feelings; these things are a part of life. And learning how to deal with normal levels of conflict can build a child's self-esteem and social competence. But when a child witnesses abuse and cruelty or suffers at the hands of an abusive parent, he learns that the world is cold, uncaring, and unsafe. He feels helpless and alone and will sometimes channel all the anger and aggression he feels toward his abusers onto his own victims. When an abused child abuses (or bullies) another child, he feels powerful in a way he doesn't at home. The abused child wants his victim to suffer the same way he did. He wants him to feel small, unloved, and worthless. And this is how the cycle of violence is perpetuated.

The next time a bully pushes your child to the ground and demands to be the first kid on the bus, you might reflect for a moment on how that kid came to be a bully. Perhaps he isn't an eight-year-old monster without feelings or humanity. Perhaps he is a victim, too. That's not to say his behavior is acceptable—it is not—but that bully may only be emulating conduct that he has seen, or suffered, at home.

Lack of a Positive Role Model

Because children learn through observation and experience, they need to have positive role models in their lives. A child can learn through example to have a can-do attitude, integrity, self-discipline, courage, compassion, and a positive regard for the people around him. Children can learn to contribute to their families, schools, and communities. Often, this same process can make them vulnerable to learning all the wrong things from less-than-ideal role models. A child can just as easily learn negativity, violence, and contempt for his fellow man.

So who can the average child look up to? Certainly not a sports figure as an increasing number of them have criminal records or are involved in other forms of scandal. So who then . . . movie stars? Teen television celebrities? Pop music icons? Not many would make the A-list of positive role models for kids. That leaves it up to parents and close family members, and perhaps teachers and coaches.

Question?

Does your child have positive role models in his life?
Your child needs to be exposed to adults who model positive, responsible, caring behavior. For instance, if you want your child to learn how to resolve conflict in a healthy, civil manner, he needs to see adults who can do the same.

Violent Television

Does a steady diet of violent television teach children about violence, subsequently causing them to behave in a more violent fashion? A few studies do show at least the suggestion of a link between televised violence and imitative and/or aggressive behavior. For example, The Kaiser Foundation report states that eight out of ten parents have seen their children imitate both positive behaviors (sharing, helping) and negative behaviors (hitting, kicking) they had seen on TV. And by the time the children in the study reached the age of six, almost half of their parents reported seeing imitative behaviors their children had seen on TV. Now this isn't all that surprising, considering that children learn through observation (remember the Bobo doll) and modeling. Monkey see, monkey do. This form of learning would be predominantly positive if all television programming was of the Mister Rogers variety. Unfortunately, it is not.

Most young children watch an average of two to four hours of television per day. And when you include the time spent playing video games, this can add up to around thirty-five hours of screen time per week. Kids are watching at younger and younger ages, and television consumes more time than any other socializing influence except the family. The Parents Television Council, a conservative media watchdog agency, estimated in a 2007 study that the average child "sees over 1,000 acts of murder, rape, and assault on TV each year."

Alert!

The National Institute of Mental Health details the three major potential effects watching violence on television can have on young children: (1) children may become desensitized to the pain and suffering of others; (2) children may become fearful and afraid of people and the world around them; and (3) children may behave in a more aggressive manner toward others.

Television is not all bad; and not every child who is exposed to televised violence will be affected negatively. There are many other factors at play, such as genetics and family environment. And there are many researchers who criticize the studies that link television violence to real-life violence and aggression. These critics point to a lack of statistical scientific proof that watching televised violence actually increases a child's propensity for violence. One theory is that children who are more genetically predisposed to aggressive tendencies actually prefer more violent television shows. Another is that children who watch violent television may come from homes where there is a high level of child abuse or neglect. So the argument becomes which came first, the chicken or the egg? Are certain children more aggressive to begin with, and is the innate higher level of aggression causing more violent behavior? Or is it the exposure to the TV violence that ups the aggression? At the moment, the evidence is not adequate to claim definitively that exposure to violent television is a significant source of violence.

Essential

If you have young children, be wary of the G rating in movies. Many films (Disney and otherwise) have a few scary moments and contain violent scenes that may not be appropriate for your preschooler. To see detailed descriptions of the content of animated movies, go to *www.kids-in-mind.com* or *www.screenit.com.*

As a parent, you have likely seen television's direct effect when a news report frightens your child or a scary movie gives her nightmares. Television does have some effect, but it's your job as a parent to minimize the negative effects as much as possible. It is important to keep abreast of the television rating system and allow only age-appropriate viewing. You can utilize the v-chip system to block out unacceptable or inappropriate content. Television is an invited guest in your home; treat it that way and you can keep it from being a negative and harmful influence.

 Fact

Studies on the effects of violent television viewing and aggressive or violent behavior are not nearly as consistent as most antimedia reports suggest. A study conducted by Freedman in 2002 found about 200 existing studies on television and violence, and they were evenly divided between those that find some small effect and those that either find no effect or even a positive one.

Violent Video Games

The Columbine High School massacre of twelve students and one teacher sparked great controversy among researchers and scientists about whether or not violent video games contribute to violent behavior in teens. Such a tragedy invokes anger, confusion, and outrage, and it is understandable for society to want to look for someone or something to blame for the unspeakable act. So were Eric Harris and Dylan Klebold adversely affected by the video games they played? Were they so desensitized by violence that they could casually enter their school and murder their peers? Was it all externally motivated or is there a genetic or social component to the violent behavior they exhibited?

If violence is, in fact, caused by video games, then the solution to a less violent world would be to eliminate the games. Obviously, that's too simplistic a solution. Violence and aggression are caused by the interaction of a dozen different variables.

 **Fact**

The Virginia Tech Review Panel—a state-appointed body responsible for reviewing the Virginia Tech massacre on April 16, 2007, in which Virginia Tech student Seung-Hui Cho shot and killed thirty-two people before committing suicide—concluded that Cho was not a player of video games. Cho reportedly was not involved in video-game playing in college and only played nonviolent games in high school.

Historically, society has always searched for a quick and easy answer for the world's ills. Novels have been banned, music has been maligned, and television and movies have sparked moral outrage. Every generation has found things to blame for teen rebellion, violent behavior, and moral degradation.

There is no doubt that many video games on the market today are violent. Parents mistakenly assume that just because video games are marketed to kids, they are appropriate for kids. This is not so. Video games have ratings similar to movie and television rating systems. Many of the games with questionable and excessive violent content are rated M (for mature) or A (for adult), and an impressionable tween or teen should not be allowed to view or play video games with an M or A rating.

Alert!

Bully is the name of a video game that is set in a high school. Critics of the game say that while it does not include guns, blood, or gore, it is violent and should be rated M (for mature) instead of T (for teen). The main character shoots slingshots, takes over cliques, and uses firecrackers and stink bombs against bullies. Supporters of Bully report that the game mirrors the kinds of moral choices kids may have to make about bullying in real-life settings.

Lawrence Kutner and Cheryl K. Olson, cofounders and directors of the Massachusetts General Hospital's Center for Mental Health and the Media, wrote a book called *Grand Theft Childhood: The Surprising Truth about Video Games and What Parents Can Do*. The book covers research findings from Kutner and Olsen's $1.5 million study (funded by the U.S. Department of Justice) on youth violence and gaming that was coordinated at the Harvard Medical School between 2004 and 2006. This study involved surveys from more than 1,200 middle school students and over 500 parents, and interviews with dozens of teen and preteen boys and their parents.

The study found that the majority of young male subjects regularly played violent, M-rated video games. What they didn't find was a significant correlation between playing these games and a general increase in violent behavior. Furthermore, Kutner and Olsen found that the motivation for playing video games for most kids isn't a result of reclusive or antisocial tendencies. Kids usually play video games for excitement and escape from boredom and stress. They also note that kids in the study were capable of recognizing and separating real-world violence from fantasy in-game violence. However, the authors do caution that an obsessive or excessive interest in M-rated violent video games could point to other more troublesome or deep-seated psychological issues. And video game addiction is something parents should always look out for.

Despite the inconclusive studies and arguments among researchers about whether or not video games contribute or cause an increase in violent behavior, recommendations remain in place for parents.

- Monitor your child's video-game playing.
- Limit the amount of time spent playing video games.
- Be aware of the ESRB rating system and follow the age-appropriate guidelines.

If you have a child who is prone to increased violent or aggressive tendencies, reconsider allowing him unsupervised access to the violent games. And if you do see a link between the games your child is playing and his behavior, don't hesitate to ban the games. You are the parent—it's your job to monitor and assess risk levels for your child.

Prior Victim of a Bully

Like almost everything else in life, learning happens through experience. Sadly, one of the most destructive things a child can learn is that violence is an acceptable way of life, that violence can get him what he needs or wants and that violence is power and aggression is the only way to achieve that power. The interesting thing about the bully who was the prior victim of bullying or abuse is that he chooses to hurt others in exactly the same way he was hurt. He knows how it feels to be on the receiving end of hurt and humiliation, yet he still chooses to dish it out to others. These kids adhere to the I'm-hurting-so-you-will-too school of thought.

As mentioned earlier, a recent study showed that 97 percent of kids who bully had also been the victims of bullying. Kids raised in aggressive and violent homes have learned to be aggressive and violent. And if these kids don't get help, some of them will bully and abuse their offspring, who will then go on to abuse and bully their peers and offspring, and the cycle will go on and on and on.

To be fair, many kids who are abused or bullied do not go on to become bullies themselves. They endure the abuse until it subsides or they find other ways to handle it. Those who do go on to bully are simply perpetuating the cycle of violence.

School Failure

Many, but not all, bullies struggle in school. Since it is known that a large percentage of bullies are abused at home or are being abused by another peer, school may not be a top priority. Trouble concentrating, lack of interest in school, and abnormal peer interactions are all possible side effects of being abused. If the abuse is intense, a child can shut down and have difficulty performing even the basic skills needed to progress from academic year to academic year. If this happens, the bully may be held back a grade and now becomes a bully who is older and bigger than almost all of his peers.

Victims are also at risk for school failure. A victim of bullying can become so withdrawn, so anxious, and so fearful that she is no longer able to function in school. Her mind may become so focused on avoiding her bully and wondering and worrying when the next attack will occur that she becomes literally frozen with fear at school. Her motivation evaporates, her grades plummet, and she is victimized yet again.

Peer Rejection

Making and maintaining friendships is a vital social skill for children to master in the early grades at school. Kids who have the skills to make friends easily and to keep those friends are the least likely to be bullied. Children are considered popular when the majority of the class likes and wants to play with and be partnered with them for activities. Popular kids usually have positive and competent social interaction and communication skills. Moderately popular children are well liked by some kids and disliked by a few. These children generally have decent social skills but aren't quite as socially savvy as the popular kids. They might be class clowns or labeled the rowdy ones. Unpopular children are often disliked by a majority of the class. They have trouble with basic classroom rules and are often immature. They tend to be self-centered and lack proper social interaction skills. And overlooked children are the wallflowers. They might be shy, have low self-esteem, or just have slow-developing social skills. These children aren't usually liked or disliked, as they rarely claim much attention in the classroom.

In truth, bullies and victims can come from any category. But knowing where your child stands in the eyes of her peers can help you assess her risk of being a bully or bullied child.

School Climate

One of the main reasons the majority of bullying remains under the radar in schools is because of the dangerously tolerant atmosphere. When superintendents, principals, teachers, and school personnel tolerate episodes of bullying, it affects the quality of the learning experience and jeopardizes the safety of all the students, not just those directly involved. And when bullies learn that their behavior will be overlooked and there will be no serious consequences, they feel free to continue to abuse their fellow peers. When the victims of bullying learn through experience that there are no serious consequences for bullying, they too realize that the bullies are free to continue to abuse them. In an environment where adults are expected to care for and protect children, this apathy is unacceptable. Anyone working with children who sticks their head in the sand—or worse, enables bullies to continue to abuse other children—is contributing to a harmful school climate.

But to change a school's climate from one of dangerous tolerance to consistent intolerance is a task that must involve administrators, teachers, school personnel, parents, and students. Everyone must be educated as to exactly what bullying is, what types of bullying exist, the roles that bullies, bullied kids, and bystanders adopt, and the devastating effects bullying can have on bullies, bullied kids, bystanders, and the overall school climate. Chapter 21 will detail exactly how administrators, teachers, parents, and students can work together to enact this type of change.

CHAPTER 8

Common Bullying Myths

A myth is often described as being a fictional, unfounded, or false notion. In short: untrue. But ask any parent about bullying and chances are they will say, "Bullying is a normal part of growing up." "It's good for kids, toughens them up." or "There isn't a problem with bullies at my kid's school." Sadly, despite decades of bullying research to prove all of these statements wrong, these myths persist. Well, the time has come to learn the truth.

Myth 1: Bullying Is a Normal Rite of Passage

What would you call a kick to the backside that catapults a ten-year-old boy across the classroom? Normal? What about a twelve-year-old snipping off the ponytail of her unsuspecting ex-best friend? All in good fun? Or what if a handicapped boy was being repeatedly ridiculed by a group of his classmates? Would you call it kids' play?

Unfortunately, these types of rite-of-passage behaviors are occurring day in and day out in schools across the country. And with approximately 30 percent of kids engaged in bullying or being bullied, there is a real chance your child could be among them. And even if your child is one of the lucky ones and isn't a target of verbal aggression, physical assault, or peer rejection, your child will undoubtedly witness (as 70 percent of children do) many such events throughout his years in school. Bullying is a serious problem; one that can, and does, affect every student. Bullied kids may suffer anxiety, depression, low self-esteem, and academic difficulties. In the long term, kids who bully are at higher risk of depression and relational issues, and have higher rates of adult criminal behavior. And bystanders who witness bullying behavior feel ill equipped to intervene, and yet feel guilty for not helping.

Picture this: your child comes home from school with a black eye and a bruised lip. Would you dismiss it by saying, "Don't worry about it, kiddo. Everyone goes through it"? Probably not; you would be dialing the principal before you even grabbed an ice pack out of the freezer.

After decades of research, many of the common bullying myths have been debunked. Yet somehow a large percentage of the population continues to downplay and discount the seriousness of the bullying problem. Stripped of all the misconceptions—it's harmless—misrepresentations—it's just a little roughhousing—and excuses—it's hard to tell what's really happening between kids on the playground—bullying is still abuse. Just because the violence happens between children doesn't make it any less serious. In fact, it can make it more so because of a child's developing sense of self.

 **Fact**

Dan Olweus, one of the world's leading experts on bullies and their victims, has said that teachers' attitudes, behaviors, and routines play a significant role in the prevalence of bullying behavior. When a teacher fails to come to the aid or assistance of a bullied child, the teacher is enabling the activity to continue and can inadvertently create a victim mentality in a child.

All of this is happening in the one place (besides your home) that your children should feel safe; in the hallowed halls of academia, where your child should be focused on growing and learning and socializing with his peers. He shouldn't be worried about when he will get the next sucker punch or wedgie ripper; he shouldn't have to worry about being attacked in the bathroom or stuffed in a locker; and he shouldn't have to worry about being taunted and teased or humiliated every day.

Myth 2: Kids Need to Learn to Defend Themselves

If you recall from Chapter 1, there are three criteria that must be met for a behavior to be considered bullying: an imbalance of power, intent to harm, and threat of future harm. Therefore, when someone says, "Bullying will toughen a kid up" or "It will make a man out of him," it makes no sense. There is an inherent power differential, either real or perceived, that almost guarantees the victim won't be able to stand up and fight his bully. And that's intentional on the part of the bully; bullies choose their victims for the very reason those victims can't or won't fight back. Bullied kids tend to be quiet, passive kids, friendless kids, or kids who are physically or psychologically weaker than the bully. Bullies, on the other hand, are aggressive kids with high self-esteem who lack empathy for others. So a quiet, passive, friendless child is picked on by a stronger, more aggressive kid with an attitude, and he's supposed to defend himself? All by himself? Does this seem like a fair fight?

Another way we place responsibility, or blame, on the victim is by believing the bullied child did something to deserve it. Wearing odd clothing, not attending to personal hygiene, having a strange or obsessive hobby, acting out in socially unacceptable ways, and being overly emotional can all lead to bullying.

Having a strange hobby can sometimes place a kid in the line of bully fire. A child who is fascinated with bugs, who can rattle off the names and characteristics of a hundred different insect species, is probably not going to be looked at with admiration. Most kids will immediately label her weird, and she may find herself the recipient of a bug-related nickname. A socially acceptable hobby, on the other hand, can gain admiration from one's peers. A girl who can name and list the batting averages of every professional ball player on her home team is viewed as having an amazing memory—and no one will accuse her of having a personality problem.

Alert!

If your child has chronic bad breath, unkempt hair, body odor, or dirty clothes he can become the object of peer ridicule. And the older kids get, the more judgmental and cruel they become. Provide the self-care items your child needs to keep clean and encourage her to take pride in her appearance.

A child who has social "quirks" might also be more likely to fall prey to a bully. A social quirk might be a stutter, a severe reluctance to speak up, or an emotional frailty. A child who is overly emotional provides a bully with instant entertainment. Anytime the bully wants to put on a show, all she has to do is call out the emotional child. Being able to make another kid cry is high on the list of favorite bully activities. It makes a bully feel powerful because she's in control of another child's emotions.

Essential

Be sensitive to the need for your child to fit in and look similar to everyone else. If your child tells you "Everyone is wearing these sneakers" or "All of the girls wear their hair this way," she's probably telling you the truth. Try to allow (within your budget) a few of these must-have items.

A study published in *School Psychology International* reported that six out of ten students agree that some bullied kids "brought it on themselves." That is a scary statistic, considering that bullying is never acceptable, no matter what. The physical appearance or relational skills of a bullied child should never come under fire, and blaming the victim should not be allowed. Clearly, this is a problem that needs to be addressed.

Myth 3: Children Who Are Bullied Always Tell an Adult

Most children do not tell an adult when they are being bullied. In fact, most studies show that only about 25–50 percent of kids report being bullied. This leaves parents scratching their heads and asking, "But why? What are they afraid of?" Well, it's not a simple, straightforward answer, but here is what researchers have found.

Kids Are Afraid of Retaliation

Lauren has been the recipient of "poison" letters—mysterious folded notes that appear in her locker. They read, "You think you are all that, but you are nothing!" "Some girls are nice to your face but they really hate you and talk about you behind your back." "You're a %@!#&! We hate you!" "You are a %@!#&, %@!#&, %@!#&!" Lauren is crushed. She has no idea who hates her enough to put poison notes in her locker. After a few days, the notes get nastier and Lauren decides to show the notes to her teacher and her mom. Lauren's mom meets with the principal and Lauren's teacher speaks to the class. For a few days the notes stop and Lauren is relieved; a week later, Lauren opens her locker and out pours a hundred poison letters.

Kids Have a Fear of Being Dismissed

Todd was born with an abnormality in one leg. As the result of multiple surgeries, Todd has an odd gait that makes him clumsier than other kids his age. Rogan, the class bully, takes advantage of Todd's weakness and trips him almost every day during gym class. Todd does the right thing and tells Mr. Krause, the gym teacher, each time it happens, but Mr. Krause just tells Todd to slow it down. Todd eventually realizes that Mr. Krause isn't going to help him.

When adults who are supposed to care for and protect children from harm fail to do so, kids have nowhere to turn. They feel scared, helpless, and alone.

 *Fact*

The Maine Project Against Bullying surveyed third-grade students from 165 schools. Students reported that 71 percent of school-based bullying incidents were ignored by teachers or other supervising adults. That means that three out of four students who need assistance and support are being denied help.

Kids Have a Fear of Being Blamed

Charlie sits in the back of the class and rarely participates in class discussions. Cameron sits beside Charlie and constantly bullies him. Cameron likes to mess up Charlie's Friday spelling test papers with bubble gum. It never fails: No matter how hard Charlie tries to protect his paper, Cameron sticks a big wad of pink chewing gum onto Charlie's paper. And every Friday, Charlie tries to peel it off and winds up ripping his paper. Every Monday, Charlie gets his test back and sees his grade has been docked ten points for messiness. One Friday, Charlie screws up the courage to ask the teacher to move his desk. The teacher asks why and Charlie tells her the truth—that Cameron puts gum on his spelling tests. The teacher tells Charlie that gum isn't allowed in school. The teacher then asks Cameron if he has gum in his mouth. Cameron says, "No ma'am," so the teacher sends Charlie back to his desk.

Charlie finishes his test that morning and stands up to turn it in—clean for the first time all year! He takes a step backward and SLAM! His desk tips over (Cameron kicked it over). The teacher looks up with a scowl and orders Charlie to go sit in the time-out space. Later that day, the teacher lectures Charlie about his unacceptable behavior and says, "Being angry because I didn't change your seat is not a good reason to act out. If it happens again, I'll have to call your mother."

What did Charlie learn? Charlie learned that he won't be taken seriously and he won't be helped. What's worse is that Charlie learns that telling can actually make the situation harder because now the teacher thinks he's the troublemaker!

Kids Fear Being Labeled a Tattletale

A group of fourth-grade girls were bullying Lili. They would say, "Only pretty girls can wear jewelry," and they would take her bracelets and necklaces. When she wore barrettes, they would say, "Ugly girls don't need barrettes," and they took her barrettes. The day the mean girls took her favorite headband, Lili told the teacher. The teacher questioned the girls and searched their lockers. The teacher found the headband and gave it back to Lili, but it wasn't over. After telling, the shunning got worse. The girls told everyone that Lili was a tattletale and that she couldn't be trusted. They whispered, "Snitch," whenever Lili walked by, and every time someone did or said something out of line, one of the girls would loudly announce, "Better watch out! Lili will tell on you!" Lili did the right thing, but now she wishes she had never told.

Kids Have a Fear of the Situation Escalating

Tyler was being harassed by two older boys. They took his lunch money and made him carry their textbook-laden backpacks. Tyler hated it and he hated them. Even though Tyler was embarrassed that he was being bullied and scared that the older boys would make good on their threats to pummel him if he told, he eventually told his parents and hoped for the best. Tyler's mom immediately called the parents of the other boys and informed them of the situation. The other boys' parents were defensive and unapologetic. When Tyler ran into the boys the next day at school, they dragged him into the bathroom and beat him with their book-filled backpacks. They told him they'd kill him if he told again. Tyler was so afraid of what would happen next, he refused to return to school.

None of these situations would have been able to persist or escalate if system-wide adult support and intervention had been in place.

Myth 4: People Are Born Bullies

Bullying is learned behavior. If you recall from Chapter 7, children learn through social experience and modeling. It's also true that there is a biological component that must be taken into account. For instance, all human beings have aggressive tendencies, and children are born into the world with varying levels of innate aggression. If children are not taught how to successfully and constructively deal with their aggressive tendencies, they will behave aggressively. It might take more consistent effort and instruction to teach a child with a higher innate level of aggression how to control his impulses, but it can, and should, be done. But even with a higher level of innate aggression, a child still needs to learn how to bully.

Children learn how to play baseball by practicing with their parents and friends and by watching games on television. They learn how to recite the alphabet by singing along with mom and dad and watching Sesame Street. And they learn how to shove and smack someone while calling them insulting names by watching how mom and dad fight. Kids watch and absorb all they see around them, and they will model the behavior of the significant people in their lives. If the behavior is negative, abusive, and bullying, the child will learn to be a negative, abusive bully.

Alert!

For bully behavior to be effectively transmitted to a child, three conditions must be met. First, the role-model must be someone the child is emotionally attached to. Second, the role model's behavior must be met with success—might is right. Lastly, the role model's bullying behavior must be legitimized by being accepted by those around him.

Myth 5: Bullying Doesn't Happen at My Child's School

When you ask about bullying problems in your child's school, these are the statements you'll likely hear from teachers and administrators. "We don't have a bullying problem in our school." "Sure, kids at our school have conflicts, but we don't have a problem with bullies." "When problems arise, the teachers handle them on a case-by-case basis."

Fact

Over a twenty-five year period, the Secret Service and the Department of Education identified thirty-seven incidents of school-based violent attacks committed by forty-one individuals. School shootings are rare, but when they happen, they have a devastating effect on students, parents, educators, and the entire nation.

What you *want* to hear is a statement like this: "We know that bullying is a widespread and serious problem in our nation's schools. Therefore, we train our teachers to recognize and intervene in bullying situations, we conduct an anti-bullying program with our student body, we have administrative policies in place to deal with kids who bully, we provide parents with assistance and support, and we do our best to foster a caring, supportive, and cooperative school climate."

If you think bullying doesn't happen at your child's school, just ask your child, "Have you ever seen a child being picked on at school?" You will probably hear about a handful of episodes that stand out in your child's mind. One child might recall being upset when he saw a fifth grader repeatedly pour Gatorade into a classmate's backpack. Another might recount the scary experience of watching helplessly while a bullied boy got shoved under a bus seat and trapped there by some bigger kids. A third may confess that other kids have been throwing rocks at him on the playground while they call him "retard." Just asking your child that simple question will probably be an eye-opening experience.

Myth 6: Bullies Are Loners with No Social Skills

This is a popular misconception, and it's likely due to the fact that the loser stereotype is easy to accept. It gives us a reason for why the bully is bullying. He's bullying because no one likes him and he's angry about it and wants to force other kids to be his friend, however misguided that may be. Remember Skut Farkus from *A Christmas Story*? He was a classic loser bully with cold eyes, braces, a mean face, and an evil laugh. That violent arm twisting he did to Ralphie and his friends looked painful and humiliating. It's no wonder Skut had only one friend.

But the loser bullies are actually few and far between. Studies conducted by leading bullying researcher Dan Olweus show that bullies possess high levels of self-esteem and can be as popular as their nonbullying peers. This phenomenon is likely caused by the bully being periodically reinforced for his aggressive and hostile behavior by a small group of his peers. This reinforcement fuels the bully's sense of power and self-worth. Add to this mix the glorification of violence on television, in video games, in movies, and in music and they, too, can reinforce the acceptance and approval of the bully's actions.

Some of the most popular movie bullies have proven to be popular, often well-liked characters. Johnny Lawrence, the king of the Cobra Kai in the 1984 movie *The Karate Kid* was a handsome, popular (yet vicious) bully. Andrew Clark, the "jock" in the 1985 film *The Breakfast Club,* was a popular athlete who bullied a weaker student and caused serious injury. And Regina George, of the 2004 movie *Mean Girls*, is a hot, popular girl with a mean streak a mile wide; but still, all the other girls want to be her or at least be friends with her.

Myth 7: Bullying Is a School Problem

Bullying isn't just a school problem, it's a social problem. It is a problem that every individual in the United States deals with in some capacity. Bullying is everywhere. It's on the preschool playground, in the schools, in colleges, in relationships, in the workplace, in the military, in politics, in the elder-care system. It's nationwide, it's systemic, it's epidemic. Child bullies who don't receive the proper intervention and treatment simply grow up to be grownup bullies. Who hasn't been on the receiving end of a bully boyfriend or girlfriend, a bully boss or coworker, a bully friend or acquaintance, a bully salesperson or telemarketer, and the list goes on. And who hasn't seen news reports of overly aggressive sports figures, officers who use excessive force during an arrest, or abuses of military authority. Aggression and violence are ingrained in American culture.

 Essential

Millions of adults are bullied. In a 2007 nationally representative poll conducted by The Workplace Bullying Institute, it was found that 37 percent of the U.S. workforce, or 54 million employees, have been bullied some time during their work life.

This problem isn't going to go away anytime soon. That is a fact. But if change is implemented at the lowest level, where kids learn that violence and aggression is completely unacceptable, a real societal change might result. This means change has to begin with the family. Too often, by the time kids who bully reach school age, they have already been exposed to years of violence and aggression. To expect teachers to undo years of social conditioning is unrealistic. But it's not unrealistic to expect teachers to convey to even the youngest children that taunting, teasing, and aggressive behaviors will not be tolerated in school.

CHAPTER 9

Warning Signs That Your Child Is Being Bullied

There are many common physical, psychological, and educational clues—both subtle and overt—which suggest a child is being bullied. Bullied kids have a difficult time seeking help and don't often tell their parents when they are being bullied—for a variety of reasons (shame, feeling helpless, being afraid) that will be discussed later in this chapter. Knowing this, it's your responsibility as a parent to be on the lookout for any signs that your child may be the victim of a bully.

Physical Clues

Kids develop and grow physically, socially, emotionally, and academically so rapidly that it's hard for the average parent to keep up with all of the sudden and unexpected changes, especially since each stage of development comes with positive and negative changes. Preschoolers can be emotionally unstable, explosive, and prone to odd physical ailments. Grade schoolers can be excitable, impulsive, and physically unsure of themselves and their rapidly growing bodies. Middle school students can be sullen and uncommunicative, and they can be aggressive on a fairly regular basis. And high schoolers are frequently moody and withdrawn, secretive and antagonistic. And all of this is perfectly normal.

This is why it's difficult to pinpoint the difference between growing pains and the beginning of a serious problem. The most important thing to watch for is any change in your child's behavior that isn't attributed to normal developmental changes. If your child is normally a cheerful, friendly girl and she suddenly starts to resist going to the birthday parties of her classmates or no longer wants to stay after school for extracurricular activities, it's time for a talk. If your son adores playing baseball, yet comes home after a game angry and upset and refuses to talk about it—there might be a problem. And if that same son tosses his cleats in the trash and announces, "I hate baseball, and I quit!" chances are good that there is something emotionally hurtful going on and you need to gently ask your son what happened to sour him on his beloved baseball.

Parents are in a difficult situation with bullying, particularly with older children. You might get a younger child to open up about any abuse or mistreatment he is receiving by simply asking, "Are there any kids at school who are mean to you?" With older kids, it gets trickier. Older kids may want to handle it on their own, they may be embarrassed to tell you what is happening, or they may be concerned about how you will react. Denial might be their first line of defense. Studies show that the best time for intervention is when the bullying first starts. Many kids can successfully stop the bullying if they are supported, coached, and assisted in their efforts. Unfortunately, the longer the abuse goes on the harder it is to stop. So the first step for you, as a parent, is to be on the lookout for any of these physical signs.

Here is a list of the physical symptoms commonly seen in victims of bullying:

- A sudden loss or increase in appetite
- Difficulty falling sleep, night terrors, or sudden and unexplained bed wetting
- Fear of using the bathroom at school causes him to run to use the bathroom the minute he gets home
- Going right to his room to change after school or play to hide torn or heavily soiled clothes or unexplained scratches and bruises
- Asking for, begging for, or stealing extra money for lunch at school or after-school snacks

- Daily stomach aches, headaches, or simply refusing to go to school
- Trying to bring a knife, pocketknife, or box cutter to school for protection
- Showing "victim" body language: refusing to make eye contact, slouching, or mumbling when he talks
- Books, notebooks, or other personal items may be damaged
- May suddenly prefer the company of adults
- Might exhibit new nervous habits such as biting nails, tics, stutters, etc.

Fact

According to the National Education Association, 160,000 kids stay home from school each day to avoid the torment of being bullied. Kids will fake illnesses and random ailments in an effort to escape being harassed and picked on. Keep in mind that the stress of being bullied can cause actual physical illness and ailments.

Psychological Clues

Besides the obvious physical clues that your child may be the victim of bullying, there are many not-so-obvious signs of victimization. Many of these can be mistaken for normal tween or teen drama and moodiness, but if your child exhibits several of these, it's time to figure out what is going wrong in his life.

- Acts moody, sullen, or withdraws from family interaction
- Depressed, distressed, overly emotional, anxious, sad, secretive, explosive outbursts, irritable, angry, or generally acting unlike his normal self
- Puts himself down and says things like, "I'm stupid," "Nobody likes me because I'm a loser," "I wish I were invisible."

- Happy on the weekend, but unhappy and upset on Sunday evenings, Monday mornings, or at the end of a holiday
- Gets upset or moody after receiving a phone call, e-mail, or instant message
- Seems overly concerned with personal safety issues
- Loss of respect for authority figures

Educational Clues

The educational clues are often the most difficult to figure out. It might be a few weeks, or in some cases a few months, before you find out that your child's grades have dropped or that there has been a change in your child's behavior in the classroom. If your child is exhibiting any of the physical or psychological clues of being bullied, it might be a good idea to initiate contact with your child's teacher to receive some instant feedback.

- Loss of interest in school work, refuses to participate in class, or has grades that dropped for no apparent reason
- Chronically late for school or for class
- Lack of motivation
- Teacher reports your child is distracted or antsy in class
- Feigning illness to avoid going to school
- May want to drop out of activities and events once enjoyed
- May want to stay close to teachers and avoid his peers
- May want to change his routes to and from school or class or beg to be driven to school to avoid the bus

If you see some of these signs and symptoms of bullying, act quickly. Find out what is happening in your child's life and take action. Waiting will not improve the situation.

Most Likely Targets

Any child could be the target of a bully, but research shows there are certain qualities and characteristics that increase a child's chances of becoming a victim. In the past, researchers thought that kids were picked on for mainly physical abnormalities such as being overweight, wearing glasses, or being exceptionally smart. Though some children with these characteristics will be bullied, the majority are not. Researchers now know that the traits that make a child more likely to be bullied center on his emotional and social vulnerabilities, not his physical attributes.

 Essential

The good news is that you and your child can do many things to improve his confidence and social skills. There are exercises and activities that can increase your child's self-esteem and self-control. In Chapter 13, you will learn specifics on how to bully proof your child, and Chapter 14 will provide you with strategies for teaching your child social and assertiveness skills.

Things like being cautious, sensitive, or socially isolated can up your child's chances of being bullied. Lacking appropriate social boundaries, being emotionally oversensitive, radiating low self-confidence, refusing to defend oneself, not having a good sense of humor, being uncomfortable in group settings, behaving in a submissive manner, and preferring to be alone can all catch the attention of the schoolyard bully. The bully is looking for a passive, easy target and those kids who fit the vulnerable profile will be the first to be picked on.

How to Respond (Dos and Don'ts)

It doesn't matter whether your child comes to you and tells you she's being picked on, called names, has been physically assaulted, or if she confesses to being bullied only after you directly question her, how you react is going to have a significant impact on how your child thinks and feels about what is happening to her.

Do:

- **Thank her for telling you.** "I'm so glad you trusted me enough to tell me. I really want to help you."
- **Be a good listener.** Stay calm and listen to what she has to say without interrupting. Encourage her to tell you everything she's thinking and feeling.
- **Let her know that it's not her fault.** "This is not your fault. You did nothing to deserve this, and I want you to understand that I will help you put a stop to it."
- **Validate her right to physical and emotional safety.** "You have the right to feel safe at school."
- **Validate her feelings.** "You must be feeling sad and scared. I remember how being treated that way hurt when I was a kid."
- **Tell her you love her.** It sounds trite, but kids really want and need to hear their parents say that they love them.
- **Share your experiences.** "When I was in the fifth grade, I was bullied by a boy named Doug." Telling your child that you were a victim or a bystander can help her feel that she's not alone. You can share the details of how you got through it.
- **Ask her what would make her feel safe.** Be prepared for her to say, "I want to stay home with you." If that's an option for a day or two, consider it. It might give the two of you a chance to really talk about the problem. If staying home isn't an option, brainstorm ways your child might feel safer (e.g., driving her to school instead of taking the bus, opting out of gym class until you can meet with the gym teacher, going with you to meet with her teacher).

- **Tell the school.** Meet with her teacher and the school principal. Find out what anti-bully interventions and education are in place. Discuss what actions will be taken to ensure your child's physical and emotional safety. Be sure to follow up to be sure the decided-upon actions are being implemented.
- **Keep the lines of communication open.** Have a daily or weekly check-in with your child to discuss how the day or week went in terms of the bullying problem. Encourage your child to discuss her feelings.

What Not to Do

Once you discover that your child is being bullied, the last thing you want is for your child to clam up and refuse to speak with you about what she is going through. If you follow the list of "dos" you should be okay, but here are a few "don't" suggestions for keeping the situation moving in a positive direction.

Don't:

- **Don't ignore it.** Ignoring it won't make it go away. You may be uncomfortable dealing with the situation due to some old bully trauma of your own; if that is the case, get your child to a counselor or schedule a meeting with the school's guidance counselor to get your child the help and support she needs.
- **Don't tell your child to tough it out, ignore it, avoid the bully, or fight back (she might get hurt).** Your child needs your help and your intervention; she doesn't need to be brushed off or to have her pain and humiliation devalued.
- **Don't talk to the parents of the bully.** Unless you know the parents well and are sure they would respond in a constructive manner, it's best to let the school deal with the parents of the bully.
- **Don't accuse the teacher of failing to do her job.** She may not have seen the bullying or realize the seriousness of the situation. Initially, she may be defensive because she may think you are questioning her adequacy as a teacher or her level

of supervision. Give her the benefit of the doubt and keep an open mind by working together with her to protect your child.

Steps to Take if Your Child Is Being Bullied

When confronted with the heartbreaking realization that your child is being bullied, parents often realize that they have no real concrete and constructive idea of how to handle the situation. Parents who fear they will make the situation worse often become paralyzed with indecision and wind up doing nothing. But doing nothing is probably the worst thing you could do for your child. Below, find a step-by-step action plan to help you and your child.

Don't Wait
The first time your child mentions that she's being bullied, or the first time you suspect it, take action. The longer you wait, the worse it usually gets. Talk with your child, and keep talking with her. Be sure you understand all the details of her situation, and be certain she understands that you will do everything in your power to help her.

Work as a Team
Consulting your child and getting her input about what decisions will be made and what actions are to be taken throughout the process will help empower your child. This doesn't mean that she has to agree with all of your decisions (your primary job is to keep her safe), but she does need to be informed.

Assess Her Immediate Safety
If she is being physically attacked, you will need to intervene right away. This might entail staying out of school until a meeting can be arranged with the teacher and/or principal. Tip: Telling school officials that your child won't be returning to school until the matter is resolved can speed up the process. Help her remain safe; put safeguards in place to ensure she isn't in a situation where bullying can occur. Point out the safe places and people your child can go to if she's being bullied.

Assess Your Own Level of Competence

Some parents may not feel comfortable advocating in an objective and firm manner for their children. Do you have emotional baggage from your own childhood school experiences? Are you uncomfortable around authority figures? If so, it might be wise for your spouse or another close relative to speak up on your child's behalf.

Demand Action

Don't be put off with a let's-wait-and-see-what-happens attitude. Ask that specific actions be taken to protect your child. These actions may vary depending upon individual school policy. For mild bullying, the principal having a talk with the bully might suffice. In moderate or severe cases, moving the bully (or your child, if you prefer) to another classroom might be necessary. Be sure to keep a written record of the incidents and who was involved. This information can come in handy if the bullying intensifies and you need to take legal action.

Get Involved

Ask the teacher if you can schedule some time to volunteer in your child's classroom. Witnessing firsthand the interactions between your child and her peers can be helpful as you move forward. Invite a friend or two from your child's class to a play date. Plan something fun. Hopefully, this can help build your child's network of friends. The more friends a child has, the less likely she is to be bullied.

Suggest an Anti-Bullying Program

If you discover that your child's school does not have an anti-bullying program for the teachers and students, approach the PTA or PTO about organizing one soon. If that can't be arranged, try to find a professional with experience in bullying who would agree to come into your child's classroom to present a workshop on bullying. (See Appendix C for a list of national anti-bullying programs.)

Keep on Top of It

Once a child has been bullied, her chances of future bullying increase. Schedule regular phone calls to your child's teacher to assess how your child is coping. Keep volunteering, and offer to cover playground and lunch room duty on occasion. Invite your child's friends over to play whenever possible. And don't get too busy to really listen to what your child has to say.

Parents can sometimes hesitate to make waves with teachers, administrators, or the school system. This is part of the reason bullying continues to thrive in schools. If every parent with a child who was being bullied made waves and insisted on action and accountability, bullying would be far less common. You know the old saying the squeaky wheel gets the grease; well, it's true. If your child is being bullied, speak up! And keep speaking up until your child gets the attention and protection she deserves. No child should feel unsafe at school.

Alert!

Researchers suspect that a fair percentage of teen suicides are attributable to harassment by peers and vicious bullying. This phenomenon now has its own label: bullycide. Today, research is being done to determine how many suicide cases are attributed specifically to bullying.

In some cases (but certainly not all), extreme action may become necessary. Consider an intervention timeline along these lines:

Empower your child to solve the problem. If she is unsuccessful, meet with your child's teacher. If you and the teacher are unable to stop the problem, meet with the principal. If your child is still being bullied after the principal intervenes, meet with the school board and the superintendent. If after meeting with all school officials your child is still being targeted, report it to the police and retain a lawyer. If threat of legal action and bad publicity don't result in the kind of action necessary to protect your child, it's time for drastic measures. After all, your child's health and safety are your number one concern. If the problem still persists and your child agrees, change schools or move to a new school system. If that doesn't work, consider home schooling.

Bullying is peer-on-peer abuse, and you have to be willing to take it as far as you need to take it in order to protect your child. Abuse is abuse; just because it is abuse perpetrated between children doesn't make it less harmful. If your child was being sexually abused, how far would you go to protect your child? The answer is probably, "As far as it takes." Bullying is physical, emotional, and educational abuse and it shouldn't be ignored.

CHAPTER 10

The Consequences of Bullying

The consequences of bullying are far reaching, and they affect everyone involved. Some bullied kids suffer short-term (anxiety and fear) and long-term negative effects (depression, low self-esteem, and compromised educational and employment opportunities). Some children who bully also suffer from short- (maladaptive social interactions) and long-term problems (increased criminality, dysfunctional relationships, and alcohol and substance abuse). Let's take a look at the impact bullying has on a child.

Physical

When there is something unusual or different happening in the life of a child, it usually shows up as a physical red flag. For example, a child who experiences a death in the family might have insomnia, bed wetting, or night terrors. A child who has parents going through a divorce might have stomach aches and headaches that send him to the school nurse every day. Bullying causes great physical stress on a child; it sends his nervous system into a constant flight-or-flight state. If your child is being bullied, his mind senses the acute threat and sends his body into overdrive. He may experience:

- Sharpened senses
- Dilated pupils

- Increased heart rate
- Increased respiration rate
- Increased metabolism (for increased energy)
- Kidney and digestive systems temporarily shut down
- Sweat glands open to cool his overworked system
- Endorphins are released (the body's natural pain relievers)
- Normal judgment is impaired and primitive responses take over

Historically, the fight-or-flight response was necessary for survival. If the body wasn't instantly prepared to either stand and fight or flee the enemy, death might result. Today, the stakes aren't nearly so high, yet the body still activates the state of hyper arousal to even a low-level threat. Unfortunately, this can take a toll on your child's body. Continued stress with prolonged arousal can compromise a child's immune system and leave him vulnerable to infection by bacteria and viruses.

Continued stress can also cause:

- Loss of or increase in appetite
- Sleep disorders (insomnia, nightmares, night terrors, bed wetting)
- Psychosomatic illness (stress can literally be expressed as phantom pain or illness)
- Stress-induced headaches and stomach aches
- Skin disorders
- Nervous habits (nail biting, knuckle cracking, pulling out hair) and/or tics
- Psychological problems (anxiety, depression, post-traumatic stress disorder)

Chronically bullied kids don't look or behave the same as normal children. When a child is hurting, it affects his entire being. It is reflected in his eyes, expression, tone of voice, posture, and overall attitude. Add in the physical injuries they may sustain (cuts, scratches, bruises, black eyes, bloody lips, etc), and victims are fairly easy to identify.

Emotional

The emotional effects of bullying are the most difficult to see and can often be the longest lasting. When a child is bullied and suffers from chronic stress, he becomes unable to relax and can eventually suffer from emotional burnout. This means your child internalizes his anger and sadness and, over time, becomes increasingly socially dysfunctional and isolated from his peers. The more isolated he becomes, the greater chance of the bullying continuing and even intensifying.

 Fact

According to a 2007 report in *Science Daily,* researchers from Penn State confirmed that children exposed to one-time bullying episodes might experience a spike in cortisol (the stress hormone) levels, whereas chronic exposure to bullying is associated with hypocortisol (lower than normal levels). Hypocortisol can have a numbing effect that might make a child more likely to take his own life or strike out against others.

Bullied kids experience inner turmoil and emotional angst on a daily basis. Try to put yourself in a bullied child's shoes. Imagine that every day you must go to a place where everyone picks on you, is mean to you, and says and does hurtful and humiliating things to you. Imagine that you have no control over it and that it makes you feel like a colossal failure every single day. School is, in essence, a child's job; imagine having to go to work every day knowing that you are failing at your job, that you aren't wanted, and that people want you to quit. It sounds downright awful, doesn't it? It's no wonder bullied kids suffer from these emotional aftereffects:

- Moody, sullen, and withdrawn
- Depressed, distressed, and irritable

- Unexplained explosive outbursts
- Acting in a way that is different from his normal behavior
- Overly emotional, anxious, sad, or secretive
- Verbally beats himself up ("I'm an idiot." "I'm a loser." "I suck.")
- Suddenly obsessed with personal safety issues
- Shows warning signs of suicide (talking about death, saying he wishes he were dead, giving away his possessions, not caring about anything, or a sudden change to cheerful, which could mean he has made the decision to end his life and is happy about it)

Over time, these emotional effects of bullying can impede a child's normal emotional development. A child can become unable to establish and maintain appropriate social and interpersonal relationships with his peers. He may develop full-blown depression or an anxiety disorder.

Children tend to blame themselves when they have been bullied. When a child succumbs to self-blame, it can lead to decreased self-esteem and confidence, which will eventually lead to a loss of self-worth. Once a child feels helpless and hopeless, he may turn to suicide as a way out. Parents need to be aware of the progression of this emotional down cycle; it can be prevented with the proper support and intervention.

Educational

There are numerous ways bullying impacts a child's educational opportunities. When a child is being bullied, we know that the majority of his physical and emotional strength is diverted into surviving each day. A bullied child is on hyper alert and is doing everything he can to manage his emotions, avoid the bully, and get home safely. That is his main concern. Unfortunately, this leaves very little time or attention for his studies.

As his grades drop, his parents and the teacher start to pressure him to do better and the stress a bullied child is under increases even further. Eventually, something has to give, and it's usually the academics. A bullied child can't concentrate in class, he doesn't want to participate in class, and he certainly doesn't want to participate in after-school activities—he wants to be invisible. In extreme cases, academic failure can result. How sad that one bully can jeopardize a child's future educational and employment opportunities. Because if a child can't achieve his potential, he misses out on educational opportunities that may lead to further education that then leads to a better job or further advancement in his chosen field.

 **Alert!**

If your child seems sad, depressed, withdrawn, or upset encourage him to open up and talk. Ask him specific questions about how he's feeling, and tell him you love him and are concerned that he might try to hurt himself. If you are worried he is thinking about suicide, call 1-800-273-TALK (8255) to find a crisis center in your area.

Short-Term Effects of Being Bullied

The short-term effects of being bullied can vary from child to child. In the short term, many bullied children experience:

- **Anger**—"Stop picking on me!"
- **Frustration**—"Why are they picking on me?" "Why can't I get this to stop?"
- **Anxiety**—"I'm so afraid of what will happen today."
- **Learned helplessness**—"I wish I could stop them, but I can't, so I won't even try."
- **Depression**—"I hate school. I hate life. I hate me."

Being bullied is very stressful for kids. It is stressful for everyone. Can you recall a time when you were bullied as a child? Maybe it's a vivid recollection of so-called friends giggling and snickering behind your back or the memory of hunger pangs and wounded pride as you handed over your lunch money each day. Sadly, many of you may have witnessed (and perhaps been victim to) the more physical type of bullying: tripping on the school bus, shoving on the playground, and sucker punches that led to blackened eyes or bloody noses.

Even if you weren't bullied as a child, there is a good chance you may have been on the receiving end of adult bullying. Many adults can tell incredible stories of having a bully for a boss, neighbor, or spouse. The difference between being an adult victim and being a child victim is that a child has no opportunity to extricate himself from the situation. A grownup can quit his job, move to another neighborhood, or get a divorce. A child is stuck going to the same school day after day, year after year. A child is powerless to change his situation without the help of those who love and care for him.

Going to school becomes all about logistics for a bullied child. He will plan and strategize how to avoid running into the bully. He will risk being late to class, he will skip eating lunch to avoid being a public target, and he will wait until he arrives home to use the bathroom. A bullied child can suffer severe physical problems from engaging in these types of behaviors. He can become nutritionally deficient from not eating or suffer from bladder and kidney infections from holding in the urge to urinate.

A bullied child will endure constant levels of anxiety that can, over time, wear down his immune system. He will be sick more often and miss more school than his nonbullied peers. And a bullied child cares less and less about his studies as the bullying wears on. He becomes so emotionally and psychologically caught up in avoiding and enduring the bullying, that he can no longer function properly in the classroom; he can't concentrate and he loses interest in his studies. Once the bullied child's academic performance is compromised, it adds even more tension and stress to his already-overworked nervous system. The failures add up and the bullied child can become severely depressed and experience suicidal thoughts and feelings. Escape can seem like the best (or only) option. Also dangerous is when a child's depression is mixed with anger and revenge fantasies. This can lead to an even greater trag-edy—like the one seen at Columbine High School.

Long-Term Effects of Being Bullied

The long-term consequences of being a victim also vary greatly from person to person. Most victims of bullying, who have the proper support systems, will survive the experience and go on to lead normal and productive lives. Others may not fare quite so well. Research has shown that it is not necessary to be physically harmed to suffer lasting damage. Black eyes and broken arms hurt, but only temporarily. The physical wounds will heal; it's far more difficult to heal the damage that can be done from years of emotional and psychological abuse. Repeatedly being told that you are worthless, incompetent, and a loser can take its toll, until one day you internalize it and believe that you are a worthless, incompetent loser.

Once a child believes that he is a loser, he will begin to self-sabotage. He will no longer try to change his situation for the better. It's a phenomenon called "learned helplessness." Learned helplessness is a psychological term that means once a child has come to believe that nothing he does will change his situation (even if it isn't true), he will no longer try. He has learned that he is helpless and will simply accept his fate. Learned helplessness can lead to hopelessness, depression, and in some cases, suicide.

Being labeled an outcast and an outsider can shake the confidence of even the most self-assured youngster. And that's because much of what passes as confidence and self-assurance is actually a reflection of the positive reinforcement he receives. When people around him reinforce his belief that he is a good, worthy, and desirable person, he believes it. On the other hand, if people are telling him that he is stupid, cowardly, and no good; eventually he will believe that.

Long-term shortfalls of self-esteem can cause deficits in every area of a child's life. And long-term isolation and lack of positive peer interaction can cause difficulties in establishing and maintaining healthy adult intimate relationships.

Alert!

Some common long-term effects victims of bullying may experience include chronic low self-esteem, difficulty with interpersonal relationships, avoidance of social interactions and new or unfamiliar situations, difficulty trusting people, reduced occupational opportunities, residual feelings of anger and bitterness, or continued bullying and victimization.

How Parents Can Help

If your child is being bullied, the most important thing you can do is provide a place where your child can receive all the unconditional love and support she needs. Studies have shown that kids can withstand and weather even cases of moderate to severe bullying if they have a strong support system at home. This might mean that you have to be there for your child more than the average parent, but if it can temper the effects of bullying on your child's emotional, psychological, and physical health, it is worth it. When a child can say, "My family loves me. My family thinks I'm special," it can negate the effects of the bully sending a message of, "Nobody likes you. You are worthless."

A second way to help is to encourage and foster your child's friendships. Having friends to confide in, and receiving support and advice from peers, tends to lessen the impact of bullying. Even one good friend can significantly decrease the negative effects of bullying. If the bully doesn't succeed in permanently harming your child's self-esteem and sense of self-worth, then relatively little lasting harm can be done.

CHAPTER 11

Boy Bullies

"Snakes and snails and puppy dog tails, that's what little boys are made of." Well, that old saying couldn't be more wrong. Little boys are made of all the same things little girls are made of—with perhaps a dash more testosterone thrown in for good measure. Little boys are kind and sweet, honest and helpful, smart and strong. Little boys are wonderful . . . until one becomes a bully. And then a bully boy might very well be made of snakes and snails and puppy dog tails—or at least a little spite and meanness.

The Boys-Will-Be-Boys Myth

Digging in the dirt, roughhousing with the neighbor's dog, and playing tackle football in the backyard are all traditional boy behaviors. Rough and tumble is accepted, even expected of American boys. Boys are supposed to be tough and they are supposed to be tough on each other. Most young boys spend a great deal of time trying to figure out the rules of masculinity and how to live up to them. But the masculinity bar is set high; far too high for most boys.

American boys see ultramasculine superheroes like Batman, Superman, and Spiderman, and they envy the strength, power, and courage they possess. Many boys worship these mock mortals and desperately wish they could grow up to be just like them. The reason is simple: Superheroes have already proven their masculinity. They are real men; only they aren't. But boys don't get the message that Superman is not human, he's from the planet Krypton, or that Peter Parker (who in his prespider life was an unpopular nerd) was bitten by a radioactive spider, which gave him superhuman spider-like powers. Which leaves Batman as the only superhero who does not have superpowers. What Batman (a.k.a. Bruce Wayne) does have is intelligence, resourcefulness, insight, and years of extensive and grueling training to make up for a lack of superhuman powers. That Batman sure does set the masculinity bar exceedingly high.

 Essential

The book *What Stories Does My Son Need? A Guide to Books and Movies that Build Character in Boys* by Michael Gurian focuses on the role stories and movies play in shaping boys' characters and in teaching moral lessons. He identifies and summarizes 100 movies and 100 books. Gurian includes questions for parents to ask when discussing these books and movies with their sons.

Even nonsuperhero role models can be intimidating. Everyone from muscle-bound professional athletes to perfect male-specimen action-adventure TV and movie heroes can make the path to masculinity seem unattainable. The media gives young boys the impression that in order to be accepted and successful, they must be tough, strong, and invincible. This is a real shame, since the actual qualities that are valued most in males are caring, compassion, the ability to provide for himself and his family, and solid inner strength; not brute strength or the ability to scale tall buildings in a single bound.

From a very young age, boys do seem to be more physically active and focused on developing dominant skills, while girls practice and hone their intimate skills. But is this nature or nurture at work? Are boys and girls born different or are they simply socialized to behave differently? The jury is still out on the exact interaction between biology and environment, but it is known that the variation within a sex group (such as males) is far more variable than the difference between sex groups. Meaning, the variance in human males runs the gamut from very feminine males to very masculine males. Same goes for females: they range from very masculine females to very feminine females. This is why it is important to foster your child's individual growth and development instead of simply expecting your child to reflect the appropriate gender stereotype.

The boys-will-be-boys stereotype is particularly damaging to boys who don't fit the traditional mold. Those boys realize they are far from the ideal male stereotype, and for them it can have serious consequences for their fledgling identities and self-esteem. For parents, it is a hurdle to raise a boy who can see men as three-dimensional figures instead of one-dimensional cardboard-cutout action figures. Boys need to understand from a young age that stereotypes are just that—type casting. Just because a stereotype exists doesn't mean he needs to buy into it. Boys need to be taught to be caring and compassionate, that it's okay to express emotions, and that they don't need to be tough guys to be masculine.

When a boy internalizes the tough-guy persona and strives to live up to it, there is a distinct danger that he will become a bully. The pressure to act like a man might prompt an otherwise passive boy to act out and bully a peer. But the real trouble starts when the bully boy is rewarded for his toughness with laughter and admiration from his classmates. The bully boy realizes that acting like a man is making other kids see him as more masculine, and he likes the feeling. The shame of it is that acting like a man in a child's mind is usually akin to exaggerated tough-guy behavior. The distinction between being a protector (typically male behavior) or an aggressor (typically bully behavior) gets blurred.

Adults excuse a large percentage of bullying behavior with a sigh and a shrug and a boys-will-be-boys attitude. Society has set a dangerous and destructive stage for young boys by placing that boys-will-be-boys stereotype on aggressive behavior. And what does that say about boys who choose not to act aggressively? That they are not masculine? Of course, an adult realizes that line of reasoning is ridiculous, but does a boy? Probably not. So until society changes (and don't hold your breath), teach your child how to recognize and confront aggressive impulses, allow him to display emotion and inner turmoil, and help him see through damaging macho stereotypes.

Excusing a boy's excessively aggressive behavior with the boys-will-be-boys ideology may prompt more aggressive behavior, not less. Furthermore, when a child is socialized to believe that his aggressive tendencies are predominantly or entirely innate or biological, he will believe that he doesn't have the power to control them. That is false.

The Danger of Stereotypes

Gender stereotypes begin the day a child is born. The family and friends flood the hospital room and exclaim, "Look at that big, strapping boy!" "What an adorable little linebacker." "He's a handsome little devil" or "Oh . . . she's so sweet and dainty." "Look at her delicate little hands." "What a precious little angel." The comments are immediately gender stereotyped, and will set each child up to be viewed as belonging to a certain set of characteristics and to follow the gender guidelines established by society long ago. Girls are expected to be pretty, nurturing, and kind; boys are expected to be confident, capable, and strong.

To prove just how influential gender stereotypes are, researchers dressed a group of male babies in pink and handed them to adults who were told they were girls. The adults referred to the "girl" babies as sweet, cuddly, cute, etc. And when adults were given girl babies dressed in blue, the adults called them slugger, tough, strong, etc. It's easy to see how subconscious and entrenched these age-old stereotypes are. Be mindful of your own expectations and tendencies to reinforce stereotypes. Here are a few dos and don'ts to keep in mind:

- ❏ Do keep your behavioral expectations the same for boys and girls.
- ❏ Do snuggle, color, and read with your boys and wrestle, roughhouse, and play video games with your girls.

- ❑ Do encourage nurturing and compassionate behavior in both boys and girls.
- ❑ Do encourage assertive and confident behavior in both boys and girls.
- ❑ Do limit the media and its stereotypical gender images in your home.
- ❑ Do love your child regardless of where he or she fits on the gender scale.
- ❑ Don't view aggression as more acceptable for boys than for girls.
- ❑ Don't ignore aggressive or violent behavior in either girls or boys.
- ❑ Don't forget to praise your child for positive social behavior, regardless of whether it's considered stereotypically masculine or feminine.
- ❑ Don't force your child to display stereotypical masculine or feminine behavior. If your son wants to play house, let him. If your daughter likes to hunt for frogs in the mud pond, be all for it. And conversely, if your son is obsessed with trucks and trains and your daughter wants to wear a pink, sequined princess dress every day of her young life, that's fine, too.
- ❑ Don't impose your stereotypes on your child. You may have been captain of the football team, but your son may prefer music or the arts. Respect your child's individuality.

Physical Aggression

What is physical aggression? *Merriam Webster's Collegiate Dictionary* defines it as "a forceful action or procedure (as an unprovoked attack) esp. when intended to dominate or master." As you see from this definition, aggression isn't synonymous with violence, which is defined as, "exertion of physical force so as to injure or abuse (as in effecting illegal entry into a house)." Violence includes the intent to injure or abuse, aggression does not. Aggressive impulses are the urge to dominate and control, not necessarily to hurt. This is an important distinction to make as you observe young boys at play.

 Fact

Social learning theory has been the basis for many mentoring programs like the Big Brothers Big Sisters program. The idea is that when you pair a child with an older child or adult, the child will observe, learn, and model his behavior after the positive behavior of the adult. Some bully prevention programs have begun to adopt similar mentor-type strategies.

An active boy is not always an aggressive boy. If you watch boys playing you can easily see that many boys like to run, jump, and roughhouse. Boys like physical play; they like to move their bodies and burn off excess energy. They will chase each other, kick balls, and play tag until they are exhausted. This is normal—scientists know that boys are predisposed to higher levels of activity. This is a direct result of being exposed to androgens (male hormones) before birth.

So what accounts for the way some boys will turn straws into guns, juice boxes into bombs, and sticks into light sabers? How they will fight and kill the bad guy and go looking for more bad guys? How they worry their parents with talk of shooting, stabbing, and cutting the head off their enemy? Researchers aren't sure, but what they do know is that boys in all cultures roughhouse, mock fight, and are drawn to play that centers around the themes of power and domination. But that play doesn't often translate into real-life violence. All human beings have normal aggressive impulses and the potential for violence, only a small percentage have chronic difficulty controlling them.

As a young boy sees it, when he is killing the bad guy he's not engaging in socially unacceptable behavior, he's simply protecting the people he loves and making the world a better place. This type of play is helpful and can give a young boy the chance to work out his aggressive tendencies in a socially acceptable manner. He is learning to control and channel his impulses through his fantasy play. Intervention is necessary only if another child at play is injured or afraid. Otherwise, pretend aggressive play can be a healthy emotional outlet for young children.

 Essential

For more information on gender-based male stereotypes, read *Real Boys: Rescuing Our Sons from the Myths of Boyhood,* written by William Pollack; *Boys Adrift: The Five Factors Driving the Growing Epidemic of Unmotivated Boys and Underachieving Young Men,* by Leonard Sax; or *Raising Cain: Protecting the Emotional Life of Boys,* by Dan Kindlon and Michael Thompson.

Here is how you can support your son's active impulses and channel aggression through positive, proactive channels:

- **Allow some fantasy.** If your son wants to pretend he is a superhero and uses violent imagery to kill the bad guys and crush the enemy, don't try to prevent it. Remember, it is play acting, not reality. If your son can defeat the bad guys in his mind, he will feel more powerful and be less likely to act it out for real.
- **Encourage active play.** Let him run around and engage in physical and competitive play. Just be sure to monitor closely to be sure no one is being treated in an aggressive or unfair manner.
- **Limit the amount of screen time.** Set limits on the amount of television, computer, and video-game viewing. Boys need activity; get him outside to play, and make sure the television he watches, the computer he navigates, and the video games he plays are all supervised and age appropriate.
- **Foster your son's interests.** If he's a huge Batman fan, let him run with it. Whatever it is that he likes (trucks, baseball, bugs,

or even Barbie dolls), show an interest and you will teach your son that you value his interests because you value him.

- **Keep the lines of communication open.** Boys want and need to talk to their parents just as much as girls. If your boy has a tough time opening up, try talking while engaged in another activity like building a model airplane or a playing a video game.

- **Model appropriate behavior.** You are your son's first teacher and a powerful and influential role model. Model constructive and socially acceptable ways to handle frustration and aggression and your child will learn from it and do the same.

Boys Bullying Girls

The boys bullying girls phenomenon has confused researchers and scientists for years. Boys bullying other boys makes perfect sense to most individuals because the survival of the fittest and king of the hill mentalities have always existed in schoolyards and in adult life. Boys competing with boys to be the biggest, fastest, or best is an age-old dynamic. Society expects boys to be competitive, and because of that need for social dominance, society has tolerated the idea that the strong will do whatever it takes to survive and the weak will not.

But boys already have dominance (mainly physical dominance) over females. Boys are generally bigger, stronger, and faster than girls. So why do boys bully both boys and girls? Simply because they can seems to be the standard answer. A bully always seeks a victim who is less powerful, less strong, and less able to defend themselves than the bully. The bully wants a victim who won't fight back, who will quietly acquiesce, and one who will cower with fear. So when picking a victim, a boy bully will target either a quiet boy who lacks confidence or a girl. In the bully's mind he will be successful either way.

In essence, the bully acts in direct conflict with the greater society. Society values protecting those who are weak, not exploiting them; but a bully has contempt for all who are weaker than himself, therefore he makes no distinction between the sexes. For a younger child, the bullying takes traditional forms and the boy bully will push and shove and verbally abuse a girl. As he gets older and hits puberty, the bullying and harassment can take on sexual undertones. The bullying may become sexual bullying and entail rude and crude verbal taunts and unwanted physical advances.

 Fact

Sexual bullying affects both genders and can be defined as repeated harmful or humiliating actions that target a person's sexuality. This can include name calling; crude comments about appearance, attractiveness, or sexual development; uninvited touching; sexual propositioning; pornographic material; sexually graphic graffiti; and in extreme cases, sexual assault.

Why Boys Bully Other Boys

It has been established that boys bully other boys mainly for reasons related to power and control. A bully wants to mark his territory and make it known that he's the top dog in the classroom, in the grade level, or at the school. Power and domination are common themes in the pretend play of young children, and most young kids leave it in their pretend play world. But some kids, the ones who become bullies, never seem to resolve this urge for power and domination. It might be because they feel powerless in an abusive home, they feel angry at being challenged in some way by life, or they may simply enjoy being the king of the hill.

How Parents Can Help

It can be summed up in three words: love your boys. Don't expect your three-year-old to suck it up when he falls down and scrapes his knee. Kneel down, hug him, and give his boo-boo a kiss, just like you would do for his sister. Don't tell your six-year-old to toughen up or call him a mamma's boy when he strikes out at t-ball and cries. Give him a few minutes to compose himself, give him a hug, and remind him how proud you are that he did his best. And don't expect your ten- or twelve- or fourteen-year-old to act like a man. He's not a man, he's a boy; and boys need your love, acceptance, and support. Pushing a child to behave in ways that deny his feelings, emotions, and inner struggle to love and be loved will inadvertently create a hostile and overly aggressive child.

Researchers know that many boys who bully are mistreated and abused by their parents, other authority figures, or their peers. It makes sense when you examine and understand the developmental process. Kids model their behavior after the important people in their lives. So don't let your child learn how to use aggression and violence to hurt others. Instead, help him develop his full potential to grow into a caring, compassionate, and confident young man.

CHAPTER 12

Girl Bullies

The word "bully" conjures up the mental picture of a brawny boy with a deep voice and a premature five o'clock shadow. This bully knocks kids into lockers, shoves his way to the front of the lunch line, and commandeers the homework of a bespectacled underclassman. He's big, he's strong, and he's incredibly intimidating. Now imagine a girl bully. What does she look like? It might surprise you to discover that she probably looks and behaves like Regina George, the leader of the "plastics" clique in the movie *Mean Girls*.

Verbal Bullying

In Chapter 2, the old adage sticks and stones may break my bones, but names can never hurt me was mentioned as being false. Specifically, and in regard to girl bullying, this saying is exactly backward. Cuts and bruises heal, but internal, emotional scars from being called "fat," "lard***," "ugly," "cow," "horse face," "slut," "whore," "filthy skank," and so on reverberate in the minds and memories of girls and women everywhere. Verbal insults and vicious taunts are hard to forget. And being called cruel and hurtful names can affect a young girl's fragile and developing self-esteem. Being called horse face would make even a pretty girl question her attractiveness, and being labeled a slut can impact the quality of her intimate relationships.

Verbal bullying starts at a very young age and is popular with both boys and girls, but somehow girls seem to hone and perfect the skill. This isn't surprising, considering the advanced verbal skills that girls possess in comparison to boys. Physical aggression and bullying are more common than verbal bullying in the early years because young children have less developed social skills. When you are three-years-old, it is easier to strike out physically than to craft a clever and insulting verbal barb. Verbal aggression and bullying become more prevalent as girls begin to develop their verbal skills.

 Essential

Odd Girl Out: The Hidden Culture of Aggression in Girls, written by Rachel Simmons, skewers the notion that girls are the kinder, gentler sex. In her book, Simmons examines the dangerous repression that girls face from a society that expects them to be sweet and docile, which can, in turn, cause a "hidden culture of silent and indirect aggression."

Eventually, as a girl's verbal development progresses, indirect bullying (otherwise known as relational aggression) increases. This increase can be a direct result of enhanced verbal and social skills, but it might also be that girls recognize that relational aggression (gossiping, excluding, and rejecting) results in a higher likelihood of success and a lower likelihood of getting caught and getting in trouble. Why bother calling a girl a derogatory name when you can work behind the scenes to destroy her reputation and know that by doing it this way, you won't be caught.

Research shows that girls progress through certain developmental stages faster than boys because of their relatively more advanced social and verbal skills. And it is, in fact, true that the level of relational aggression escalates as girls get older and verbal and social skills mature. Let's take a quick look at the three types of relational aggression girls use against each other:

- **Social bullying**—This is when a girl is humiliated or demeaned in front of her peers. A target of social bullying may hear insults and put-downs as she walks down the hall, or the other girls at the lunch table suddenly spread out and claim there is no more room. These actions are harmful and hurtful because tweens and teens are desperate to fit in.

- **Relational bullying**—When one girl intentionally damages the social status of another girl, it's called relational aggression. Girls are social creatures who want and need to have friends. A relational bully will do everything in her power to undermine this. She will tell other kids to shun the target, spread untrue vicious rumors about her, give her the silent treatment, and treat her like a social outcast. This is particularly devastating to a young girl's self-esteem because making and developing friendships is an important tween and teen developmental task. Relational bullying is difficult to detect because it's subtle and sophisticated, and it's often done out of earshot of the adults.

- **Emotional bullying**—This is when a girl uses manipulation to get what she wants. She might say things like, "You can't be my friend if you don't sit with me on the bus." "You can't be friends with me and Sally. You have to tell Sally you won't be her friend." The emotional bully demands exclusivity from her target and will use emotional blackmail to continue to control her.

 Fact

Read *Queen Bees and Wannabes: Helping Your Daughter Survive Cliques, Gossip, Boyfriends, and Other Realities of Adolescence* by Rosalind Wiseman. It focuses on adolescent girls, but with cliques forming at younger and younger ages and girls bullying and being bullied as early as preschool, it's a book worth reading.

Bully girls gossip, tease, taunt, reject, exclude, shun, and form mean-girl cliques. They can make other girls' lives so unpleasant that, years later, when they are adults, they can easily recall every horrible detail. If you recall from Chapter 2, this type of female bullying is specifically called relational aggression. Relational aggression is when girls use relationships instead of fists to hurt and humiliate each other. They use words and social exclusion to inflict wounds as painful and deep as a razor blade.

When Girls Get Violent

Are American girls getting more violent? It seems so when you read the headlines about six Florida teens videotaping the half-hour long beating of a classmate or the story about the ten- and eleven-year-old Pennsylvania girls who allegedly dragged a ten-year-old classmate off the monkey bars and stomped repeatedly on her head and legs. What has changed? According to a 2006 Federal Bureau of Investigation report, between 1980 and 2005, arrests of girls increased nationwide, while arrests of boys decreased. An increase in girls being arrested, along with high-profile cases of violent female behavior, has prompted many recent sensational media headlines.

But do these arrests signify a real change in girls' behaviors, or are they attributed to something else? Could the increases reflect changes in public tolerance and stricter law-enforcement policies? The National Crime Victimization Survey, in contrast to FBI arrest statistics, shows very little change in the gender gap for assault crimes and the Violent Crime Index over the past two decades. And reports conducted by the Centers for Disease Control and Prevention show that between 1991 and 2001, the number of girls getting into fights showed a 30 percent decline.

Regardless of which statistic is, in fact, a correct reflection of the status of girls' rates of violence, there seems to be no question among researchers that the level of violence has escalated. The exact cause of this remains unknown, although there are several hypotheses.

"Girl power" has been a significant theme in the past decade or so. From the popular kindergarten cartoon *Powerpuff Girls* to teenage cartoon crime fighter *Kim Possible* to *Buffy the Vampire Slayer* to *Alias*'s butt-kicking spy Sydney Bristow. These popular role models make violence and aggression acceptable in an otherwise physically tame female world. But regardless of the way the media portray women, we still can't discount the role biology and socialization has on female behavior. And realistically, the increase in female violence may in actuality be the byproduct of a more technologically connected world.

When beatings can be recorded with a cell phone and posted online, they gain widespread publicity. When the actions of girls can be detailed in online slam books or on MySpace pages, the information is out there for all to see. In the past, violent behavior by girls may have been downplayed or underreported. It was unacceptable for girls to be aggressive and violent; therefore, the incidents that did occur may have been handled quietly and swept under the carpet. Today they are posted online for millions to see.

So are girls really more violent today than they were decades ago or are we just shining a light on the behavior for the first time? The problem lies in that researchers are uncertain whether or not there actually is an increase in girl violence or whether society is just responding differently to it when it occurs. Although more information and analysis is needed, the U.S. Department of Justice suggests that girls' violence occurs in the following situations, for the following reasons:

- **Peer violence.** Girls fight with other girls to gain status (such as in the quest to become more popular or better respected), to defend their sexual reputation (if another girl insults or spreads rumors about a girl, she may physically retaliate), and in self-defense against sexual harassment (a girl may physically attack a boy who is sexually harassing her).
- **Family violence.** Researchers have discovered that girls fight more frequently at home with parents than boys do. Girls' violence against parents is multidimensional. For some girls, the violence represents striking back against what they view

as an overly controlling structure (e.g., extreme authoritarian parents); for others, it is a defense against or an expression of anger stemming from being sexually and or physically abused by members of the household.

- **Violence within schools.** When girls act out aggressively or fight in schools, they may be doing so as a result of the teacher labeling them as violent and aggressive, self-defense, or out of a general sense of hopelessness and despair.

- **Violence within disadvantaged neighborhoods.** Girls in disadvantaged neighborhoods are more likely to engage in violence against others because of the increased risk of victimization (and the potential for violent self-defense against that victimization), parental inability to counteract negative community influences (widespread violence in the neighborhood), and lack of opportunities for success (mainly due to poverty).

 Essential

For information on the increase in girl violence, read *See Jane Hit: Why Girls Are Growing More Violent and What We Can Do About It* by James Garbarino, PhD. Garbarino's book examines how the message "aggression works" is being internalized and acted out by American girls.

Group Bullying

One of the interesting differences between boy and girl bullying is that many girl bullies bully in groups. There may be a "head" bully that orchestrates or starts the bullying, but her social circle is right there behind her backing her up. Girl bullies seem to feel braver and safer bullying from within the confines of their tight-knit social group.

A common method of girl bullying is exclusion and social isolation. These techniques require a group of "insiders" in order to be successful forcing someone into the "outsider" position. There must be an "us" and a "them" or a "we" and a "you" for rejection and shunning to be carried out effectively.

In Rachel Simmons's book *Odd Girl Out: The Hidden Culture of Aggression in Girls,* Simmons says, "When the politics of popularity devastate girls' relationships, the loss is multilayered. A girl is abandoned by someone she loves and trusts. The loss signals her low social value, an event that shrinks her self-esteem and for which she blames herself. She learns a new, dark understanding of relationship as a tool. And where the abandonment is public and followed by cruelty, there is public scorn and shame."

Alert!

The book *Best Friends, Worst Enemies: Understanding the Social Lives of Children* by Michael Thompson, Lawrence J. Cohen, and Catherine O'Neill Grace not only describes the social lives of kids, but the appropriate roles of parents, teachers, and school administrators.

This quote sums up the feeling of rejection and hurt a girl feels when a group of girls turn on her and excludes her from their tight-knit circle. The victim becomes an instant outsider and the group has the shared goal of keeping her out. The girls within the group are scared; they see what the bullied girl is going through and worry that someday it will be them. In order to prevent that from happening, even normally nice girls will behave in cold, cruel ways. The fear is often so strong; girls will actually admit that they are glad that someone else is being targeted because as long as another girl is being bullied, they are safe.

Why Girls Bully Other Girls

Being a female is an inherently competitive situation. And unfortunately, this competitiveness starts at a very young age. Early on girls get the message that they must be pretty, smart, and sweet. And they can't simply be pretty, smart, and sweet, they must be prettier, smarter, and sweeter than the next girl.

Beauty pageants, fashion magazines, and popular media all portray women as being incredibly beautiful and impossibly slim. These so-called "ideal" women set real girls and women up for failure. And fear of failing at being perfect is what fuels the competitiveness seen among girls at such tender ages. Girls often equate being perfect with being popular; and if perfection is what it takes, then so be it. Simmons writes that popularity is, "a cutthroat contest into which girls pour boundless energy and anxiety. It is an addiction, a siren call, a prize for which some would pay any price. Popularity changes girls, causes a great many of them to lie and cheat and steal. They lie to be accepted, cheat their friends by using them, and steal people's secrets to resell at a higher social price."

Girls compete for relationships, and the competition can be merciless. They rate each other on a scale that measures how many friends a girl has, how popular they are, how pretty they are, and how committed they are to each other. And because it's a competition, someone has to lose in order for someone to win. A bully will ensure that she's the winner by choosing the loser or losers. The popular bully girl will expect and require that the other girls in her group back her up in bullying a less popular girl. The bully threatens the other girls with exclusion; if they don't comply and carry out the bully's punishment, they risk the same (or worse) punishment.

Today, girls bully frequently and with increasing cruelty. And while the average girl bully tends to bully only other girls, she picks her target the same way a boy bully does. She will look for a girl with less power and personality, lower social status and grades, or who is less attractive. Similar to boy bullying, girl bullying seems to be a display of strength versus weakness. The female bully or queen bee retains her top of the social ladder status by undermining other girls and creating fear in her social circle so they acquiesce to her wishes. It's a rather warped, yet disturbingly effective, survival of the fittest of the young female social jungle.

 Essential

Try not to let your own experience with girl bullies prejudice you from responding to your daughter's unique situation. Times change, and what worked or didn't work when you were young may not be helpful. And be careful not to internalize your daughter's experience; the focus should be on her, not you.

The Good-Girl Persona

Research has found that the girls who most frequently engage in relational aggression are the feminine, popular ones who look the part of an all-American cheerleader or prom queen. They are slim, pretty girls who have all the right clothes, shoes, and makeup. They rule the school and are invited to all the important parties. Every girl wants to be them and every boy wants to date them.

But some of these girls are hardly sugar and spice and everything nice. They can be mean, controlling, and spiteful. Girl bullies are called mean girls, RMG (really mean girls), queen bees, alpha girls, bitchy broads, and any number of other catchy phrases. It is interesting (and telling) that aggressive girls and girl bullies aren't simply called bullies.

How Parents Can Help

The most important thing you can do is talk to your daughter. Listen to what she has to say and what she thinks about the things that are happening around her. Encourage communication any way you can.

Ask questions, talk to your daughter's friends, and be available when she's in the mood to talk. Initiate conversations in the car, at the dinner table, and while having late-night snacks. Drop in when she's working or doing homework in her bedroom. Pull up a chair and ask what she's working on. Be interested in the events and activities that your child is exposed to.

Encourage your child to talk with the other adults in her life. Get to know the parents of your child's friends and create a social safety network. The more grownups who are aware of what is going on in your daughter's life, the better off she will be. Teach her to respect herself and how to stand up for herself. Be sure to model healthy assertiveness and prosocial behavior so your daughter can see how it is done. Celebrate your daughter's accomplishments and acknowledge her efforts. And don't forget to love her for who she is—not who you want her to be.

 **Fact**

> *Mean Chicks, Cliques, and Dirty Tricks: A Real Girl's Guide to Getting Through the Day with Smarts and Style* by Erika V. Shearin Karres is a book written for tweens and teens who may be struggling with backstabbing, gossiping, bullying girls. The book breaks girl predators into groups (The Bully, The Snob, The Traitor, etc.) and provides tips on how to handle each type of aggressor.

Always discourage violent and aggressive behavior, and if you see these types of behaviors developing, don't hesitate to get your daughter help. If you think your daughter might be bullying, step in and educate her on the social and relational pitfalls bullying may cause. If she can see that bullying is also harmful for the bully, it might be an eye-opening experience. If she continues to bully, seek professional help. With the legislation being constantly changed and updated, your daughter runs the risk of being accused of a crime if her behavior continues or escalates.

If you see warning signs of bullying such as anxiety, mood changes, or depression, seek out more information. If you discover your daughter is a victim, be there for her. Support her. Help her understand the dynamics of social/emotional/relational aggression, and work with her to decrease the stress and negative effects.

 *Question?*

Would you recognize the signs of depression in your daughter? According to the National Institute of Mental Health, some symptoms of depression include persistent sad, anxious, or "empty" feelings; irritability; restlessness; loss of interest in activities or hobbies; difficulty concentrating, remembering details, and making decisions; insomnia; overeating or appetite loss; and persistent aches or pains, headaches, cramps, or digestive problems that do not ease even with treatment.

Girls look up to the women in their lives, and they look for cues as to how to behave in certain situations. Make sure you are providing a good role model for your daughter by doing the following things:

- **Behave ethically**—Hold yourself to a high moral standard.
- **Take responsibility for your actions**—When you make a mistake, admit it.
- **Keep a positive attitude**—The power of positive thinking can improve any situation.
- **Model a healthy, balanced lifestyle**—Take care of yourself.
- **Serve others**—Volunteer to help those less fortunate.
- **Take care of your emotional health**—Find constructive ways to relieve stress.
- **Value education**—Continue to learn and grow.
- **Be reliable and trustworthy**—Be someone your daughter can count on.

- **Value friendships**—Enjoy, support, and cherish your female friends.

The Ophelia Project

In 1997, The Ophelia Project was founded as a direct effort to increase parental and community support for girls. The project is now one of the nation's leading authorities on identifying and addressing relational aggression (behavior meant to hurt someone by harming her relationships with others). Today, The Ophelia Project serves girls, boys, and adults in its continued efforts to stop relational aggression. The Ophelia Project pairs with educational, civic, and community leaders in an effort to create safe social climates where relational aggression and bullying are not tolerated.

The Ophelia Project's services and programs include:

- **CASS (Creating a Safe School):** As the Ophelia Project advances new anti-bullying programs, it creates safe social climates through this prevention-oriented, school-based initiative.
- **Original curricula development and leadership training:** The Ophelia Project provides educational materials and events in an exciting pilot project designed and launched in collaboration with the Girl Scout councils.
- **National Opheliate:** The organization cultivates grassroots change by mobilizing volunteers across the country and empowering them to operate an affiliate in their own communities.
- **Workforce Dynamics:** This powerful program specifically targets relational aggression in the workplace.

What makes the Ophelia Project unique is that it strives for systemic, long-term change. The programs aren't designed to be a quick fix for the problems facing children and schools today. The focus is on long-term cultural change, and The Ophelia Project is trying to achieve that change by altering the destructive social norms that perpetuate the cycle of covert relational aggression in children, youth, and adults.

The program trains peers as leaders and believes peer mentoring relationships can be very effective at changing the attitudes and overall climate in a school setting. The majority of these programs are successful when conducted in existing social settings. YMCA's, Girl Scout troops, and other existing clubs and organizations partner with The Ophelia Project to enact change.

If your daughter's school is experiencing problems with relational aggression, consider looking into the program. For additional information, visit *www.opheliaproject.org*.

CHAPTER 13

How to Bully Proof Your Child

Have you ever sat and watched a group of children playing on the playground? Can you spot the kids who seem popular and well liked? The kids whom everyone crowds around and who seem to know exactly what to do and say to gain the approval, acceptance, and attention of their peers? And can you spot the kids who hover on the outskirts of the activity? The kids who desperately want to be included in the fun, but instead look away, trying to pretend they don't care?

Teaching Social Skills

It can be heartbreaking to realize that your child is on the outskirts of his social group, and you may be thinking that there isn't much you can do to help. You wouldn't be alone in your thinking; many parents believe that popular kids are born with a special gene that makes them socially savvy, that kids are destined from birth to be either popular or unpopular, liked or disliked. Truth be told, there is no popular gene, and sought-after kids aren't born with any special social gift. Popular kids developed their interpersonal skills over time and with the help and guidance of the grownups around them.

You may be rolling your eyes at the thought of having to actually teach your child new and better social skills, but if your child is having trouble with bullies, taking the time to raise his social IQ could make a world of difference. Take a minute to think about just how many things you teach your child. Besides physically caring for your child day after day, there are hundreds of things you need to teach him, such as walking and talking, singing and dancing, reading, writing, arithmetic, baseball, swimming, and soccer. You teach him how to make his bed, do laundry, and eventually, how to drive. But what many parents overlook is the need to teach kids the art of friendship. Not many parents realize that teaching a child friendship-making skills is a very important thing.

 Fact

> Social and interpersonal skills can be improved at any age and at any stage of development. With a little help and guidance from you, your child can learn the skills he needs to navigate almost any social situation with competence and confidence. The trick is to approach it like any other learning experience and practice, practice, practice.

Many a parent could spend less time out in the backyard teaching their child how to toss a baseball or football and more time coaching him on how to make and keep friends. How many parents do you know who make a concerted effort to teach their child how to be a good friend? Socially savvy kids have parents who bring them to the playground and say, "Go over to those kids, introduce yourself, and tell them you would like to play with them." Popular kids have parents who expose them to many varied play situations and who help them practice and perfect approaching other kids. Socially savvy kids have parents who plan and encourage play dates and the occasional sleepover. These kids have parents who not only encourage academic and athletic skills; they value, encourage, and reinforce social and interpersonal skills.

Ways to Improve Your Child's Self-Esteem

Every parent wants the best for her child. The most common response to, "What do you want for your child?" is "I want my child to be happy and healthy." And for the most part, it's relatively easy to keep kids healthy. After all, an entire industry is devoted to children's health. We have lotions and potions, pills and tablets, vaccines and checkups. When a child is sick, there are doctors to see, specialists to consult, and hospitals where kids can receive the best care—healthy is covered. But what about happy? How do you ensure your child's happiness? There isn't a pill or elixir to instantly cure unhappiness, but there are ways you can insulate your child from unhappiness. Not all unhappiness, mind you, but the kind of unhappiness that comes from having low self-esteem and little self-worth.

Let's start by defining and understanding self-esteem. *Merriam Webster's Collegiate Dictionary* defines self-esteem as, "a confidence and satisfaction in oneself." Don't be fooled by the recent self-esteem backlash that has researchers and psychologists criticizing kids with overly high self-esteem. No doubt you saw these types of headlines: "Parents who praise too much" or "A generation of kids with swelled heads from too much false praise." If your child is struggling with self-esteem issues, you can safely ignore the hype that too much self-esteem is bad for kids.

Self-esteem is a necessary and vital psychological skill that kids need to feel competent and confident in their ability to handle all aspects of life. And having positive self-esteem is the cornerstone of living a happy life. When a child feels good about who he is, he is more capable of handling the ups and downs of life. Luckily, the level of your child's self-esteem can be raised, and with a little help from you, he can keep improving his self-esteem until it is as positive as it can be. Do you know whether your child has high or low self-esteem? Here's how to find out.

Behaviors commonly associated with high self-esteem include:

- Your child socializes well with other children.
- Your child can say no to his peers.

- Your child can enter a roomful of strange children and find someone to play with.
- Your child is mainly relaxed and good natured.
- Your child maintains good personal hygiene.
- Your child can lose a game gracefully.
- Your child is determined not to give up easily.
- Your child is aware of his strengths and weaknesses.
- Your child can accept constructive criticism.
- Your child has friends.

Behaviors commonly associated with low self-esteem include:

- Your child resists new experiences and new situations.
- Your child keeps to himself and is socially withdrawn.
- Your child is often tense and can have drastic mood swings.
- Your child doesn't care about his appearance.
- Your child is a sore loser and gets upset at even the thought of losing a game.
- Your child has trouble standing up for himself and rarely expresses his wants and needs.
- Your child gets frustrated and gives up easily.
- Your child focuses on the negative and makes statements like, "Nobody likes me," "I'm a loser," or "I wish I could just disappear."
- Your child is sensitive and can be easily hurt by the slightest criticism.
- Your child has very few or no friends.

Chances are good your child doesn't fit squarely in either the high or low self-esteem categories. But while he may incorporate traits of both lists, he will likely fit better into one over the other. And if your child shows more of the behaviors associated with the low self-esteem list, it is time to take action.

Temperament

Every baby is born with a unique temperament. A temperament is that part of the personality genetically based or inborn. A child's temperament is made up of a set of traits that determine how he will relate to the world and the people in it. These traits are usually fairly stable and should not be viewed as either good or bad. It is not possible to change your child's temperament, but you do need to understand it. Simply understanding your child's temperament can help you anticipate what situations may be potentially difficult for your child. And it will help you tailor your parenting strategies to compliment your child's temperament.

Rita is the mom of a seven-year-old girl named Rachel. Rachel is a quiet, calm girl who isn't fond of noise and activity. Rita, on the other hand, is an outgoing and active woman who has an insatiable lust for life. Rita has dozens and dozens of close friends and is always looking to make more. Rita likes to throw large, loud parties as often as she can. When Rachel's birthday comes along, Rita suggests inviting Rachel's entire second-grade class over for a Mexican-themed birthday bash. Rachel refuses and Rita gets upset. Rita thinks there is something wrong with Rachel and she worries that if Rachel doesn't "loosen up" she will be an outcast at school. Rachel feels like her mom wants her to be something she isn't and it makes her feel like a failure, which is negatively affecting her self-esteem.

Rita takes Rachel to see a counselor and is stunned to discover that Rachel is perfectly normal. The counselor helps Rita see that her expectation that Rachel is supposed to be just like her is causing problems in their relationship. The counselor helps Rita understand that Rachel has always been a quiet, introverted person—and that it is just fine. The counselor encourages Rachel to tell her mom exactly what type of party she wants for her birthday (Rachel wants to invite her best friend over to watch a movie and to sleep over). Rita realized she was trying to force Rachel to have the type of party she wanted, not the type of party Rachel would prefer. Rita and Rachel now have a terrific relationship because Rita understands, appreciates, and respects her child's unique temperament and personality traits.

You can inadvertently undermine your child's self-esteem when you fail to appreciate and honor his uniqueness. This is important to remember as you read through the rest of this chapter and the next. The strategies discussed are meant as guidelines on how to improve your child's self-esteem and social skills. But don't forget to factor in the specifics of your child's personality and overall temperament.

 Essential

There are three basic types of temperament: easy, slow-to-warm up, and difficult. Easy children are flexible and adapt easily to new situations. Slow-to-warm children are cautious and favor routine over novel situations. Difficult children are high strung and intense. Approximately 65 percent of kids fit into these categories; the remaining 35 percent are a combination.

Strategies for Improving Your Child's Self-Esteem

Read through the following list of strategies and select the ones that will help your child the most. Take your time and don't rush your child through them. Developing a higher self-esteem takes time and positive experiences and it won't happen overnight. Set aside a consistent time each day to go over and work on one or more of these suggestions, and before long, you will start to see positive changes in your child.

FIND YOUR CHILD'S AREAS OF STRENGTH
AND COMPETENCE

One important component of self-esteem is not overlooking or undervaluing what your child can do well. It may not be what you want him to be good at, but what you want doesn't matter at the moment. Just because you were the quarterback of the football team doesn't mean your son will follow in your footsteps. Your son may play football to appease you, but may secretly love origami or have a passion for astronomy. Don't miss out on opportunities to uncover special interests and talents in your child simply because you are pigeonholing him into a smaller, younger version of yourself. Your child is not a chip off the old block; he's an individual with his own talents and competencies. Discover what those talents are and encourage your child to develop them.

 Essential

Create a brag book or scrapbook for your son. Solicit positive statements from family members and friends. Ask loved ones and others who know and interact with your child to write something positive about your child in his book. Realizing what others like and admire about him can have a powerful and positive impact on your child's self-esteem.

Make a list of the things you think your child is good at. Also, include his positive traits and anything you think makes him special and worthy of praise. Show this list to your child and ask him if there is anything else you should add to the list. Once the list is complete, hang it up in a place where he can see it every day. When he's feeling down or depressed, have him read the list aloud. Regular reinforcement of your child's positive traits and value can help him weather the difficult days.

Ask your child what he is proud of. His answers might surprise you, and they may give you some insight into what he values and thinks is important in his life. Your son may be proud of himself for things that are entirely different than the things you are proud of him for. Understanding what is in your child's heart will make it easier to steer him in a direction that will foster his self-esteem instead of undermining it.

PROVIDE SPECIFIC PRAISE AND ENCOURAGEMENT

When praising your child, try to avoid ambiguous or nonspecific phrases, such as, "You're a good boy." "Good job." or "Nice work." These types of phrases don't mean much to a child, and they do very little to improve a child's self-esteem. In order for praise to be effective, it needs to be specific: "I like the way you held your sister's hand in the parking lot to keep her safe. That was very responsible of you." "I noticed how hard you have been working at soccer practice. Your effort is really paying off and I can see that you are getting better."

Overwhelmingly, kids hear negative comments far more often than they hear positive ones. Parents are quick to order, command, nag, and reprimand, but often forget to praise and compliment. Unfortunately, human nature is to focus on the negative instead of the positive. Think about it—your child is playing quietly in the other room and you say nothing. A few minutes later, he's bouncing a super ball off the wall and you yell at him to knock it off and quiet down. Why is it that parents generally only speak up when it is to reprimand or control the behavior of their child?

If you have a child with self-esteem issues, you need to retrain your automatic responses and take the exact opposite approach. You need to notice when your child is doing something right or well and you need to compliment him. Do this often for both big and little behaviors. It takes a bit of getting used to, but once you see how your child shines when you praise him instead of criticizing him, you will see the benefit.

 Fact

Use some of these phrases when praising your child:
"I'm so glad you are my son/daughter." "You are really good at _____." "I am proud of you for _____." "I like the way you _____, keep it up." "I love you." "_____ was a smart idea." "I appreciate the way you _____." "Thank you for being you."

If your child behaves in a manner that needs disciplining, stop and think about your words and actions before you react or punish him. Try to remember that to discipline your child is to teach him. So don't place hurtful or insulting labels on him. Don't say things like, "Why don't you use your brain?!" "How can you be so stupid?" or "What's wrong with you?" These types of statements will damage his self-esteem and make him feel bad about himself. Set rules, and when your child breaks them, implement a consequence in a nonjudgmental way. If your child was supposed to clean his room on Sunday and come Monday you notice his room is a pigsty, inform him of the agreed-upon consequence (e.g., no playing outside until it's clean). There is no need to call him lazy or irresponsible.

KEEP UP THE EXERCISE

Be sure your child engages in enough physical activity. Physical activity can raise self-esteem in kids. Regular exercise can release endorphins (feel good hormones) that will help your child manage stress and bad times. When your child can manage his stress better, he will feel more competent and better about himself. Regular exercise will also help him maintain a healthy body weight and a healthy body image; having a healthy body weight and image will naturally improve his self-esteem. Allow your child to choose the method of exercise he prefers, but require that he does exercise.

FIND AREAS THAT NEED IMPROVEMENT

Ask your child to make a list of anything in his life that he would like to change. You might be surprised by what you find out. Try not to judge—this is his list, not yours. Look the list over carefully and pick out the things that you and your child can control. If your child hates that his skin breaks out, bring him to the dermatologist. If your child wishes he knew how to play the guitar, borrow a guitar and try to set up some informal lessons. If he wants a new hairdo, encourage him to be adventurous.

If there is something your child can't change, try to see if you can turn the negative into a positive. If your child hates his size 13 feet, point out that shoes in an unusual size are always in stock. If your child hates that he's the youngest of four, point out that your parenting skills have gotten better with each successive child, and that your youngest gets the benefit of advice from his three other siblings; an only child isn't so lucky. The point here is to get your child talking about what things can be changed and what things can't be changed. If something can't be changed, it might be time to readjust his thinking about that particular issue. A child can't change the fact that his parents are divorced, but he can learn to look for a bright side of the situation. This teaches your child to look for a silver lining in even the darkest of situations.

DEVISE A PLAN TO IMPROVE AREAS THAT NEED IT

Once you and your child have discussed what types of things he wants to improve, you will need to make a step-by-step plan to follow. Start small. Say, for example, that your child wants to feel more comfortable joining a group of children on the playground at school. Start by asking him what he does now. He may tell you that he does nothing, that he doesn't approach kids who are already engaged in play. If that is the case, take him to the playground to watch how other kids do it. Spend an afternoon just sitting and watching the interactions of kids on the local playground. Point out what the other kids are doing, and talk with your son about how the other kids go about joining in play. Be sure to let him tell you his hopes and fears. And don't discount his fears; address them and tell him that it's normal to be nervous. Share with him how you feel when arriving at a dinner party where you don't know anyone or how you felt when you attended your first PTO meeting.

The next step would be to organize a small get-together. Ask a few neighborhood families or friends to come by with their children. Let your child practice the things you saw and talked about at the playground with kids he already knows. Praise the efforts he makes. Remember, your child won't master a new skill right away. It will take practice and time. Be sure to debrief afterward and talk with your son to see if he felt his efforts were met with success. If not, it's back to the drawing board to devise a new plan. Tip: When teaching new social skills to your child, it may be better to gather a group of children who are slightly younger than your child. This way, he can practice his skills on a younger, less judgmental crowd.

Encourage socialization. The more your child socializes with other kids, the better he will get at mirroring and emulating their behavior. If your child is exposed to kids with healthy, positive self-esteem, your child will have a better chance of learning positive behaviors from them. Teach your child how to self-monitor his behavior. When you debrief with your child, he is learning to look at his behavior objectively and as an outsider. This will help him learn to monitor and adjust his behavior to achieve the most positive outcome. With your help and over time, he will learn to do what works and to avoid doing what doesn't work. This level of self-awareness is a valuable social skill.

Alert!

For a successful play date, follow these guidelines: Impose a time limit (one to two hours for young children, two to three for older kids). Invite an even number of kids (that way no one gets left out). Set some ground rules. Supervise, but don't participate. Offer refreshments (check with parents beforehand about allergies). Have a backup plan (keep various indoor and outdoor games handy).

This process of becoming more self-aware will also develop your child's decision-making skills. He will learn to evaluate situations in a logical manner, make better decisions, and he will slowly gain confidence in his decision-making skills.

TEACH YOUR CHILD HOW TO ENGAGE IN POSITIVE SELF-TALK

Tell your child that almost everyone feels badly about himself every now and again. It's human nature, and it's normal. Teach him that when he feels down or depressed, he can use self-affirmations to improve his state of mind. Affirmations are statements like, "I can do it; I know I can," "I'll be okay," "With practice, I'll get better soon," or "Nobody's perfect." Tell him that grownups self-affirm all the time and that it will usually make him feel a bit better.

TEACH YOUR CHILD HOW TO LEARN FROM HIS MISTAKES

It is important for children to know that everyone makes mistakes—even you. Your child needs to know that you aren't perfect and that you don't expect him to be perfect, either. Tell him stories about when you made big and small mistakes. Share with him how you felt about the mistake at the time and how you feel about it now. This can help your child put a little perspective on what he sees as his own colossal mistakes. He needs to understand that mistakes are okay—you simply learn from them and move on.

 Essential

More examples of positive self-affirmation: "I will get through this." "Tomorrow will be better." "It is okay that someone doesn't like me." "I like me." "This will pass." "I am strong." "I choose to be the bigger person." "I refuse to let this bother me."

Some parents teach their kids that do-overs are okay. A do-over is when you and your child mentally erase whatever mistake was just made and start over fresh. For instance: If your child was helping you cook and accidentally put the wrong measurement of ingredients in the casserole, don't let it become a big deal. Announce that it's time for a do-over, toss the ruined casserole, and start over with a smile. Don't mention the wrecked casserole. The main rule of a do-over is that it isn't spoken about again—period. This allows your child the freedom to make mistakes without it negatively affecting his self-esteem.

Tip: You can use this for your grownup mistakes as well. One savvy mom, who had had a lousy day, suddenly couldn't bear the normal bickering of her kids in the backseat of her car. She lost her cool and hollered at her kids for a good five minutes. When she realized what she'd done (taken her own frustrations out on her kids), she drove back to the school where she'd just picked them up, announced she needed a do-over, and proceeded to have a lovely ride home with her amused kids sitting quietly in the backseat.

TEACH YOUR CHILD IT'S OKAY TO LAUGH AT HIMSELF

Humor can do marvelous things for the human psyche. It is a known stress reliever and it can improve your mood. And teaching your child that it is okay to laugh at himself will be invaluable to him in the long run. The best way to do this is by being able to laugh at yourself and your own trials and tribulations. If your child sees that you don't have to take everything so seriously, he will follow your lead and let up on himself as well. Point out to your child that the funniest things are often the most embarrassing, mortifying, or traumatic things when they first happen. But as time goes by, you are often able to see the humor in the situation. "We'll laugh about this someday" is a good perspective to keep.

 **Fact**

Here are a few nonverbal ways to show your child you love and are proud of him: wink at him; pat him on the back, head, or shoulder; give him a high-five; create a private gesture that means, "I love you"; smile at him; give him a spontaneous bear hug; laugh with him; play with him.

Teach Your Child How to Be a Friend

The ability to make and keep friends is a skill often taken for granted. Most parents just assume that when young kids hit kindergarten, they will naturally make friends and hone their fledgling social skills. But for some kids, fitting in and making friends doesn't come naturally or easily. And when your child comes home from school one day and says, "Nobody likes me," it can break your heart.

Thankfully, social competence can be improved, and there are many things you can do to foster and develop your child's friendship-building skills. These skills are important now and in the future. A child who has friends is usually healthier and happier and experiences less stress. She has more opportunities to practice developing social skills, which will, in turn, lead to stronger friendship and relationship bonds as she matures.

Researchers have recently determined that likable children tend to behave in a similar and typical fashion. These behaviors and strategies can be taught to your child. Here's how you can help.

Blend in

Be sure that your child doesn't stand out from the crowd. Make certain that your child wears the same type of clothing and has a similar hairstyle to the other children her age. This goes against the "be an individual" and "be yourself" philosophies, but kids who need to practice social skills need to first look like they fit in. Kids are judgmental about appearance, so don't give the other kids a reason to reject your child.

Be Positive

Coach your child in the art of being nice and approachable. Teach her to smile and say hello to other kids. Friendly kids are like magnets; they will attract other kids. You can go even further and teach your child to give each child she plays with a compliment. Sincere compliments make other people like you and want to be around you.

Display Open Body Language

Teach your child to stand up straight and look other children in the eye. Teach her to keep her body language open and friendly (no crossed arms, averted eyes, or scowling faces). Go back to the playground for another observation if your child needs some pointers on how to project positive body language.

Find a Child with a Similar Personality or Interests

Your child's best chance of establishing a solid friendship lies in picking someone who has a similar temperament or common interest. If your child loves to do arts and crafts, look for a child who also enjoys arts and crafts. If your child is a soccer enthusiast, look for a child who plays soccer who may also have a personality that is similar to your daughter's personality. Spending time engaged in a favorite activity can allow a friendship to grow and deepen over time.

 Essential

To learn more about friendship skills, read *The Unwritten Rules of Friendship: Simple Strategies to Help Your Child Make Friends* by Natalie Madorsky Elman and Eileen Kennedy-Moore, *Nobody Likes Me, Everybody Hates Me: The Top 25 Friendship Problems and How to Solve Them* by Michele Borba, EdD, and *The Friendship Factor: Helping Our Children Navigate Their Social World—and Why It Matters for Their Success and Happiness* by Kenneth H. Rubin.

Ask to Join In

If a group of children are at play, have your child approach one single person. Have her ask, "Can I join in the fun?" Your child stands a better chance of a yes answer when she addresses a single person; a crowd is a tougher sell. If the child says yes, the remainder of the group will likely go along with it. Be sure your child understands that the other child may say no. Teach her that if that happens, she can simply say, "Okay, maybe next time."

Be Helpful

A trait that is known to make kids more popular is being helpful. Teach your child to be sensitive to other kids needs and to offer assistance. It's hard not to like the people who help you out.

Be a Good Listener

Teach your child to listen to what other kids have to say. Being an active listener is an important skill that will serve her well for the rest of her life. It will also help her determine which kids she truly wishes to pursue a friendship with and which kids she'd rather not. A good way to help her become a good listener is to model good listening skills yourself.

Encourage and Foster One Good Friendship

If your child can find and foster one good friendship, it will make a world of difference. Just having a single friend can insulate and protect your child's social confidence and developing self-esteem. Once your child has found a potential friend who has similar interests and a compatible personality style, it is time to coach him on how to strengthen the relationship. Here is what he needs to do:

- **Be willing to take a chance.** In order to have a good friend, you must be a good friend. Your child must be willing to take the initiative and invite his friend over to play, and he must be willing to go play at his new friend's house. Being open to new experiences is necessary.
- **Be honest.** Your child should let his new friend know that he likes him and that he enjoys spending time with him.
- **Don't keep score.** Let your child know that a friendship is rarely equal. There will be times when his friends needs help and support and times when he needs help and support.
- **Be willing to apologize and to forgive.** Everyone makes mistakes and chances are good that your child or his new friend will make a few mistakes along the way. Teach your child to say "I'm sorry" if he hurt his friend's feelings. And teach him to be gracious and to forgive when his friend hurts his feelings.
- **Have fun and stop worrying.** Keep inviting your son's friends over. Find out his friends' interests and plan activities both boys would enjoy. Relax and have fun.

Allow Your Child to Join a Group

An excellent way to expose your child to a variety of kids is to join a local club or group. Here are a few options to consider:

- **Hobby club**—chess, computers, arts and crafts
- **Music club**—listening to music, playing instruments, karaoke

- **Sports team**—soccer, hockey, gymnastics, swimming, ice skating
- **Drama club**—acting, putting on plays
- **Dance**—hip hop, jazz, ballet
- **Girl Scouts or Boy Scouts**
- **Religious youth groups**—missions, retreats, meetings
- **Exercise club**—walk together or hit the gym
- **Classes or lessons**—cooking, art, acting, writing, golf, roller skating, knitting, sewing, scrap booking, or classes just for fun like jumping rope or bubble blowing

 Essential

Books for kids on how to make and keep friends include *How to Be a Friend: A Guide to Making Friends and Keeping Them* by Laurie Krasny Brown; *Fab Friends And Best Buds: Real Girls On Making Forever Friends* by Erika V. Shearin Karres; and *A Good Friend: How to Make One, How to Be One* by Ron Herron, Val J. Peter, and Father Flanagan's Boys' Home.

Enroll Your Child in a Self-Defense Class

If your child is being bullied, consider enrolling him in a self-defense course. The goal is not to teach your child how to act out against a bully (that is never a good idea); the goal is to empower your child to successfully escape or resist an attack. A self-defense course can teach your child to be aware and assertive in a threatening situation. It can also teach your child verbal confrontation skills and physical strategies meant to de-escalate, slow down, or stop an attack. A good self-defense course can increase your child's confidence and help him feel more capable of defending himself should the need arise.

Teach Basic Prevention Skills

If your child is the victim of bullying, teach her these basic strategies for staying safe:

- Do whatever it takes to avoid the bully.
- Stay close to teachers and other adults.
- Stay close to friends and try not to be in situations where she is alone.
- If she is approached by a bully, she should quickly walk away and find help. If the bully follows her, she should speak loudly and tell the bully to stop bothering her.
- Do not fight back unless she feels that she needs to do so in order to protect herself (you don't want others to accuse your child of being the bully).
- Stay calm and find the nearest adult who can help.
- Report the incident to you.

CHAPTER 14

Social Skills and Assertiveness Training

Social skills go beyond the basics of saying "please" and "thank you." And good interpersonal relationships are made up of more than a friendly "hello" and a firm handshake. It's rather astonishing that the average parent will spend a small fortune on piano lessons and soccer fees—and will often require their children to spend countless hours practicing these skills—but will barely give a thought to teaching their child the skills that are most important for leading a life filled with successful interpersonal relationships and emotional good health.

Why Your Child Needs Social-Skills Training

Human beings are social creatures. Since the beginning of time, relationships and interpersonal interactions have been the foundation for social health and happiness. Kids generally fall on a continuum of social competence. Kids at one end of the scale seem to be gifted with relational and interpersonal skills; others at the opposite end of the scale have a noticeable deficit of relational abilities. However, the majority of kids fall in the middle range.

Have no fear; social aptitude, like any other skill, can be studied, practiced, and improved upon. If your child is lacking in the social-skills department, she can be coached to develop stronger and more appropriate skills. It is an effort well worth making if it helps your child navigate through her world with more competence and confidence. Studies have linked social competence with better academic achievement, stronger friendships, and higher self-esteem. And in later years, social competence can increase career and marital success. It is a win-win situation.

Question?

Does your child have nonverbal learning disability (NLD)?
Kids with NLD (among other things) have trouble processing nonverbal information (such as facial expressions, tone of voice, and overall body language). They hear the actual words that are being said, but miss the nuances and subtleties of nonverbal communication. With over 90 percent of communication conveyed nonverbally, this can pose a serious social barrier for your child.

The Most Essential Social Skills for Kids

In dealing with children, there are some fundamental social skills that, when developed, will lay the foundation for your child to develop the more sophisticated skills he will need as he matures. The three most essential social skills for a young child to learn are:

The Ability to Make Friends

Childhood is all about making friends and playing with those friends. A large chunk of a child's time is spent in play activities. This play time allows children to practice and experiment with various kinds of relationships with different kinds of kids. The hope is that when kids play, they will learn how to interact effectively and will develop the skills necessary for making friends at every age. Unfortunately, this doesn't always work out as planned. Some kids will need your help and guidance to develop the skills that may appear to come naturally to other kids.

To Have Confidence in Herself and Her Abilities

If you watch kids on the playground, the kids who seem to have the most friends are usually the kids who display the highest level of self-confidence. Kids with confidence feel good about themselves and expect that others will like them and want to play with them. This confidence and positive attitude serves as a social magnet for kids. How can you instill this confidence in your child? It's simple: Find something your child is good at and allow her to become even better at it. Praise her, and love her unconditionally. Follow the guidelines in Chapter 13 on building self-esteem and you will be helping your child gain confidence.

 **Fact**

> Harvard psychologist Howard Gardner names "interpersonal intelligence" in his original list of the seven types of intelligences. Gardner defined interpersonal intelligence as, "the capacity to understand the intentions, motivations and desires of other people." Gardner says that interpersonal intelligence is what allows people to work effectively with others.

Ability to be Resilient

Resilience (the ability to bounce back from life's little and big disappointments) is a vital life skill. If your child can learn to look at the bright side of a bad situation, it will protect his self-esteem. And the better your child gets at handling problems and conflicts, the more confidence he will gain in himself and his ability to cope.

Take ten-year-old Jamison, for example. When Jamison ran for class president, he was certain he would win the election. Election Day came and Jamison didn't win. Jamison went home that day, went online, and studied up on the strategies and philosophies of winning presidential campaigns. Instead of crying and moping around wondering why his classmates didn't like him enough to vote for him, he focused on what he'd done wrong with his campaign. Jamison was going to be ready with a winning strategy when next year's election arrived.

Andrew, Jamison's classmate, also lost the campaign. Andrew was so upset that he refused to go to school for the rest of the week. He couldn't face his classmates because he felt like a loser. Andrew stayed in his room and cried every day. He vowed that he would never again put himself out there to get hurt again.

Jamison chose to ignore the negative and looked at the positive of the situation. He decided he would study up and be better prepared next time. Andrew chose to see his loss as a personal failure. Andrew's self-esteem and confidence will suffer as a result of his inability to cope with his disappointment.

Body Language

One of the best ways to help your child improve her interpersonal and social skills is to teach her the basics of effective communication. Researchers know that some kids who get bullied tend to broadcast via their body language that they don't feel good about themselves. They don't make eye contact, they slouch and look downtrodden, and they seldom smile and look happy. There is argument and disagreement in the psychological community about whether the victim body language was there first (before the bullying began) or whether it developed as a result of being bullied. Either way, it is something you can train your child to be aware of.

The use of the word "train" is intentional because it can be hard to retrain your child to engage in new and different behaviors. Humans are creatures of habit, and displaying poor body language may have become a habit for your child. You will need to be patient and prepared to consistently point out proper body language and positively reinforce it when you do see it.

Eye Contact

Failure to make eye contact is usually an indication that your child is insecure. Think about it for a moment: When a person makes eye contact with you, it sends a signal that the person is confident, honest, and forthright. When someone refuses to look you in the eye, human nature is to become suspicious and uncertain of the intentions and state of mind of the other person.

You can practice this skill at home. Start a conversation with your child and teach him to hold eye contact for a few seconds at a time. Slowly build up the amount of time your child can maintain eye contact until he can confidently hold a conversation while looking directly at you. Have him practice this skill as often as possible. This skill will help him in all his social interactions.

Alert!

Be wary of overdoing these lessons with your child. There is a fine line between holding eye contact to signal interest in what that the speaker is saying and staring in a way that makes other people uncomfortable. Explain and demonstrate the difference to your child.

Posture

Confident kids hold their heads up high and greet the world with enthusiasm. Bullied kids tend to draw in on themselves in an attempt to disappear. But you can teach your child to hold his head high, square his shoulders, and sit and stand up straight. You might want to practice these things in front of a mirror with your child; he may be able to understand the impact of his slouch better if he can see it in the mirror.

Take him to a public place and study the people who pass by. Ask him who seems confident and friendly and who doesn't. You may see people who stand with their arms crossed—this signals "keep away" and can seem hostile to another person. Point out these subtle actions and body postures to your child. Watch television together and study the body language of the characters on a show or in a movie. Look for examples of great body language and explain to your child why we react more positively to open, confident, and friendly postures.

Facial Expressions

This is the trickiest component of body language for kids to learn. Kids are usually open books (meaning you can see exactly what they are feeling simply by looking at their face). If your child is unhappy, his face is a scowl. If he is sad, his face holds a crestfallen expression. If he's happy, his face is lit up with joy. No doubt you can read him like a book. Problem is, so can everyone else. For a bullied kid, this is not good. A bullied child is frequently upset, angry, and scared. These types of facial expressions will put off other kids. They will see your child as unfriendly, hostile, or unapproachable and this will make it harder for him to socialize successfully.

 **Fact**

UCLA professor of psychology Albert Mehrabian is known for his research and publications on the significance of verbal and nonverbal communication. Mehrabian's work concluded that the spoken word consists of a mere 7 percent of all communication, 38 percent is conveyed through tone of voice, and the remaining 58 percent through body language. This is known as the 7 percent-38 percent-55 percent rule.

Stand your child in front of a mirror and have him close his eyes. Ask him to think of a recent unpleasant or hurtful event. Ask him to open his eyes to see his facial expression. Then ask him to close his eyes again and think of the best and happiest moment of his life. Have him open his eyes and look at his reflection. Did he notice the difference between the two expressions? Discuss the importance of gaining mastery over his facial expressions. Explain to your child that people are attracted to relaxed, happy faces. Tell him that when people smile and are aware of keeping a pleasant expression on their face, other people see them as positive, happy people.

Cut out pictures from magazines of happy faces, angry faces, sad faces, scared faces, etc. Have your child use these pictures to practice making different faces in the mirror. Once he realizes that he has some control over what others think he's thinking and feeling, he will feel more in control.

Voice Quality

When your child is communicating via the spoken word, there are many things that must be taken into account. For instance, how she says something can be more important than what words she uses to say it. Here are a few aspects of speech your child should be aware of.

Tone and Pitch

Every parent at some point will feel like saying, "I don't like your tone of voice." And what that means is that your child has spoken with what you term "attitude." Attitude is hard to describe, but every parent knows it when they hear it. It is a word or phrase spoken with sarcasm, disdain, or contempt. Kids have to be careful about the inflection they use when speaking, as it can often be misinterpreted or misunderstood. This is clear when you tell your child you don't like her tone and she responds by saying, "What tone?"

Volume

When kids get agitated or angry, their voices get louder (or softer). When kids get louder, other people stop listening and tune them out. When their voices get softer, they are overlooked and ignored. You can teach your child to either tone it down (by gently and consistently pointing out the escalation) or dial it up (by requiring her to speak at a normal volume level in order to get what she wants or needs). Don't forget that this will take practice and patience.

Rate

Kids get nervous, and one of the best indicators of their nervousness is the rate at which they speak. Nervousness speeds up your nervous system and sends your body processes into overdrive. Just think how your heartbeat and breathing quicken when you are required to speak in public. It is important to teach your child to slow down and speak at a normal pace. Your child's speech can't be understood if she rushes to get the words out. Have her practice taking deep breaths and counting to five before speaking.

Clarity

Your child needs to be clear about what she is saying in order to be effectively understood. This is when what you are saying becomes important. Teach your child that adults and other kids are not mind readers; they can't be expected to understand what she says unless she makes it perfectly clear. Your daughter might tell the teacher that Cindy is bothering her when what she really means is that Cindy (who sits behind her) is plucking individual hairs out of her head one at a time and it hurts. And your daughter might tell Cindy to knock it off when what she really means is, "If you pluck one more hair out of my head, I will tell the teacher, the principal, and my parents."

Conversational Skills

A child who can initiate and sustain a conversation will usually be successful in his interpersonal relationships. But again, it is a skill your child may need to brush up on.

Greetings

Being able to walk up to another child to say hello can be a daunting task for a young child. In fact, it can be a daunting task for some adults. But this is a skill that is vital for a young child to learn. And it will be nerve wracking and uncomfortable the first few times he attempts it. Encourage your child to role play with you. Pretend you are a new classmate and have your child approach you and say hello. Once your child is comfortable with it, take him to the playground and have him try it a few times. Be sure to congratulate him for every successful attempt.

Introductions

Once your child is comfortable greeting other children, he should try to introduce himself. Begin again by role playing the situation with family and friends. Once he is confident, he can introduce himself. Take him to the playground or a party where he doesn't know many people and have him practice greeting unknown kids and introducing himself. When he can approach another child to say, "Hi, my name is Kevin," he will be ready for the next step.

Sustaining Conversations

The next step is to engage the other child in a conversation. This is trickier than just introducing himself. To engage another child in a conversation, your child will have to ask a question. Here are a few examples:

- Do you live around here?
- I like your shirt. Is it new?
- That is a great sandcastle. Was it hard to build?
- Do you come to this playground often?

If your child can think of an open-ended question, that would be even better.

- Why do you like this playground?
- Why did you decide to build a sand town instead of a sand castle?

Friendship Skills

Kids who have lots of friends seems to understand that friendship is a give and take, that friendship requires effort, and that sometimes you need to think of the other person before you think of yourself. So how can you teach your child friendship skills?

Compliment Others

Everyone loves to be complimented—it is human nature—and the kids who have the most friends seem to be at ease with complimenting the academic skills, physical prowess, physical appearance, or social savvy of other kids. Popular kids understand that complimenting others doesn't take anything away from themselves, and when they admire something about another child, they tell them.

When was the last time you received a spontaneous and unexpected compliment? How did it make you feel? Pretty good? And how did you feel about the person who issued the compliment? Did you feel positive feelings for them? If the compliment was genuine, you probably did have a good feeling toward the person who complimented you. Share this phenomenon with your child and help her understand how making others feel good about themselves will reflect positively on her.

Offer to Help

Researchers have discovered that helpful people are usually well liked. Teach your child to pitch in and help whenever someone needs it. This is not to say you should encourage your child to be a doormat; it simply means that offering help to someone who needs it is viewed positively by all.

Ask to Join In

When your child sees kids who are doing something she thinks she would enjoy, encourage her to join in. At times, she will be able to simply join the activity. Other times, she may need to ask permission to join in (such as when a game is already established and in process). Help your child understand that the worst that will happen is that a child might say no. Let her know that it isn't the end of the world; she can simply say, "Maybe next time" and walk away. Once she achieves a few successful yes responses, she will feel more confident approaching kids at play.

Show Appreciation

When kids include your child in an activity or game, let her know that the gracious thing to do is to say, "Thank you. That was fun." Showing appreciation is yet another way to create a positive social climate for your child.

Assertiveness Skills

As your child begins to develop stronger social skills and more confidence, he will be ready to start asserting himself in uncomfortable situations. Many kids aren't naturally assertive and need to be taught that it is not just okay to stand up for themselves, it is recommended.

 Fact

There are three basic relational styles. Passive people believe they have no right to express their needs and they acquiesce to the people around them. Aggressive people believe they are always right and seek to impose their will on others. Assertive people find a middle ground between aggressive behavior and passivity by respecting the needs and wishes of everyone, including their own.

The first thing to do is teach him the difference between being assertive and being aggressive. Explain that aggressive people try to force their will on others, whereas assertive people simply stand up for their own rights and feel comfortable defending themselves against aggressive people and unfairness. Assertive people don't bully or badger, they calmly state their position and refuse to submit to shoddy treatment.

Jade is a fourth-grade girl who has been taking an assertiveness-training community-education class with her mother. Jade has been victimized by bullies since she was in the first grade. The assertiveness-training class has taught Jade how to stand up for herself. The next time Diane tries to bully Jade, Jade stands up tall and says loud and clear, "No one deserves to be bullied. If you don't stop, I will walk over and tell Mrs. Spellman that you are trying to bully me." Jade asserts herself clearly and consistently for the next few weeks until the bully eventually leaves her alone.

Provide a good example for your child and don't let others bully you. Assert yourself calmly and clearly when dealing with salespeople, repairmen, etc. Stand up for your rights every chance you get and hopefully, your child will learn by example that it works.

Asking for Help

It is important for your child to be able to ask for help when he needs it. Many kids are unwilling to ask for help for a variety of reasons—they believe they won't receive it, they believe they won't be believed, they feel like they should handle their problems on their own, etc. It is your job as a parent to help your child understand that there are times when everyone needs help—even you. Tell your child about a time where you had to ask for help and be sure to include how grateful you were to receive it.

Let him know that asking for help is nothing to be ashamed of and that he should never hesitate to ask you (or another adult) for help. If he is reluctant to go to his teacher for help, set up an appointment with you, your son, and the teacher to work out a strategy that will help your child feel more comfortable seeking help.

Saying No

Many grownups struggle with the inability to say no; it is a common problem. And kids have an even tougher time saying no, mainly because they are not taught that it is acceptable to do so. Your child should feel that he has the right to say no to a request that makes him uncomfortable. If your child does not wish to attend a certain party, he should be allowed to say, "Maybe next time." If he doesn't feel like playing tag with the other boys, he should feel secure saying, "No, thank you." Part of instilling a sense of personal power in your child is giving him the freedom to control the things he does and does not want to do. Let him make some decisions and he will gain the confidence to believe he can make the right and best decisions for himself.

 Essential

Harvard psychologist Howard Gardner also lists intrapersonal intelligence in his original list of the seven types of intelligence. Intrapersonal intelligence is "the capacity to understand oneself, to appreciate one's feelings, fears and motivations." In other words, you have a realistic understanding of yourself and you use that knowledge to self-regulate.

Dealing with Bullies

As your child's confidence and self-esteem increase, he will be better equipped to deal with kids who try to bully him. Over time, as he practices his social skills, becomes more aware of his body language, improves his friendship-making skills, and improves his level of assertiveness, he will feel more competent dealing with aggressive kids and kids who bully. As he tries to deflect bullying, help him try new strategies and devise new plans to deal with it. With your help (and a plan), he will no longer feel that he's alone. You have been helping him for some time, and he will feel confident you will help guide him through this, as well.

CHAPTER 15

Parental Responsibility and Why Getting Involved Can Help Enact Change

For most parents, finding out their child is the victim of a bully is a highly emotional experience. Many parents openly speak of a visceral anger reaction. They want to rush right out to find the kid who hurt their precious child—and they want to wring her neck. Thankfully, this doesn't often happen. In truth, parents react to the news of bullying in varied and sometimes baffling ways. But despite initial reaction to bullying, parents and school personnel must work together to prevent bullying and enact positive change because even the best bullying prevention and intervention programs won't be successful unless they have the full support of the most important adults in children's lives —their parents.

Fear of Making the Situation Worse

Some parents are prepared, have done their homework, and know exactly what to do to help their child when she comes home crying and says she's being bullied. Some parents jump right into action and save the day, but many do not. It is not that they don't want to help their child; it is that they just don't know what to do. This can be especially true if the parent of a bullied child has never experienced bullying first-hand. For some parents, having a child that is being bullied is their first introduction into the bully/victim scenario.

Add to this the fear that interfering will only make the bullying worse, and it creates a certain paralysis and failure to act on behalf of their child. Parents don't know what to do, are afraid of doing the wrong thing, and wind up doing nothing. It is true that bullying can intensify as a result of parental intervention, but it can (and frequently does) get worse without any adult intervention. And doing nothing sends the message to your child that you either can't or won't help her.

 **Fact**

Here are a few books on how to help your bullied child: *When Your Child Is Bullied: An Essential Guide for Parents* by Jenny Alexander; *Helping Your Socially Vulnerable Child: What to Do When Your Child Is Shy, Socially Anxious, Withdrawn, or Bullied* by Andrew Eisen and Linda B. Engler PhD; *10 Days to a Bully-Proof Child* by Sherryll Kraizer, PhD.

Embarrassed by a Bullied Child

Some parents have identities that are tied into having the "perfect" child. These are parents who long to have the smartest, prettiest, or most popular and athletic child. They want so badly to have a perfect child that they fail to see the actual child they do have. They overlook their child's inadequacies and problems because they don't want to admit their child isn't perfect.

These are the parents most likely to tell their child that bullying is a rite of passage (it's not), that everyone goes through it (they don't), and that it will go away if you just ignore it (that's not likely). These parents are more worried that someone will find out about the bullying than they are about protecting their child.

Kids Beg Parents Not to Tell

This is a fairly common scenario. Many kids fear that if other kids or the bully find out they told an adult, the bullying will get significantly worse. This leads them to beg their parents not to tell anyone what they told them. This can be a difficult judgment call for parents. On one hand, the parents want to respect their child's wishes and are grateful their child came to them to tell them he was having a problem; but on the other hand, the parents wish to protect their child from further harm or humiliation. It's a tough position to be in—one which parents must weigh carefully.

 Essential

Here are a few good anti-bullying books for kids. Grades K–2: *Best Enemies* by Kathleen Leverich and *The Very Bad Bunny* by Marilyn Sadler. Grades 3–8: *The Meanest Things to Say* by Bill Cosby and *Bad Girls* by Cynthia Voigt. Grades 9 and up: *How You Can Be Bully Free* by Allan L. Beane and *Dear Mr. Henshaw* by Beverly Cleary.

If your child is not in any physical danger, if the bullying is mild, and if your child is upset but not devastated by what is happening, it might be okay to honor your child's wishes. You should start coaching your child on potential ways to handle the bully and work on building his confidence and self-esteem. Purchase books on bullying for you and your child, and keep an open dialog so you are aware of exactly what is happening with the situation. Keep close tabs on your child and be attentive to any emotional, psychological, or educational changes in him. It's not uncommon for kids to go through a brief bullying situation. It could actually help to build his self-esteem if he is capable of handling the situation. But at the first sign of escalation, be prepared to step in. It is also a good idea to meet with your child's teacher (in confidence if necessary). It is important for the teacher to be informed of the situations and problems occurring in her classroom. This simple step may be all that is needed to give your child a little behind the scenes help.

In comparison, if the bullying is physical in nature, is moderate to severe, and seems to be affecting your child's mood or behavior, don't wait; get him help immediately.

Parents Fear Being Seen as Overprotective

Parents are sometimes reluctant to step in and demand changes in their child's classroom or school out of a fear of coming across as overprotective. Occasionally, this is realistic. There are some parents who complain about every slight altercation and mishap. Frankly, there will always be spontaneous spats, brief exclusions, and occasional outright fights between kids. Kids disagree, argue, and they fight. Kids will have good days and bad. They will have years where they have many friends and everything is great, and they will have years where they have just a few friends and encounter some social difficulty. These things are normal and expected in the course of a school career. While it is important to bring major things to the attention of school personnel, small transitory things are not generally a cause for major concern.

If your child is being picked on, excluded, or assaulted on a regular basis, you should not worry about being seen as overprotective—you need to be protective. Your child's safety and well-being should always come before your discomfort. It can be difficult to make waves and upset the applecart, but if you don't, then who will? Who will step in to protect your child when you waste time worrying about being seen as overprotective? There are far worse things to be thought of than overprotective.

Parents Want the Child to Stand Up for Herself

This is the most misguided type of parent. This parent wants his child to be able to stand up to the child or children who are bullying her. The fundamental problem with this type of reasoning is that if kids who are being bullied could stand up to the bully or bullies, they would. But it is understandable that some adults believe this is a viable option for their children. After all, in countless movies (*The Karate Kid, Back to the Future, Stand by Me*) the bullied child triumphs over the bully in the end by standing up to or fighting him. The audience cheers and all is well in the world. In reality, that type of cinematic triumph of good over evil is rarely as dramatic and successful.

What usually happens in real life is that the child tells her parents she is being bullied, the parents tell the child to toughen up and fight back, and the child realizes her parents think she's a coward. That makes her feel even worse. She also realizes that she is now on her own, that her parents will not help her with her problem, and that can be a very lonely and frightening situation for a child to be in.

Reasons Why Bullying Should Always Be Reported

One of the main reasons bullying continues to exist is because it is so underreported. Kids don't tell, and that is a grave problem. They don't tell for a variety of reasons, and until society changes, kids will continue to keep quiet. Parents and educators need to find a way to remove the stigma that bullied kids experience. Bullied kids need and deserve our attention and our support. Kids who tell should be viewed with admiration and respect, and they should be immediately given the help they need.

Kids won't receive the help they need until all of the adults involved in a child's life are acting in unison. When kids are no longer ashamed to be a victim, when they stop trying to live up to parents' unrealistic expectations, when they believe that adults understand what they are going through, and when they truly believe they will receive the help they need, only then will they consistently tell.

Until that time arrives, it is up to parents to report all instances of bullying to the proper social personnel (and sometimes to the authorities). Schools need to understand the full scope and breadth of the problem. If every parent who had a bullied child spoke up every single time the bullying occurred, schools would have no choice but to dedicate more time and attention to preventing the problem. And some will argue that teachers and school personnel have too much to do already, and that any time spend on implementing anti-bullying programs and education will be time taken away from academics. In truth, bullying is seen by kids as a big problem, and most will admit that they would be much happier and better able to learn if they didn't have to worry about bullying. A climate that tolerates bullying is detrimental to the learning environment. To put an end to bullying would a great social, psychological, and educational benefit to all children.

 Fact

The National Youth Violence Prevention Center reports that, "almost 30 percent of youth in the United States (or over 5.7 million) are estimated to be involved in bullying as either a bully, a target of bullying, or both." In all likelihood, that number will climb even higher when kids are no longer too afraid and too intimidated to report what is happening to them.

What Works in Bullying Prevention?

Researchers are just beginning to piece together strategies proven to be successful in bully prevention. It is a long road and one which society has only begun to travel. In the past, bullying wasn't seen as a big problem. Today, researchers have proven that bullying is not only a big problem; the problem is so large it is now considered a widespread social problem. But despite the recognition of bullying as a social problem and a growing awareness of its negative and harmful effects on children, not enough is being done to prevent bullying.

The past decade has at least provided some clues as to what types of strategies and programs might work to lessen the prevalence of bullying. Many more studies need to be done, and much more attention needs to be paid to this matter, but let's take a look at what researchers and school personnel believe to be strategies for successful reduction in bullying behavior.

 Essential

According to renowned researcher and bullying expert Dan Olweus, PhD, bullying behavior and various other inappropriate and antisocial behaviors can be reduced by as much as 50 percent when effective anti-bullying education and prevention programs are implemented in schools. Other studies, such as Ferguson, Kilburn, San Miguel & Sanchez, 2007, report significantly less influence overall across all anti-bullying programs.

Honest Assessment of the Bullying Problem

Adults are not always aware of what is going on inside and outside of the classroom. A significant percent of school bullying occurs under the radar, and because of this the level of the bullying problem in schools can be seriously underestimated. Researchers have found that administering an anonymous survey to students in a given school can provide more accurate information on how often kids are being bullied, what types of bullying are occurring, and where in the school most of the incidents occur. School personnel can then devise a plan of action depending on the specific problems and trouble spots in the school. These surveys can also provide baseline information that the school can use as a comparison after implementing prevention strategies now and in the future.

School Climate Change

As mentioned before, a climate of tolerance for bullying behavior enables the activity to continue. In order for a school to decrease the level of bullying, a change must be made in the overall climate of the school. School personnel (including paraprofessionals, bus drivers, cafeteria workers, etc.) must become intolerant of bullying behaviors and those behaviors must be consistently identified, addressed, and met with appropriate consequences. A change in perception must occur so that students no longer view bullying as cool and begin to realize that bullying is undesirable and decidedly not cool. Everyone involved (school personnel, parents, and students) must view bullying as inappropriate and unacceptable. Only then, when the social norms and perceptions have been altered, will change happen.

Integrated Bullying Prevention

One of the biggest misperceptions in bullying prevention is that students can learn about bullying with a single program, or at one grade level, or in one class (like health), and it will do the job of educating the students. This thinking is inadequate. Studies have shown that the best bullying prevention and intervention programs incorporate many activities and programs that include all adults and students involved in the school system. These programs need to be administered every year on the student level, the school personnel level, and the parent level. Everyone must work from the same framework and set of guidelines. And everyone should be aware of and have some input into the bullying prevention policies, rules, and activities.

Parents and educators should be provided with education programs on how bullying affects children and how it adversely affects their learning environment, how to identify bullying behavior, how to respond if they observe or are informed of bullying behavior, and how they can work with other adults in the school system to prevent the bullying from occurring again in the future.

Students should also be provided with education programs on how to handle bullying situations when they are the bullied child, a bystander, and the bully. Students need to understand the negative consequences that bullying has on them and others. Students should be given the ongoing opportunity to make suggestions and provide feedback on bullying prevention to school personnel. And they should feel comfortable doing so.

 Fact

A report released by the organization Fight Crime: Invest in Kids, identified three proven bullying intervention and prevention programs: The Olweus Bullying Prevention Program (first developed in Norway and now implemented around the world); Linking the Interests of Families and Teachers (LIFT), a ten-week antiaggression program; and The Incredible Years, designed for children two to eight years of age.

These things will be impossible unless every person is willing to adopt and enforce the new policies and procedures. Every person needs to see the value in continuing, supporting, and periodically upgrading the school's existing bullying prevention programs and interventions. Only then will real change be enacted.

Supportive Parents and School Personnel
Even the best bullying prevention and intervention programs won't be successful without a "buy in" from the most important adults in children's lives. The school system can be putting forth 100 percent effort in the prevention of bullying, but if parents undermine, or worse, oppose the bullying prevention efforts, the situation is doomed to failure. On the flip side, if parents are 100 percent on board but the teachers or school personnel are reluctant to consistently address and

enforce anti-bullying policies and procedures, even the best program (and parental intentions) will fail. Only when both parents and school personnel work together to prevent bullying will positive changes be seen.

Character Education for all Students

It can be difficult to change a school climate that has traditionally tolerated bullying behavior. Bully, victim, and bystander behaviors may be strongly entrenched in the social norms of a particular school culture. Bullying may be viewed as cool and bystanders may view interfering or intervening as uncool. It can be tough for bully prevention educators to reverse this erroneous way of thinking. One way educators have been doing this is to provide character education to all students. These programs emphasize things such as respect, responsibility, fairness, caring, and fostering a sense of community and inclusion. Character education is geared toward creating a change in the social norms that have allowed bullying to continue in every classroom and on every playground.

In character education, kids are taught that respect for each other is positive and proactive; that each individual should take responsibility for his or her own behavior and for ensuring that the behavior of others is consistent with school expectations and rules; that everyone deserves to be treated with dignity and respect; and that a community is only as strong and as functional as its members. When kids are given permission and support from their peers and the adults around them to protect each other, they will usually step up and do the right thing.

When kids understand that silence and staying out of it only makes the situation worse for victims, bullies, and themselves, they are more likely to intervene. There is strength in numbers, and if kids are unified in their disapproval and condemnation of bullying behavior, it will dramatically decrease.

Safe Reporting Procedures

Kids need to feel like they can report bullying and abusive behavior in a confidential and safe environment—especially at the outset of a bullying prevention and intervention program. Some kids won't trust the system, and fear putting themselves and their reputation on the line. There should be an anonymous reporting system in place—such as a box where kids can drop notes or a phone line they can call to report bullying problems—until the climate has sufficiently changed enough for kids to feel comfortable going directly to school personnel or parents to report a bullying situation.

 Essential

The Olweus Bullying Prevention Program (recognized by the federal government as a model program) recommends that schools adopt these four rules about bullying: (1) We will not bully others; (2) we will try to help students who are bullied; (3) we will try to include students who are left out; (4) if we know that somebody is being bullied, we will tell an adult at school and an adult at home.

Graduated Sanctions

Schools that develop simple, clear rules about bullying behavior have an easier time enforcing those rules. Students are aware of exactly what types of behavior won't be tolerated, teachers and school personnel understand the proper sanctions for students who engage in bullying behavior, and parents are clear on what repercussions and punishments will be enforced should their child bully another child.

Zero tolerance policies have been less than effective so far in the pursuit of bully-free schools. Zero tolerance tends to make students and teachers reluctant to report bullying behavior because of the extreme punitive nature of a zero tolerance policy. If a student knows that his classmate will be expelled from school if she reports a bullying incident, she may hesitate to act or not act at all. And teachers may be less likely to reprimand and report a student who engages in bullying behavior if that teacher thinks the zero tolerance policy is too extreme.

Another problem with zero tolerance is that many of the children who bully (especially the younger offenders) are simply engaging in learned behavior. With early intervention, many bullies can be taught not to bully. Expelling a student for a first offense is extreme and is essentially sending the student to another school where he will likely continue the behavior.

Alert!

Critics of zero tolerance policies suggest that these policies are inconsistent with healthy childhood development. Childhood is a time of growth and development, and it should be a time to practice and develop cognitive, social, and academic skills. Zero tolerance imposes harsh punishment without allowing for positive instruction, further guidance, or rehabilitation.

Graduated sanctions allow for appropriate punishments and consequences that can modify the bully's behavior. Add counseling and peer mentoring to the mix, and help can be provided for the bully (help should always be provided to the victim). The sanctions should escalate in scope and may very well end in expulsion if other, lesser sanctions have failed to correct a bully's behavior. The graduated sanctions should be clear and should be provided to every school employee, student, and parent.

Consistent Enforcement of Sanctions

It is vital that school personnel consistently enforce bullying sanctions. The sanctions will be completely ineffective if they are not enforced equally across the board. No child can be exempt from the sanctions—not the popular kids, not the athletes, not the kids who have parents working in the school system. The consequences for bullying must be enforced without discrimination. If the school fails to do this, the students will not trust in fair treatment, the program will not be successful, and bullying will continue.

Increased Supervision in Trouble Spots

In every school there are certain places where bullying occurs frequently. In some schools it's the playground, in others it might be the bathrooms. If administrators can identify the most likely places bullying occurs (this can be done via anonymous student surveys), they can increase the level of supervision in these areas. It may take some creative maneuvering (and some parent volunteers), but this should be seen as a necessary and important aspect of bullying prevention.

 Fact

Some schools are adopting district-wide definitions, policies, and sanctions regarding bullying and are including them in student, teacher, and parent handbooks. A handbook is a book or booklet that outlines information on academic, procedural, and student-affairs policies, rules, and procedures.

Continued Education and Intervention

With staff turnover and a new batch of students entering the school each year, bullying prevention and education programs must be conducted on an ongoing basis. And with the national attention bullying in schools is starting to receive, there are new studies and valuable research being conducted and released on a regular basis. This new information should be incorporated into existing programs. The goal is for schools to have access to the best and most effective anti-bullying programs and be able to keep abreast of new finding, suggestions, and recommendations.

CHAPTER 16

Cyber Bullying

A decade ago, a chapter on cyber bullying would not have been included in a book of this nature because tweens and teens were limited to bullying the old-fashioned, in-person way. Since then, the rapid advance of technology has allowed kids to broaden their bullying horizons to the point where cyber bullying is now a serious issue. Cyber bullying is generally defined as deliberate ongoing intimidation, harassment, or threats conducted via any type of communication technology including e-mail, instant messenger (IM), chat rooms, social networking sites, cell phones, pagers, and more.

Types of Cyber Bullying

Despite progress in defining and identifying cyber bullying, confusion remains surrounding exactly what constitutes cyber bullying. It might help to first understand some of the various ways your child could be the target of a cyber bully.

Harassment

In order for a behavior to be labeled as harassment, it must be repetitive and offensive. And for it to be considered a form of cyber bullying, it must occur online. Online harassment is common among kids who use e-mail, instant messaging, text messaging, and social networking sites. Harassment is probably the simplest way to bully another child online. A bully can send hundreds of hostile e-mail messages and can enlist the help of her friends to do the same. A bully can launch a "text war" and send hundreds of nasty text messages to another child's cell phone. Not only will the victim have to sort through hundreds of hate-filled messages, she will have a huge bill to pay for all the text messages she receives. Parents beware.

 Fact

Cyber bullying, by definition, must occur between minors. When adults engage in behavior that fits the definition of cyber bullying, it is called cyberharassment or cyberstalking. It is not that an adult can't be bullied; it is just not defined as such in the adult world.

Marta accused Sonia of trying to steal Marta's boyfriend. Sonia denied it because it wasn't true. Marta refused to believe Sonia and told Sonia to watch her back. When Sonia arrived home from school that day and logged onto her e-mail account, she had 760 messages. Sonia opened the first one and read, "You are the biggest whore in school and everyone knows it! We hate you, you slut!" Sonia opened a few more; each e-mail was meaner and more derogatory than the one before it.

Though mortified, Sonia told her parents and her parents tried to discover if Marta was the one behind the e-mail attack. Unfortunately, the person sending the harassing e-mails had opened an anonymous e-mail account. Sonia's parents were unable to find out who was harassing their daughter. Despite not knowing who opened the account, they were able to notify the sender's ISP (Internet Service Provider) and get the account shut down. This stopped the horrible e-mails—but not for long. Within hours, Sonia's mail box was once again filled with hate.

Harassment is usually long lasting and one-sided. The harassed child might know who is harassing her, or she may have no idea who is behind the attacks. Many kids who suffer this type of cyber bullying must repeatedly change their e-mail address, their online username, and their cell phone number. And even then, a tech-savvy bully can find other ways to taunt and torture.

Question?

Are you familiar with the term "griefer?"
A griefer is an online bully who tries to harass, embarrass, or push around kids playing online multiplayer video games such as Star Wars Galaxies, SOCOM, and Halo 2. Griefers have video-game companies concerned that kids who are taunted will cancel their subscriptions. Many companies are employing new methods to find and sanction griefers.

Flaming

Flaming can be described as a contentious or heated online exchange between two or more kids. It usually begins as a normal interaction in a chat room, on a discussion board, or even during an instant-messaging session.

Giovanni was a science buff who enjoyed participating in chat-room discussions that were set up specifically for kids with a penchant for science. One day, Giovanni disagreed with a comment that another student made about green living. The other student responded with a rude and insulting comment and proceeded to continue to post nasty follow-up comments to Giovanni. Soon, several more students were "flaming" Giovanni. When Giovanni tried to defend himself, the flaming got worse.

Flaming usually occurs in a public online environment with many users present. It can be restricted to just two users, or it can include many users. Flaming can get very personal, be very intense, and can cause strong emotional reactions. It many instances, it is of relatively short duration, but if your child continues to participate in that particular chat room, it can continue to be an ongoing situation.

Denigration

Merriam Webster's Collegiate Dictionary defines the word "denigrate" as, "to cast aspersions on; belittle." When a child is the victim of denigration, it means that someone has spread a lie or started a malicious rumor with the intention of maligning the victim's character and reputation. This can be carried out numerous ways: an e-mail or instant message containing false accusations and statements could be sent out to other students; a slanderous statement could be posted on a website or social networking site; a nasty passage could be written about the victim in an online slam book; or a photo of the victim could be digitally altered and posted online or sent via e-mail to others with the sole intention to humiliate and embarrass the victim.

Impersonation

This is where one child poses as or impersonates another child (the victim). Great harm can be wreaked if a child's online identity is stolen and it is made to look like the victim sent hateful or hurtful communications to others.

Vicky had a fight with Chloe and the two friends didn't speak for a week. As time went by, Vicky got angrier and angrier and decided she wanted to get back at Chloe for starting the fight and breaking off the friendship. Vicky pretended to make up with Chloe and then suggested they go home from school together so they could go online to update their MySpace pages. When Chloe logged into her MySpace account, Vicky paid close attention and discovered Chloe's password.

That night, Vicky logged onto Chloe's MySpace page (as Chloe) and changed everything on her page. Vicky wrote mean and spiteful things about Chloe's friends, insulted Chloe's boyfriend, and posted a very unflattering photo of Chloe taken at a recent sleepover. Vicky then went to Chloe's e-mail account and sent a mass e-mail to all their mutual friends with a live link to Chloe's MySpace page. The e-mail said, "Look what I really think of you all. . . ."

When Chloe arrived at school the next morning, she had no idea why everyone was mad at her. No one would speak to her and most of her friends were calling her bitch and loser. Finally, one girl told Chloe that people were angry because she dissed them on her MySpace page.

Chloe had no idea what she was talking about until she went home and logged onto her MySpace page. What she saw there horrified her. Vile and hateful things were written about all her close friends, and the terrible picture of Chloe in her underwear was almost too much to bear. Chloe was mortified and had no idea how to fix the situation. She took down the page and sent an e-mail denial and apology to her friends, but the damage was done.

 **Fact**

According to the Pew Internet & American Life Project—a nonprofit fact tank that explores the impact of the Internet on children, families, communities, the workplace, schools, health care, and civic/political life—39 percent of tweens and teens who used social networking sites such as MySpace and Facebook had been the victims of some type of online bullying.

Fake e-mails and bogus instant messages can be sent, personal profiles can be altered on social networking sites, and phony blogs and community posts can be created. The number of ways kids can impersonate other kids is mind-boggling. And the damage can be significant. In extreme cases of Internet impersonation, a particularly vengeful perpetrator can post the victim's name, phone number, e-mail address, or real address on a pedophile or hate-group website. If the perpetrator insults the members of the hate group or baits the pedophiles, it can put the victim in serious physical harm—threatening her safety and even her life.

Trickery

This is a popular strategy for cyber bullying. It can be accomplished fairly easily and can damage the victim's social standing significantly.

Andrea was desperate to belong to the "in" crowd. Andrea dressed like the popular girls, tried to walk and talk like them, and joined all the same extracurricular activities. Andrea tried everything, but the popular girls continued to ignore her. One day, Andrea received an e-mail from Ashlyn, the most popular girl at school. Ashlyn asked Andrea about a recent homework assignment. Andrea was thrilled to be able to help Ashlyn and she hoped that the popular girls would now let her in to their group.

Over the next few weeks, Ashlyn e-mailed Andrea to ask her opinion on various girls. Ashlyn told Andrea that they were holding informal "auditions" for girls who wanted to become part of the popular crowd. Ashlyn would sometimes insult a particular girl, and Andrea, wanting to please Ashlyn and fit in, would bash the girl as well. Andrea felt terrible about saying bad things about some of the other girls (especially those who were her friends), but Ashlyn assured her that their discussions were private and confidential.

Ashlyn lied. When Andrea went in to school on the day that Ashlyn told her she would announce the next addition to the popular girls' group, Andrea's desk was filled with disgusting trash and nasty notes. Andrea read a few of the notes and realized that Ashlyn had lied and tricked her into saying bad things about her friends. And now those friends all hated her! Ashlyn and the popular girls were gathered to one side of the room giggling and acting innocent. Ashlyn had printed out all of the e-mails (with Ashlyn's own insulting comments conveniently deleted) and handed them out to all the girls in the class. The e-mails made Andrea look very bad in the eyes of her friends and they subsequently shut her out. Andrea lost all of her friends.

Outing

When someone shares personal information that was meant to remain private, it is called outing. Girls tend to use this method of cyber bullying more than boys due to the more intimate nature of their relationships. When two girls get in a fight, chances are good that both girls have a stockpile of personal information that they can share with others online that will hurt, embarrass, or humiliate.

Exclusion

It hurts to be excluded from cliques and groups in real life, and it can hurt just as much to be excluded from online groups. Some call online exclusion cyberostracism. A child can be suddenly blocked from sending e-mail or instant messages to one or more other people. A child can be denied being added as a friend on a social-networking site, and it can hurt as much as being blocked from sitting at a certain lunchroom table that suddenly becomes too full or a study group that has no room for one more.

 Fact

According to ComScore, a leader in measuring activity in the digital world, social networking site MySpace.com attracted more than 114 million visitors in 2007 (this represents a 72 percent increase over the year before). Facebook.com attracted 52.2 million visitors (a 270 percent increase). Bebo.com had 18.2 million (a 172 percent increase) and Tagged.com had 13.2 million (a 774 percent increase).

To be excluded from online social activity can be like a social death to some kids. Communicating online has become a natural extension of in-person socializing and when that communication is blocked or cut off, it can be devastating. The victim is left out and has to live with the knowledge that all the other kids are talking, gossiping, making plans, and having fun without her.

Exposure

This is when kids post inappropriate photos or videos online. In the past, when a kid took an embarrassing or compromising photograph of another kid, just a few people were likely to see it. It might get passed around in school or at soccer practice, but the power to embarrass and humiliate was fairly limited. Today, that photo can be posted online for millions to see, and it can hang around in cyberspace forever and come back to haunt the victim even in adulthood.

In the past, when kids would fight, it would be a similar situation. There might have been a few kids who witnessed the fight and talked about it for days or weeks afterward, but when it was over it was over. Today, fistfights and beat-downs are being recorded with digital cameras and cell phones and uploaded to video-sharing websites like YouTube. The fight is exposed to millions of viewers, who can watch it or forward it as many times as they please. This type of exposure leads to unending humiliation and victimization.

Why Cyber Bullying Has Become such a Problem

It takes a certain kind of child to bully another child. And it takes a certain kind of contempt and disregard for the victim's rights to be able to treat a fellow classmate with cruelty. But at least the traditional bully is relatively easy to identify. A traditional bully draws from a fairly consistent set of bullying methods. He will physically or verbally attack his victim, use relational aggression, or extort. Researchers have studied and pinpointed the constellations of behaviors a traditional bully will employ to bully others. Researchers know the common characteristics of bully children, and they are starting to understand how to intervene and stop the cycle of traditional bullying.

The study of cyber bullying, on the other hand, is in its infancy. This is because researchers are just beginning to understand the full scope of the problem, and because technology is advancing at such a rapid pace, researchers are not able to keep up with the types of bullying it unleashes.

Cyber bullying is not as easy to identify as traditional bullying. In the impersonal and one-dimensional world of the Internet, it can be tough to read the nuances of online communication. For example: you might read an instant message between your son and his friend that appears to be hostile. When you question your son about it, he laughs and says they talk like that online all the time, and that it's just a joke.

Or you might find your daughter in tears over an e-mail her friend sent. When you read the e-mail, you can't figure out what your daughter is upset about. Even after you ask for clarification, you are still confused. With online communication, kidding around can be mistaken for bullying, and bullying can be so subtle that it is overlooked or misunderstood by parents.

 Fact

According to the Pew Internet & American Life Project, the average eight- to eighteen-year-old spends over an hour a day on the computer and spends a total of six hours and twenty-one minutes exposed to media of some sort (television, radio, movies, video games, etc).

How, Who, and Why

Technology is a normal part of your child's life; she doesn't know any different. She doesn't recall the days before cell phones and Black-Berrys, laptops and wireless routers, social networking sites, and personal e-mail accounts. Your child has grown up in a technological world that is making rapid advances and introducing so many new gizmos and gadgets that even technophiles have trouble keeping up. Is it any wonder that parents (who didn't grow up with a dizzying array of electronic communication devices) are often unsure how to monitor and police the use of devices that they don't fully understand?

It is a known fact that some kids who bully in person also bully online. But it is also known that kids who would never bully in person will do so online—mainly because of the anonymity. And kids who are victims of in-person bullying will sometimes bully online.

The reasons kids cyber bully are too numerous to count. But some of the more common reasons are that it's a way to continue bullying that began as in-person bullying; it can happen as a result of a fight or falling out; a bullied child can seek revenge through online means; a child might enjoy hurting and scaring other kids; a tween or teen might use the Internet to carry out relational aggression; or a kid or group of kids might cyber bully for fun and entertainment—which would be the online equivalent of the old-fashioned prank phone call.

You Can't See Me, I Can't See You

The most dangerous and seductive allure of the Internet is the anonymity it affords. Unfortunately for kids (but fortunately for adults when intervention is necessary), they believe that what they do online is private. The younger, less tech-savvy kids believe that what they do online disappears once they delete it. A fourth grader might send a rude and insulting e-mail and be shocked to discover that the mother of his victim has traced the e-mail back to his parent's account. A tenth grader might be surprised to discover that the police can trace threatening messages he posted on his ex-girlfriend's MySpace page back to him.

When teens use the Internet, they sometimes believe they are invisible or that their activities are untraceable. This is not true. Most online activities can be traced. But thinking they are safe from detection, many teens will engage in online behavior that they would never perform in real life. The perceived anonymity strips them of their normal checks and balances and social controls.

Bullying another child is easier to do online because the bully isn't face to face with the victim. The bully can't see the hurt on the victim's face, and she can't hear the misery in the victim's words and tone of voice. This emboldens kids to push the envelope of cruel treatment even further than they would in person. Their inhibitions disappear without a face-to-face confrontation, and the results can range from mildly hurtful to completely devastating.

Impact of Cyber Bullying

The impact of cyber bullying is similar to traditional schoolyard bullying—it causes significant physical, emotional, and psychological distress. The consequences of cyber bullying are also far reaching and affect everyone involved. Bullied kids suffer short-term (anxiety and fear) and long-term negative effects (depression, low self-esteem, and compromised educational opportunities). And the children who bully suffer from short- (maladaptive social interactions) and long-term problems (increased criminality, dysfunctional relationships, and alcohol and substance abuse). But in addition to the customary effects of traditional bullying (which you can review in Chapter 10), cyber bullying has some unique and disturbing additional effects.

The Bullying Can Be Anonymous

When a child bullies your child at school, at least she is a known entity. Your child knows who she is, what she looks like, and can try to avoid her as much as possible. In a cyber bullying situation, your child may never learn the identity of the bully. This can add to your child's distress.

The Bullying Can Be Relentless

When your child is bullied at school, she knows that at three o'clock she can go home and the bullying will end. She knows that she is safe on weekends, holidays, and during the summer. This knowledge gives your child a few breaks from the stress and worry of being bullied. When she is being cyber bullied, there are no breaks or holidays. The cyber bully can wreak havoc all hours of the day, every day of the week.

Equal Opportunity Bullying

It doesn't take any special physical strength or social prowess to bully someone online. And it doesn't take a great deal of courage. Anyone who has a cell phone or a computer with Internet access can bully another child. The problem with this is that many kids who wouldn't normal bully a peer might be tempted to do so when it is so easy to accomplish.

Signs of Cyber Bullying

Many of the signs of cyber bullying are similar to those of traditional bullying, and it can be difficult to pinpoint the difference between normal moody kids and their growing pains and the start of a serious problem. It is important to watch for a change in your child's behavior that isn't attributed to normal developmental changes. If your son normally loves to send instant messages to his friends but suddenly starts to resist using his computer and disables the IM feature when he does go online, it's time for a talk. If your son seems grouchy and upset after playing an online game with friends or deletes his e-mail without opening it, there might be a problem. Parents need to tune in and watch for unusual behavior or responses that happen in conjunction with computer use.

It can be difficult to get your child to open up about any abuse or mistreatment he is receiving. Older kids may feel that they can handle it on their own, they may be embarrassed to tell you what is happening, or they may be concerned about how you will react. Denial is likely the first line of defense. As with traditional bullying, studies show that the best time for intervention is when the online bullying first starts. Many kids can successfully stop the bullying if they are supported, coached, and assisted in their efforts. Unfortunately, the longer it continues, the harder it is to stop. So the first step for you, as a parent, is to be on the lookout for any of these signs:

- Your child might experience a sudden loss or increase in appetite, have stomach aches or headaches, or sleep disturbances (these are stress-related symptoms).
- Your child might become secretive and try to hide his computer communications from you. Watch for signs of excessive deleting, emptying of the deleted folder, or erasing of the history file. Or he may rapidly switch screens when you are near.
- Your child may be angry, sad, or depressed after spending time online, after a cell phone call, or after receiving a text message.

- Your child may act moody, sullen, or withdraw from family interaction.
- Your child may put himself down and say things like, "I'm stupid." "I have no friends." or "I would be better off dead."
- Your child might seem overly concerned with personal safety issues.

If you see any of these signs, tread lightly, but do try to get to the bottom of the situation. Kids tend to keep traditional bullying a secret, and studies are showing that online bullying might be reported or revealed even less often.

Ways to Protect Your Child

There are many ways to protect your child from cyber bullying, and you don't have to be a technical genius to do so.

Stay Involved

Many parents think they can install filtering software on their child's computer and—voila!—the child is protected. This is far from the truth; bullying can occur in spite of the best parental-control software. Unless you know exactly who your child is communicating with online, what websites he's visiting, what communities he belongs to, which social networking sites he uses, and what types of communications he is sending and receiving, you are not doing enough to protect your child. Many parents are surprised to find out that their child is being cyber bullied or that their child is a cyber bully. It is not usually something that a parent can uncover at first glance. It can take careful monitoring and ongoing supervision to discover a problem—and by then, the harm has been done.

Have an Open-Door Policy

Keep the computer in a public family space in your home. You can keep tabs on what your child is doing, what sites he is visiting, and who he is communicating with if you can see the screen. Make sure you know all of the screen names and passwords your child uses to access his private information and online communities. Explain that you will only use these if you suspect he is in danger or that he is engaging in unsafe or irresponsible behavior. Be clear about your rules for online behavior and don't hesitate to enforce them.

Essential

There are dozens of existing social networking sites (besides MySpace and Facebook), and more are being created every day. Here are a few of them: Bebo—open to people thirteen and older; Classmates—open to all; Friendster—open to people sixteen and older; Habbo—open to people thirteen and older; MOG—open to people fourteen and older; Windows Live—open to all.

Install Monitoring Software

You can buy and install keystroke-monitoring software that will record all of your child's online activities. This will allow you to monitor the communications and online activities of your child should you suspect he's being bullied or is bullying other children.

Question?

Is your child a supercommunicator?
According to the Teens and Social Media study conducted by Pew Internet & American Life Project, 28 percent of kids are super-communicators who use every available means of technology to communicate (phone, cell phone, text message, instant message, social networking sites, and e-mail). These kids thrive on multitasking and enjoy staying in constant contact with family and friends.

Responding to Cyber Bullying

The best way to prevent your child from becoming the victim of a cyber bully is to educate her on the strategies that cyber bullies use to attack their victims. Explain the similarities and differences of cyber bullying and traditional bullying. And discuss what she needs to do if she believes she is being targeted by a cyber bully. It is important to reassure your child that you won't restrict her Internet use as a result of a bullying incident, but that you do need to be aware of it so you can help. Tell her if she hides it from you, then you will have to restrict her online use, as she will have proven that she isn't mature enough to go online.

 Fact

According to the Pew Internet & American Life Project, 64 percent of teens create online content; 58 percent of teens have created their own profile on a social networking site such as MySpace or Facebook; 47 percent of teens have uploaded photos to the Internet; and 28 percent of teens have blogs.

Early intervention is key, as it can often prevent an escalation in the bullying behavior. As with traditional bullying, do not hesitate to intervene and get help for your child. No child deserves to be bullied, in person or online. Tell your child that if she is aware of another child (or a friend) being bullied online, she should let you know. Explain to her that by witnessing the online bullying and not reporting it, she is guilty of wrongdoing. Let her know that you want her to be part of the solution, not part of the problem.

Work with your child as she matures to help her understand the permanent nature of an online reputation. Explain to her that a photo of her drinking (when she's underage) at a party or engaging in other unlawful activities will be accessible online forever. Stress the importance of proper online behavior and conduct.

Teach your child how to handle hurtful communications. Tell her it is okay to ignore them, but not to delete them. Tell her to be sure to always do the five following things if she has been the victim of cyber bullying.

Save the Communications
Save e-mails, IMs, text messages, and records of chat-room or community discussions, and print out web pages. This will give you proof should you need it in the future.

Try to Identify the Cyber Bully
It can be hard (and occasionally impossible) to track down the identity of your child's cyber bully. If the communication is an e-mail, ask your ISP (internet service provider) to identify the source of the e-mail. If that doesn't work, contact a company that specializes in finding such information. If a crime has been committed, the police may be able to track down the offender. And, if you plan to file a lawsuit, an attorney might have access to those avenues as well.

Ignore the Communications
If the cyber bully gets no response, he may give up and move on to the next victim.

Tell the Offender to Stop
Clearly and firmly tell the cyber bully to cease and desist. Inform the bully that you have reported the incident to the police and that they will investigate. Change your child's e-mail address or block the bully's communications and instruct your child to avoid visiting any sites where she has been attacked.

Report the Attack
Kids who cyber bully or harass other kids are usually in violation of the company policies of most phone companies, ISPs, and websites. Look for the "Contact Us" information for the company who provides your service and follow the steps to file a complaint. If the

school computers are involved, file a complaint with the school. If the bullying is severe or threatening, file a police report.

Prevent Your Child from Being a Cyber Bully

Your child must be clear on the guidelines and rules you set up for appropriate Internet use. He must be given a list of acceptable and unacceptable behaviors and he must know that a violation of the rules will end in restricted Internet use. You should discuss cyber bullying and inform your child of the possible civil and criminal consequences if he engages in cyber bullying. Your child should understand that the high standards of behavior you hold for him in real life are to be continued in his online life.

 Essential

Keep up to date with common Internet acronyms and you will be able to decipher your child's communications. For an exhaustive catalogue of Internet slang, go to *www.netlingo.com /acronyms.php*. Here's a few all parents should know: POS (parent over shoulder), PIR (parent in room), KPC (keep parents clueless), PA (parent alert) YBS (you'll be sorry), and LMIRL (let's meet in real life).

Explain to your child that the seeming anonymity of the Internet may make it seem okay to engage in irresponsible online behavior, but that the recipients of negative or hurtful messages or harassment can track him down and discover his identity. Also inform him that you will be held responsible for his behavior, as he is still a minor child.

Be sure he understands that even if he is attacked online, he should never retaliate. If he does, and continues a back-and-forth attack, he is also guilty of cyber bullying. Google your child's name every now and again to check for objectionable content and to find things your child may not even be aware of.

Consider installing monitoring software so you can be sure your child is not engaging in unethical or illegal activities. Some parents say this is a violation of their child's trust; one way you can confront the ethical implications of monitoring software is to inform your child that all of their Internet activity will be monitored. Simply informing your child that the software exists can immediately deter potentially inappropriate behavior.

CHAPTER 17

What if My Child Is a Bully?

Every parent worries that their child might fall prey to a bully. But what if you get a call from another parent or the school principal informing you that your child is a bully? How would you respond? Would you know how to handle it? Many parents don't realize that children who bully suffer in ways similar to their victims. Bullies are at risk for school difficulties, depression, and self-esteem issues; and in the future, they suffer much higher levels of interpersonal problems, violence, and criminal activity.

Signs that Your Child Might Be a Bully

There are numerous traits that researchers have identified that can result in higher levels of bullying behavior. Keep an eye out for these types of traits:

- Lack of empathy or compassion for others' feelings
- Needs to be in control
- Easily frustrated
- Underdeveloped social and interpersonal skills
- Quick to place blame for her actions on others
- Has a need to win or to be the best at everything
- Seems to derive pleasure from the pain and suffering of others
- Shows little or no remorse for negative behavior

- Misinterprets others' intentions as hostile or aggressive
- Attacks before someone can attack her
- Disregards most rules
- Seeks both positive and negative attention
- Hangs around with kids who are considered to be a bad influence
- Likes to hurt or injure pets
- Parents are overly punitive or overly permissive
- Has been bullied by a peer, sibling, or parent

There are many other traits that might reveal your child's potential for bullying behavior. Each child is different and your child might fit just a few of these traits or she may fit all of them. The best thing to do if you suspect there is a problem is to keep an eye on your child's interactions with other children. Watch how she relates to adults and peers, and try to figure out the situations that might cause the most trouble. Talk with your child's teachers and the principal. Ask them what their observations are and what areas your child needs to work on. Talk with the parents of your child's friends. Ask them if they have seen bullying behavior and, if so, what would they do if it were their child? Read some books on bullying and go online to see what type of information is available for the parents of a child who bullies other children. The more you educate yourself, the better equipped you will be to help your child.

Keep an Open Mind

If you suspect (or know for a fact) that your child is a bully, don't panic. You should be glad that you know and that you can now do something about it. Bullying is learned behavior and learned behavior can be unlearned. Your child, with your help, can learn why bullying behavior is detrimental to both himself and his victim. He can learn new, more appropriate, behaviors and he can learn to make amends for his past behavior.

The worst thing you can do, upon finding out that your child has been harassing other children, is to condemn him. Don't call him a bully and simply punish him; he will get angry and lash out in even more aggressive ways. Instead, you want to condemn the behavior while showing your child you love him enough to help him find more appropriate ways of handling peer pressure, his feelings, and conflict with his peers. You will need to love him more—not less—in order to guide your child toward successful and healthy peer interaction.

 Essential

If you get a call from a parent informing you that your child engaged in bullying behavior, stay calm. Don't automatically deny it, because it may, in fact, be true. All children have the capacity to bully. It is important to learn the facts of the situation and figure out the best way to handle it before you approach your child.

Intervention

Once you discover that your child is engaging in bullying behavior, you will need to intervene. Immediate intervention is important in order to protect the victim of your child's bullying, but it is also important to protect your own child. Being a bully has some very real and detrimental effects. Bullies aren't the lucky ones who sail through school because they have the ability to pick on others and rise to the top of the playground pig pile.

When bullies get labeled as such, it harms their ability to have authentic and positive peer relationships. Most kids are afraid of and intimidated by bullies. They will be nice to the bully so the bully leaves them alone, but they resent having to do this and will interact in a perfunctory and impersonal manner. Because of this, a bully won't have the opportunity to develop close personal relationships that prepare her for successful adult romantic and interpersonal relationships.

Studies show adults who were identified as bullies at a young age are at a higher risk of developing antisocial behaviors such as vandalism, shoplifting, skipping and dropping out of school, fighting, and the use of drugs and alcohol. This is why it is important for you to intervene as soon as you discover that your child is bullying her peers.

Psychological

The first step in solving the problem is to figure out what is motivating your child to bully her peers. Why is she bullying? Don't be afraid to come right out and ask her why she tripped Janet on the school bus and ripped pages out of her textbook. Ask her and listen closely to her response. Also ask questions like these to get a better picture of the overall problem:

- What was happening right before your child decided to trip Janet?
- Has your child ever tripped Janet or another child before?
- What happened immediately after your child tripped Janet?
- Were there any bystanders who saw the bullying? If so, what did they do?
- How long has your child been bullying other kids?
- Does your child feel remorse for hurting Janet?

Questions like these will give you some insight into what your child was (and is) thinking about her behavior. If your child tells you, "Janet deserved to be tripped because she walks too slowly," you know that your child is blaming the victim for her behavior. If she tells you that everyone laughed immediately after she tripped Janet, you can be sure that your child was reinforced for her negative behavior. The fact that she remembered and recounted the laughter to you implies that she was pleased by it. The laughter might also have sent the message that your daughter's behavior was acceptable and admired because the other kids on the bus didn't tell her to stop—they laughed.

If your child tells you that this was the first time she bullied another child and that she is embarrassed and ashamed by what she did, you will have an easier time teaching her why bullying is wrong. Occasionally, good kids will bully other kids in order to impress a new friend, to go along with the crowd, or to increase popularity.

Listen to her explanation and use the information to explain to her why her reasoning was faulty. Buy her an age-appropriate book on bullying and require her to read it (an excellent disciplinary approach). After she's done reading it, have a discussion about what she learned and reiterate your expectations for her behavior in the future. Discuss what the consequences will be if she continues to engage in bullying behavior.

If your child tells you that she does it (bullying) all the time, you will need to pay significantly more attention to identifying the underlying reasons for her behavior and focus on using education and consistent discipline to correct her behavior. You may discover that your child has some deep-seated psychological issues (such as a total disrespect and disregard for others' feelings and well-being), anger control issues, or that she is simply blind to her own faults. In a situation like this, you will need to seek professional help for your child. A trained counselor, psychologist, or psychiatrist may be the best person to help your child understand the true impact that bullying has on her life and the lives of others.

If you feel that your child's bullying is something you can tackle on your own, here are a few things you can do to help.

EXAMINE YOUR APPROACH TO DISCIPLINE

Do you verbally berate your child and say things like, "Stop acting like such a loser!" "What are you, stupid?" or "I brought you into this world and I can take you out!"? Do you use physical punishment? Do you push, slap, or use physical force to discipline your child? If so, your child may be imitating the behavior she learns at home.

EXAMINE YOUR PARENTING STYLE

Are you overly strict? If so, your child may have learned that she can get her way through a show of force. She will demand respect by forcing her peers to do as she says when she says it; and if they refuse, she will attack. She has learned that might is right, but lacks the sophistication and maturity to achieve the power she craves thorough constructive channels. She will bully and use destructive means to gain control.

Perhaps you have been too permissive. If so, your child may not have developed the self-control necessary to handle peer interactions without resorting to bullying behavior. If your child has not received focused guidance and corrective consequences for prior negative and inappropriate behavior, she may believe she can do as she pleases without fear of punishment. If you are guilty of some of these less-than-stellar approaches to parenting, you can make changes right alongside your child. You can learn to approach parenting with the balance of concern, interest, and firm discipline a child needs.

 Essential

For Information on better parenting practices, read *Seven Secrets of Successful Parenting: Or How to Achieve the Almost Impossible* by Georgia Coleridge and Karen Doherty; *Playful Parenting* by Lawrence J. Cohen; and *Parenting with Purpose: Five Keys to Raising Children with Values and Vision* by Robert W. Reasoner and Marilyn L. Lane.

EXAMINE YOUR RELATIONAL STYLE

Take a good look at how you treat others. Do you respect other people and treat them with kindness? Do you abide by the Golden Rule (treat others as you would like to be treated)? If you treat others with disdain and disrespect, your child will learn that this is the way to treat people. Be aware that your actions and attitudes have an enormous impact on your child. Conduct yourself with honor and dignity and your child will do the same.

EXAMINE YOUR CHILD'S PSYCHOLOGICAL HEALTH

Is your child depressed? Does she suffer from anxiety? Does she have anger control issues? Does she have a disability or learning disorder?

There are many internal factors that can affect your child's behavior. How your child feels about herself (positive or negative) can impact how she interacts with those around her. Some kids with psychological or physical problems lack the social skills to act in socially acceptable ways. But even if the behavior isn't intentional, it needs to be stopped.

Once you have figured out the possible causes for your child's bullying behavior, you will be better able to help her. And don't take it personally; most parents do the very best job they know how to do. And when parents know how to do better, they do better. View your child as an individual who needs your guidance and support in order to become a better person. Once your child knows better, she will do better. Don't waste time looking for someone (or something) to blame; simply take responsibility for your actions and teach your child to do the same.

Here are some intervention strategies:

- Accept that there is problem that needs to be fixed.
- Assess the underlying causes.
- Make it clear that you expect bullying behavior to stop.
- Implement consequences for bullying behavior.
- Be realistic in your expectations (change takes time).
- Keep the lines of communication open.
- Teach your child empathy and respect.
- Set a good example.
- Provide positive reinforcement for good behavior.
- Love your child unconditionally.
- Seek professional help if needed.

Social

Your child's social environment can provide clues into her bullying behavior. Here are a few things to consider.

WHO ARE YOUR CHILD'S FRIENDS?

Do you know your child's friends? How well do you know them? Are they nice and friendly or do they seem quiet and aloof? Some kids who bully hang out with other bullies; others act alone. Try to observe the interactions of your child and her friends. Do they seem healthy and normal or does it seem like something isn't quite right? If you suspect your child's friends are not a good influence, it might be time to begin steering your child in another direction. This can be difficult at first since many of your child's peers may view her as a bully, someone to be feared and avoided. And it might take time, change, and visible amends on your child's part for other children to accept that she has indeed changed.

DOES YOUR CHILD PARTICIPATE IN ACTIVITIES THAT FOSTER SOCIAL BEHAVIORS?

A child who bullies could benefit by participating in clubs, activities, and athletic programs that encourage respect and teamwork over individual achievement. Belonging to a group will allow your child to develop the interpersonal and relational skills she will need to form strong friendship bonds throughout her life. If your child does not belong to any such groups, now would be the time to encourage it.

School

As discussed in previous chapters, the school climate can have an extraordinary impact on the level of bullying that occurs within the school. School personnel who tolerate bullying contribute to an underlying acceptance of the behavior. If your child sees other kids engaging in bullying with no discernable consequence, your child won't fear repercussions. On the other hand, a school that does not tolerate bullying will have lower levels of bullying behavior.

Ask the school principal if your child's school conducts anti-bullying education and prevention programs. Find out what types of things are taught and when. Ask about the anti-bullying policy in your child's school. Be sure you understand the consequences your child can face for bullying. Some schools have graduated sanctions; others have a zero tolerance policy. If your child's school employs a zero tolerance policy, your child could be expelled for bullying another child. It's important to discuss these sanctions with your child. Your child needs to understand the consequences that will result from her behavior.

Teaching Your Child Friendship and Interpersonal Skills

If your child is bullying other kids, he should be coached in the areas of self-worth and proper social interaction. He may be bullying because he doesn't know how to assert himself in a nonaggressive manner. He may be uncomfortable socializing with his peers, and may act out in order to get attention and gain approval. Or your child may have difficulty handling confrontation and resolving conflicts. These things are not excuses for your child's behavior, they are merely possible explanations for why your child bullied.

Friendship Skills

If you look closely at your child's friendships, you may be surprised to discover that most of the kids he considers friends are actually no more than acquaintances. Put the friendships under a microscope and you might find that some of your child's friends hang out with him to avoid being the next target of his bullying. Other kids will avoid being near your child altogether. This means that your child doesn't really have any close friends; there are kids who avoid him and there are kids who do as he says out of fear and self-preservation.

After you halt the bullying behavior, you should focus on teaching your child how to be a good friend. You can refer to the information in Chapter 13 on how to teach your child to be a good friend. The same advice is appropriate for both victims and bullies. In addition, you can share with him these tips for fostering new friendships:

- Treat a friend the way you want to be treated.
- Show support and stick up for your friends.
- Be truthful but not unkind.
- If you hurt a friend's feelings, apologize.
- Accept your friend for who he is; don't try to change him.
- If you make a promise to a friend, keep it.
- Appreciate your friends.

Interpersonal Skills

When your child forms close and lasting friendships, he will hone and develop his social skills. Refer back to Chapter 14 to review the importance of social skills and how to develop the most important ones. If your child improves his social skills, he will have a broader number of successful strategies to use in difficult or challenging social situations. You don't want your child to fall back on his prior bullying behavior or to continue to bully simply because it is a habit. You want your child to have a number of positive, prosocial options to draw upon.

Create More Feel-Good and Do-Good Opportunities

Behavior modification is the psychological theory that you can change a person's behavior through the application of positive reinforcement and punishment. It works simply by reinforcing desired behaviors and punishing undesirable behaviors. That said; it makes sense to expose your child to opportunities where he will be positively reinforced for good behavior. Give him the chance to be successful and he will experience how good it feels to be reinforced for his positive behaviors (instead of destructive ones).

Sandra was upset to learn that her son was bullying a handicapped boy on his baseball team. Sandra had some in-depth conversations with her son about bullying and she gave him a couple of books to read. She also told him that he should be prepared to volunteer six hours of his time this coming weekend. Sandra arranged for her son to assist at a practice for the Special Olympics (an athletic competition for individuals with mental retardation or developmental disabilities). When Sandra's son found out where he would be volunteering, he was upset. Sandra held firm and required her son to volunteer.

That day, Sandra kept a close eye on her son and noticed how he smiled and noticeably perked up whenever someone complimented him on the job he was doing. He also seemed to enjoy helping the handicapped kids. Sandra realized that her son needed the opportunity to do things that brought out the best in him; he needed to do good things in order to feel good about himself.

It is your responsibility as a parent to expose your child to activies and experiences that will build his confidence and his sense of self-worth. All children have good in them; bringing it out is sometimes the difficult thing. Most kids want to be good and do good; many just don't know how to go about it. Volunteering is a great way to help your child feel good about himself and about what he can do to help others.

Engage in Constructive, Supervised Activities and Sports

This is one of the easiest and most constructive ways to channel the energy and aggressive impulses of your child. When you sign your child up for the soccer team, she will learn team-building skills while she gets to expend pent-up energy. If you sign her up for karate, she will learn self-control and the basic principles of respect while she diverts her aggressiveness into perfecting the form of her punches and kicks.

If you sign her up for drama, her self-esteem will increase as a result of belonging to a group and working toward a future goal—the end-of-the-year play. Sign her up for Girl Scouts and she learns to be more independent while learning about honor and good deeds. Let her take drum lessons and she can bang the drums to her heart's content while learning to self-motivate to a regular practice schedule.

The point here is to choose activities and sports that are well suited to your child's temperament. If your child is highly active, choose an activity with a lot of running and physical expenditure. If your child hates competitive sports, choose individual pursuits like karate or non-competitive swimming. If your child is creative, expose her to robot making, music lessons, or pottery class.

When you keep your child busy with activities she enjoys and can learn from, you are fostering her development. She will learn something from each activity or sport she participates in, and she will gain a sense of mastery and accomplishment. And the busier she is, the less time she will have to dwell on her less constructive impulses. Be careful not to overdo it; you want to relieve some of your child's stress, not add to it.

 Essential

Sit down with your child and develop a list of things he might be interested to learn or try. Don't judge, simply listen and make the list. You might be surprised to discover the types of things that capture your child's interest. Let your child choose his top three and do what you can to make it happen.

Limit Exposure to Violent Media

In Chapter 7, violence in the media was discussed. It is clear that the findings vary widely on whether or not violent media plays a significant role in the development of bullying behavior. Most parents don't question the fact that the media has some impact on their kids, but how much impact and to what degree it is positive or negative can vary greatly from parent to parent. Here's how to tell if your child is being affected by too much violent media.

Desensitization to Violence

Some children who are regularly exposed to high levels of media violence are apt to become desensitized to what they see on television. So-called reality television, violent and gory television shows, video games rated Mature or Adult, and access to inappropriate website content can all contribute to a situation where a child no longer reacts negatively (and can begin to react positively) to aggressive and violent behavior. When this happens, violence and gore no longer have shock value for the child; he views it as normal.

Numbing

Once a child is desensitized to media violence, it is only a matter of time before he is desensitized to real-life violence. He may no longer react to seeing another child in pain or suffering. If a classmate is being beat up, he will watch without feeling any sympathy or concern.

Imitation

Every parent has witnessed their child imitating something he has seen on television. If your child begins to act out aggressive and hostile behavior, you will need to intervene and limit his amount of exposure to violent media.

Intimidation

Some kids react to exposure to violent media by overreacting to the danger in the world. If your child witnesses extreme violence on television, he may fear that it is real and that it could happen to him in real life. He will become anxious and upset and feel that the world is an unsafe place and the people in it are mean and vengeful.

CHAPTER 18

Bullying Among Children with Special Needs

It is heartbreaking when any child is being harassed and bullied by her peers, but it's even more concerning when a child with special needs is targeted and abused. A child with special needs has physical, mental, emotional, or social deficits that she is unable to control. These deficits make her an easy target for teasing, taunting, harassment, and abuse. And research shows that kids with special needs are bullied at a higher rate than regular kids.

Are Schools Protecting Your Children?

Special needs kids may not even understand they are being taunted and bullied, and if they do understand, they are distressed when they realize it is because of their disability. The sad truth is that schools that are not yet able to protect mainstream kids from bullying and harassment are probably not equipped to protect special needs kids; but to be realistic, there is no such thing as a completely bully-free school. Bullying will occur—that's a fact. Kids will tease and taunt, gossip and ridicule, and push and shove. But in schools with a healthy, nontolerant climate toward bullying, peer harassment will be quickly identified and stopped. Teachers and parents won't contribute to the problem and students won't remain silent when they witness bullying and peer abuse.

Schools have a responsibility to protect your child, but you also have the responsibility to provide the school with support and encouragement for doing so. You have heard the statement, "It takes a village to raise a child." Well, it takes that same village working toward the same goal to reduce the level of bullying in school-age children. Every school is currently facing the predicament of trying to balance its legal and ethical responsibilities with its financial and educational goals.

Alert!

A few of the more effective anti-bullying prevention and intervention programs have boasted up to 50 percent decreases in bullying behavior. But at the moment, research shows that a more realistic measurement is about a 15 percent reduction in elementary schools that implement some of the better anti-bullying programs, and a 12 percent reduction in secondary schools. And even these statistics may be overly optimistic.

Some states have established anti-bullying legislation, and those clearer legal guidelines have paved the way for faster and more effective interventions and resolutions of bullying incidents. Antidiscrimination policies meant to protect special needs and disabled children are already in place and can offer an added layer of protection and defense when necessary.

Is Your Child Vulnerable?

All children are vulnerable to bullying, but special needs children are more vulnerable than so-called "normal" kids. The very fact that a special needs child has a disability makes him vulnerable to attack. It is a known fact that bullies seek out targets that are vulnerable. Bullies look for kids who won't defend themselves and who won't fight back. Special needs kids often fit this description; and many kids with severe special needs or serious social deficits would be unable to fight back even if they wanted to.

Fact

Children who have a physical or learning disability are at an increased risk for being involved in bullying situations. A 1991 study conducted by S. Ziegler and M. Rosenstein-Manner found that 38 percent of students identified as special education students were bullied.

Even kids with mild disabilities experience a higher rate of bullying. These kids might have behaviors considered socially awkward or have trouble grasping the subtle details of kid culture (like fashion trends or patterns of speech) that gain acceptance from peers. Let's face it, even typical kids have trouble gaining acceptance from their peers. For a special needs kid, the equation gets much more complicated. But there are several things you can do to help your special needs child.

Clearly Convey Your Expectations

Let your child's teachers, support team, and all school personnel know that you are aware of the additional risk your child faces in regard to bullying. Let them know that you will be actively monitoring the situation and that you want to be informed immediately of any bullying incidents involving your child.

Schedule a Special IEP or Section 504 Meeting

Express your desire to include anti-bullying education and social-skills training in your child's IEP. By requesting these things your child will be exposed to additional curriculum appropriate for her disability.

Talk to Your Child about Bullies

Using language that makes sense to your child, define exactly what constitutes bullying behavior. You will have to clearly spell it out. Some special needs kids are so accustomed to subtle forms of harassment that they fail to recognize exactly what bullying behavior is and don't realize it is wrong.

Role Play with Your Child

Tell your child what she should say when someone is unkind or hurtful. Be specific; tell her to say, "Stop saying that!" "I don't like it when you do that." or "Leave me alone!" Encourage her to tell you right away when someone is mean or hurtful.

Be Aware

Be aware of what is happening at school, on the bus, and in any special activities that your child participates in. Schedule regular meetings with all adults involved in your child's care. The meetings should be more frequent for those kids with severe disabilities who may not be able to speak for themselves. Consider volunteering—it's a great way to get an inside look at what your child experiences at school.

Watch for Changes in Your Child's Behavior

If you notice any signs of anxiety, depression, or school avoidance, step up your supervision and participation in your child's academic and outside activities. Talk with your child and ask her support team to talk with her as well. You will need to be vigilant and intervene quickly should a problem arise.

New Threat to Kids: Food-Allergy Taunts

In the past few years, there have been several media reports of children being bullied with the very food or substance that causes them to have an allergic reaction. There have been reports of a student sprinkling the remnants of a peanut butter cookie into the lunch box of a peanut-allergic classmate; reports of peanut butter being smeared on the arm of an allergic student; and threats of kissing or hugging an allergic student after eating a peanut butter sandwich. This type of behavior has been labeled allergy bullying, and it can be physically harmful and potentially lethal.

 Essential

According to the Food Allergy & Anaphylaxis Network (FAAN), a nonprofit organization dedicated to increasing public awareness, advocacy, education, and research on behalf of food-allergy sufferers, food allergy and anaphylaxis (a severe allergic reaction) is a growing public health concern. It is estimated that about 3 million children in the United States suffer from food allergies.

A food allergy creates a particular vulnerability in a child—an Achilles' heel of sorts. This identifiable weak spot can make your child vulnerable to bullying. As mentioned above, some kids will use a food allergy to taunt and threaten a classmate. They think it's funny to wave a peanut butter and jelly sandwich in the face of an allergic student to see the look of terror in his eyes. A bully will chase an allergic child, threatening to shove down his throat the food that he is allergic to. For parents, just the thought of this type of behavior sends chills of fear down their spines, because parents of kids with food allergies understand the extreme danger of such behavior.

Some parents of kids with food allergies think that parents of non-allergic kids may inadvertently foster insensitivity and, at times, contempt for allergic kids. For example:

Barbara receives a letter from her son's school requesting that no foods containing peanut butter or peanut butter products be sent in for snacks or lunch. Barbara is distressed by this news because her son, Frankie, refuses to eat anything but peanut butter and jelly for lunch. Barbara's husband walks in the kitchen and Barbara holds up the note and says sarcastically, "They should put all those kids with peanut allergies in one classroom and leave the normal kids alone! What am

I going to send in with Frankie? He adores peanut butter and jelly and now he can't have it at school! It's just so unfair!"

Barbara doesn't realize that Frankie overheard her. When school starts, Frankie realizes that he'll never be able to have his favorite sandwich for lunch and he's mad about that. When Frankie discovers that it is Doug who has the peanut allergy, he decides to make him pay. Frankie starts to harass and bully Doug every chance he gets. One day, he sneaks a bit of peanut butter into school in his backpack and smears it on Doug's pencil. Doug picks up the pencil and writes with it for a few seconds before he realizes that it has peanut butter on it. Doug has an allergic reaction and is rushed to the hospital.

 Fact

> The Food Allergy & Anaphylaxis Network reports that in the U.S., food allergy is the leading cause of anaphylaxis (a severe allergic reaction) outside the hospital setting. Recent analysis of data from U.S. hospital emergency departments also estimates that out of 20,821 visits, anaphylaxis (including 520 hospitalizations) due to a food allergy counted for 2,333 visits in just a two-month period.

The problem with this scenario is that the very children who should be protected are being targeted and picked on for things that are beyond their control. A child with an allergy is not responsible for that allergy, and nothing he does will get rid of it. When parents fail to educate their kids on the necessity of helping to ensure vulnerable kids' safety—or worse, when they ridicule or bully those kids—significant damage can occur. Kids wind up not knowing the severe and life-threatening impact their bullying and irresponsible behavior can have on their victim.

Kids might think that an allergic child might get a rash or be wheezy for a while or have a stomach ache. And it's true that many kids who have allergies have symptoms that are mild or bothersome, such as a runny nose, itchy throat, throat tightness, shortness of breath, hives, wheezing, cough, nausea, vomiting, stomach pain, or diarrhea. Some kids may not realize that an allergic child can die as a result of exposure to certain foods. And if they do know the potential consequences of their actions and choose to taunt and threaten allergic kids with the food they are allergic to, they are engaging in criminal behavior.

Alert!

Anaphylaxis (ah-nuh-fuh-lax-sis) is a sudden, severe allergic reaction that can cause a life-threatening physical reaction. Blood pressure drops, airways narrow, and a child's tongue can swell, impeding the ability to breath. Each year in the U.S., approximately 150–200 people die as a result of anaphylaxis caused by a food allergy.

Allergy and anaphylaxis education is necessary for parents, students, and school personnel. And strategies should be put into place for avoidance of food allergens and early recognition and treatment of symptoms in the event of accidental exposure. For children with severe allergic reactions, early administration of epinephrine (an adrenaline that is available in a self-injectable device) is vital. The parents of kids without allergies should try to put themselves in the shoes of parents who have kids with food allergies. Think about it: The average parent worries enough about their child becoming the victim of a traditional bully at school. Imagine that the bullying (in this case exposure to peanut butter) could be fatal for your child in mere minutes. How would you feel?

At this point in time, there is no known cure for food allergies. Because of this, it has become essential that school personnel, parents, and students understand food allergies and the life-threatening consequences of exposure. Death can occur within minutes if a student is unable to receive treatment for anaphylaxis.

Despite the fact that over 90 percent of American schools have students with food allergies, there are no current standardized guidelines for managing life-threatening allergies in schools. Support for such guidelines has been expressed by numerous organizations like the American Academy of Pediatrics, the American Medical Association, the National Association of Elementary School Principals, the National Association of School Nurses, the American Academy of Allergy, Asthma & Immunology, and more.

What Is Disability Harassment?

According to the United Stated Department of Education (2000), disability harassment is defined as, "intimidation or abusive behavior toward a student based on disability that creates a hostile environment by interfering with or denying a student's participation in or receipt of benefits, services, or opportunities in the institution's program." Disability harassment is illegal under Section 504 of the Rehabilitation Act of 1973 and Title II of the Americans with Disabilities Act of 1990. Section 504 covers all schools, school districts, and colleges and universities receiving federal funds. Title II covers all state and local entities, including school districts and public institutions of higher education, whether or not they receive federal funds.

Fact

There are several laws that protect children from disabilities harassment. Look into each one to become better educated about your child's rights: Americans with Disabilities Act, Individuals with Disabilities Education Act (IDEA), Section 504 of the Rehabilitation Act, State Penal laws (criminal law) in some states, and No Child Left Behind.

Bullying behavior can cross the line and become disability harassment if a disabled student is verbally threatened or physically harassed due to his disability. Even such things as another student repeatedly calling your child a "retard" or ridiculing him for having to ride the "short bus" are inappropriate and bullying. The law states that when a complaint is made or when the school discovers that harassment of a disabled student may have occurred, school personnel must investigate and respond appropriately. The major concern is that students who are exposed to disability harassment may suffer educational setbacks and be undermined in areas that are critical for their advancement.

What You Can Do if It Doesn't Stop

If your disabled child is being victimized by a bully, report it in writing immediately. If you have reported the abuse to your child's teachers, the staff, and the school administration, and the school district does not take reasonable and appropriate steps to stop the offensive behavior, the school district may be in violation of federal, state, and local laws. To find out more information about your rights and your child's legal rights, contact:

The U.S. Department of Education Office
of Special Education Programs
202-245-7468
www.ed.gov/about/offices/list/osers/osep/index.html

The U.S. Department of Education Office for Civil Rights
800-421-3481
www.ed.gov/about/offices/list/ocr/index.html

What to Do if Your Child Is Being Bullied

The first line of defense is being aware that your child runs a higher risk of victimization. Be aware and on the lookout for inappropriate peer behavior. Also, knowing your legal rights and the rights of your child will help you proceed with confidence if and when a problem occurs.

When faced with proof that your child is being bullied, there are several steps you should take:

1. **Be sure your child is safe.** If you suspect that your child is in physical danger, request immediate action by the school. Your child's safety should always be your number one concern.

2. **Report the incident.** Report the details of the incident or incidents in writing to all of the adults involved in your child's care. Everyone caring for your child should be alerted to the situation and asked to monitor and help protect your child. Keep detailed records of every incident involving your child and all of your communications to the school concerning the bullying incident or incidents.

3. **Ask to be updated on the resolution.** Due to your child's special situation, request that the school waste no time in remedying the situation. Ask that you be informed when corrective action has taken place. The school may not be allowed to discuss the sanctions for the perpetrator (due to privacy issues), but should be able to tell you what changes have been made to protect your child.

4. **Move up the chain of command.** If you are not satisfied that the situation has been resolved and that your child is now safe from harassment, request a meeting with your child's teacher, the school principal, and the superintendent. Be sure you understand your child's rights and don't back down in your request that the school ensure your child's health and well-being. Insist that the school personnel do everything in their power to protect your child.

5. **File a formal complaint.** If you are still not satisfied that your child is being protected, you can file a complaint with the U.S. Department of Education Office for Civil Rights. Be sure to do so within 180 days (about six months) of the incident. To access the Office for Civil Rights online, go to: *www.ed.gov/about/offices/list/ocr/complaintprocess.html*.

6. **Get legal advice.** If you are still unhappy and wish to file a legal complaint against your school district, you would be wise to contact an attorney who specializes in disabilities harassment.

Alert!

If you believe that your special needs child is being denied free appropriate public education (FAPE) in violation of the Individuals with Disabilities Act, you can file a request for an impartial hearing with the State Education Department. Note: A due process complaint must be in reference to a violation that occurred no more than two years in the past.

Is Legal Action Necessary?

In most instances, legal action is not necessary. Just the threat of a lawsuit is usually enough to spur even the most reluctant school system into corrective action. And in many cases the school district can offer parents and students a mediation program to successfully solve the problem. But, if after you have made reasonable efforts you are not getting the help and assistance you need from the school to protect your child and his learning environment, a lawsuit may have to be considered. Bullying isn't illegal in the U.S. (perhaps someday soon that will change), but to bully or harass a disabled child about her disability or in relation to her disability is illegal.

There have been numerous lawsuits filed by parents (and students themselves) against schools in the past few years, accusing the schools of failing to act on behalf of bullied children (both abled and disabled). These lawsuits are sending the message loud and clear to schools that they need to take their responsibility to protect children entrusted to their care seriously.

Fact

These are some key characteristics of successful disability-harassment lawsuits: The harassment was disability related; school officials were given written notification of the incidents; school officials did nothing or very little to protect the targeted student; the victim was exposed to a hostile environment and was deprived of participation, opportunity, and/or educational benefit.

Lawsuits are by nature adversarial. They set up an "us" against "you" situation. This is not an ideal situation for you or your child. Do everything in your power to solve your child's bullying problem within the school before resorting to legal action. But if you are getting nowhere, it might be time to join the voices in protest against continued school violence.

CHAPTER 19

When Bullying Becomes a Crime

Bulling is not illegal in the United States, but many of the behaviors engaged in by bullies can be defined as criminal assaults. Punching, kicking, shoving, smacking, and physically attacking another person is an assault, plain and simple. When these behaviors are carried out by one peer on another in a school setting, it is not usually considered a crime (unless the child involved has reached the age where he is considered a legal adult). In rare instances, violent bullying can escalate and end in the death of the bullied child either by homicide or bully-cide (suicide resulting from relentless bullying).

Do You Know the Law in Your State?

As the nation becomes increasingly aware of the dangers of bullying in U.S. schools, anti-bullying laws are being proposed in dozens of states. Some states (Delaware, Florida, Washington, West Virginia, and more) have already enacted anti-bullying laws, some states are in the process, and others have made no attempts to pass an anti-bullying law. As of June 2007, a total of thirty-five states had laws that address harassment, intimidation, and bullying at school. With a clear definition of bullying, schools will be required to enforce uniform standards of conduct.

A state that has a comprehensive anti-bullying law is at an advantage in the battle against bullying. When law backs policy it can give the policy some teeth; meaning that school-district personnel, administrators, teachers, and parents can't simply ignore the bullying problem in schools. Schools can now be required to implement anti-bullying programs and personnel will be required to address and correct situations that involve bullying within the schools. Policies can be ignored; laws are harder to ignore. And if a law is ignored, the consequences can be significant.

Alert!

In the report "Indicators of School Crime and Safety: 2007," released by the Bureau of Justice Statistics and the National Center for Education Statistics, 28 percent of students ages twelve to eighteen reported being bullied at school during the past six months. Of those bullied, 24 percent reported they had sustained an injury as a result of the bullying incident.

If you discover that your state currently has no anti-bullying law and you wish to become involved in supporting one in your state, there are several things you can do to get the process started. Brenda High, founder of Bully Police USA, recommends steps similar to these.

Start an E-mail Campaign

Contact your State Legislative Committee and Senate Education Committee and request the contact information for the chairperson. Call or e-mail the heads of these committees, explaining that you believe your state is in need of an anti-bullying law. Explain why this is important to you. Pass the contact information along to your friends and family and ask that they also call or send e-mail requests for an anti-bullying law. Ask them to forward the request to everyone they know to do the same.

Meet in Person

Set up a meeting with the committee chairs. Don't be shy. Bring along several other concerned parents. Be sure to bring copies of the written laws from several other states that have enacted comprehensive anti-bullying laws. Give these to the committee chairs and ask that they support efforts to enact an anti-bullying law in your state.

Increase Public Awareness

Hold a public meeting and invite everyone interested in keeping kids safe from bullying (parents, teachers, administrators, police, etc.). Invite a legislator to attend in order to explain how citizens can lobby for a law. Contact local media to attend the meeting and ask that they write an article or do a story on your efforts.

 *Fact*

Brenda High's thirteen-year-old son, Jared, committed suicide in 1998 in response to being bullied at school. Since Jared's death, Brenda founded Bully Police USA, and has been diligently working toward getting anti-bullying laws passed or revised. She has influenced the passage of laws in numerous states, including Jared's Law in Idaho, named after her son.

Inform Important People

Visit your state's education superintendent to discuss your hopes for an anti-bullying law. Do your homework and bring him information on how schools can implement anti-bullying programs for little cost.

Seek Support

Don't be afraid to contact the governor, congressmen or congresswomen, senators, etc. Think big; you just may find a high-profile supporter for your cause. Keep at it, keep meeting with people in public office, and don't give up. The more publicity you get for your efforts the better.

Many of the existing state anti-bullying laws began as the grassroots efforts of one or more parents of a bullied child. A few parents of children who committed suicide as the result of being bullied have successfully lobbied their states to pass anti-bullying laws in the names of their deceased children. It is a testament to what one person can do when he sets his mind to it.

Directives in Bullying Laws

There are several aspects of anti-bullying policy and philosophy that should be included in a comprehensive state anti-bullying law. As you research the existing or proposed anti-bullying law in your state, check to be sure the following are included.

- Does your state's law include the word "bullying"?
- Is there a definition in the law of what types of behaviors constitute bullying?
- Is the law specifically related to bullying? Some states have school-safety laws, but these laws may pertain to external safety issues (such as clean air circulation in vents, no lead paint, etc.) and may not refer to any protection of the children themselves.
- Is the wording broad based to include every child? Some laws define protection of specific groups of kids (special needs kids; homosexual kids; kids from certain racial, ethnic, or religious backgrounds; etc.). A good anti-bullying law would use language that protected *all* children.
- Does the law include cyber bullying?
- Is the law a mandate, or is it just a recommendation? Schools should be required, not asked, to provide anti-bullying education, intervention, and prevention.

There are many other suggestions and recommendations for what makes a good anti-bullying policy, but if your state's law includes the above, it is a good start.

 Essential

Go to the National Conference of State Legislatures website at *www.ncsl.org/programs/cyf/bullyingenac.htm* to view the Select School Safety Enactments (1994–2003). While this list is not inclusive of all legislative actions, it provides examples of recent state enactments.

Definition of Bodily Injury or Threat of Bodily Injury

It is hard to believe that if an adult punches, slaps, or shoves another adult, criminal charges can be filed; but if a child punches, slaps, or shoves another child, it's called boys being boys or roughhousing that got out of hand. It shouldn't matter whether the perpetrator is a grownup or a child, and giving kids the impression that physical violence is okay is sending the wrong message. Violence is violence and assault is assault, and one child punching another shouldn't be dismissed as child's play; it should be taken seriously, there should be consequences, and it should be prevented from happening again.

The basic definition of assault is a violent physical or verbal attack. In some jurisdictions, actual physical contact is not necessary; behavior can be considered assault when one person tries to physically harm another in such a way that the targeted person feels immediately threatened by a person or believes that person to be realistically capable of carrying out a violent attack. What this means is that one adult can file charges against another adult who simply threatened to commit violence against her. It is interesting that these protections are in place for you (as an adult), but not for your children.

Bullying can be verbal, relational, or physical in nature. And all three forms of bullying can cause serious and lasting psychological, emotional, physical, and academic harm. Bullying should never be tolerated, and it may be up to you—the parent—to hold your child's school accountable for her safety and well-being while she is at school. This is not to say that schools can prevent all instances of bullying—that is impossible—but you can expect your child's school administrators and teachers to exercise sound judgment and due diligence in the effort to protect your child from harm.

Most educators care deeply about the health, safety, and well-being of the children in their care. And most would do everything in their power to help your child should a problem arise. In fact, many students who have problems with bullying are supported and helped through these unpleasant situations, and many parents report positive responses and outcomes to the bullying scenarios their children have faced. Help is definitely out there; but on occasion, a parent can encounter a situation with a particularly vicious bully, a teacher who is unwilling or unable to help, or an administrator who is reluctant to get involved.

Dealing with Uncooperative School Officials

When you discover that your child has been victimized by a school-yard bully, it can spur you into action. You may want to do everything in your power to immediately stop the bullying, and you expect the school to work with you, not against you, in these efforts. Imagine how shocked you would be to experience the following scenario:

Wayne came home from school upset and limping. Wayne's mom, concerned, asked him what happened. Wayne broke down and told his mom that three boys had been picking on him since the first day of school. Wayne told his mom that the three boys pushed him around every day on the playground and that sometimes when he fell down from being shoved really hard, the boys would kick him and stomp on his legs. Wayne showed his mom the bruises up and down his legs.

Wayne's mother was devastated. She was heartsick that her son had endured physical abuse at the hands of his classmates for so long, and she blamed herself for not knowing about it sooner. Wayne's mom was determined to protect her child from further harm and called the school that day and set up a meeting with Wayne's teacher.

Wayne's mother was shocked when the teacher blamed Wayne for what happened to him. The teacher said, "Well, Wayne has a way of annoying the other boys." When Wayne's mom asked her to elaborate, the teacher said, "Wayne stares at them and refuses to speak to them when they ask him questions." Wayne's mom tried to make the teacher understand that Wayne is a shy kid and that if he is under stress, he can get even quieter. Wayne's mom also told the teacher that she thought it was completely unacceptable that the boys physically assaulted her son. The teacher just shrugged and said, "Wayne should fight back."

Wayne's mom set up another meeting with the principal and the teacher. At the meeting, the teacher proceeded to insult Wayne and suggest that Wayne was partly to blame for the bullying incidents. Amazingly, the principal sided with the teacher and recommended that Wayne's mom take Wayne to see a counselor, which she agreed to do, but she also pressed for information on how the school was going to protect Wayne from these three boys. The principal said he would talk to the boys and that they would keep an eye on the situation.

A week later, Wayne was still coming home upset and covered in bruises. The new bruises were even worse than the previous ones. Wayne told his mom that the boys were extra angry that he'd told. Wayne's mother went back to the teacher and the principal and showed them pictures of Wayne's injuries. She demanded that something be done to stop the boys who were assaulting her son. Again, Wayne's mom felt that she got nowhere with the school.

It can be frustrating when parents, who expect support and assistance in their bullying prevention efforts, are brushed off or given the it's-not-a-big-deal speech by educators. It is a big deal, and if your child is suffering, you must help him. Keep setting up meetings, keep pressing for action, write letters and e-mails, inform everyone who comes in contact with your child during the school day that he is being bullied, and document all of the bullying and all of your efforts to work with the school to prevent it. If, after all that, you are still not satisfied that the school is helping your child, you can file a formal complaint with the school system and/or the police.

Filing a Complaint

There are times when you will need to continue to move up the chain of command once you have exhausted your options within your child's school. If you have spoken with the teacher and the principal and have submitted written complaints to detail the problems your child is having with a bully or bullies at school, and you still feel like your child is not receiving the help and support she deserves, it is time to move on. But it can be confusing and intimidating to try to figure out the best way to proceed with a complaint against an educator or an administrator at a public school.

Find Out if There Is a Formal Procedure

The first thing to do is to contact the school-district administration office or superintendent's office to ask if there is a formal procedure for filing a complaint. If there is, follow the procedure. Make sure you keep careful records of all communications and meetings—you will need these if your issue cannot be solved at the local level and needs to be brought to the attention of the state or national education office. If your district has no formal policy, you can follow these guidelines.

REQUEST A MEETING WITH THE HEAD OF THE SCHOOL BOARD

At this meeting, bring all of your documented data and clearly explain the situation with your child and why you feel that your child is not getting the help and support she needs. Ask the head of the school board if he can help you. He may be able to intervene to get your child the help she needs. If not, keep moving up the ladder.

WRITE A CLEAR AND DETAILED LETTER

Include all of your concerns and details about why you are seeking help. Mail your letter to the superintendent of schools in your district. In the letter, request a formal face-to-face meeting. Writing the letter and requesting a meeting gives the superintendent time to investigate your accusations against the school. This way, when you meet, he will have a better understanding of the situation. When you meet with the superintendent, try to keep an open mind. There may be things he can do to help your child get the help and support she needs. Most school districts will try hard to solve to problem so it doesn't need to move to the state or national level.

Alert!

If your child is the victim of cyber bullying and has been threatened, you can file a report with the police. Be sure to bring copies or printouts of all the online communications. If you don't know who is doing the cyber bullying, the police can investigate to try to figure out the culprit.

TAKE IT TO THE STATE

If you don't get the help you need from the superintendent, call your state's Department of Education and ask if they have a formal process for filing a complaint. Follow the guidelines given and file a complaint. Try to keep your personal feelings from clouding your objectivity. State the facts of your complaint and be clear when stating your expectations. Consider consulting an attorney.

GO NATIONAL

You also have the right to file a formal complaint with the U.S. Department of Education Office for Civil Rights. There is a procedure that must be followed and a timeline under which you must file the complaint. The timeline can be as early as within 180 days of the incident. You are not required to file a complaint with your school district before filing a complaint with the Office for Civil Rights. Consulting an attorney would be wise at this point.

One caveat: If your child has been physically assaulted, you can file a police report. As mentioned earlier, assault is assault, whether it happens between two adults or two minors. Visit the police station with your child and share the details of what occurred. Be sure to have as much identifying detail (names, addresses, etc.) as you can on the perpetrator or perpetrators.

Resolution

The best outcome for all involved would be to come to a resolution that is mutually satisfactory to all involved in a bullying situation. This can usually be achieved at some point, if all the parties involved remain objective and everyone keeps the best interests of the student in mind. The difficulty lies in the fact that a parent's sole consideration is his child, whereas a principal must deal with hundreds of students and their parents, the teachers, the staff, the department of education, curriculum guidelines, and the list goes on.

It is sometimes hard to see the full picture when all you want is for your child to be safe and feel secure and happy at school. Most educators want this as well. This is a good thing to keep in mind as you go through the complaint process. Most educators and administrators want to resolve the problem at hand; but if that is not possible, it is perfectly acceptable to move up the chain of command. Word of advice: do this with objectivity and tact. If you conduct yourself in a professional manner, you will receive far greater consideration than if you were to rant and rave, insult and berate.

And if the school offers mediation as a possible solution, be open to it. Know what you want and need the school to do for your child and be prepared to express that clearly. But also be prepared to make a compromise or two in the process. This is not to say that you need to compromise on the safety or well-being of your child, but if the school asks something from you (outside counseling for your child, you to volunteer in her classroom, etc.), don't automatically refuse; consider meeting the school halfway. Successful resolution is only possible if everyone keeps a clear head and their eye on the best outcome possible—a safe and happy child.

Bullying Prevention Programs

If your child's school does not have a bullying prevention program already in place or if your child's school is using a program that is less than effective, bring this problem to the school's attention. The staff and administration at your child's school may think they are doing what is necessary by simply offering a bully prevention program each year. But, as you well know, that may not be enough. Do your homework and gather information on the anti-bullying education and prevention programs that have the best known track record for decreasing bullying in schools (refer to Appendix C for a comprehensive list of existing bullying prevention programs).

Other possible ways to raise awareness of the need for focused and continuous bullying intervention, education, and prevention are: donate books on bullying and bullying prevention to the principal, faculty, and the school library; provide printouts of the latest information and research on how to keep kids safe in schools; offer to coordinate a bullying prevention task force and seek other concerned parents who might be willing to volunteer for the task force; start a parent volunteer program to increase supervision in the school's trouble spots (where frequent bullying occurs); and keep an eye out for supplemental programs that could be offered in the school and provide that information to the principal.

CHAPTER 20

Why Zero Tolerance Policies Don't Work

Zero tolerance is a phrase that has been used often to describe the basic philosophy of you do the crime, you do the time. This means that when a specific punishment is attached to a specific crime and you commit that crime, you do the punishment regardless of personal culpability or extenuating circumstances. Zero tolerance is often applied to behaviors that society deems too dangerous or harmful to allow to be repeated. Many schools have zero tolerance policies already in place for drugs, alcohol, and weapons. But does zero tolerance work?

What Is a Zero Tolerance Policy?

A zero tolerance policy is a policy that requires authority figures to have no tolerance for the behavior in question. In schools, zero tolerance behaviors might be things such as drug use, alcohol use, selling drugs, carrying weapons, sexual harassment, or physical assault. In the case of drugs, the school will notify teachers, parents, and students that the school has a zero tolerance policy for drug use and the students and parents are officially put on notice that any student caught with drugs on school grounds will be expelled. If at some point during the school year a student is caught in possession of or using drugs on school property, he will be immediately expelled.

Many school systems have adopted zero tolerance policies for bullying, and that is a step in the right direction; but critics of zero tolerance suggest that a zero tolerance policy that includes the highest possible consequence for any and all bullying behavior is inherently unfair. Should an aggressive, chronic-offender bully receive the same punishment as a first-time offender? What if the offender is a special needs student who is incapable of understanding the ramifications of his behavior? Or what if that same special needs student is tricked by other students into bullying a classmate? What if a transfer student, unaware of the existing policy, bullies a student? Do all of these students deserve to be immediately expelled?

Alert!

According to the American Psychological Association's Zero Tolerance Task Force Report, "Before the age of fifteen, adolescents appear to display psychosocial immaturity in at least four areas: poor resistance to peer influence, attitudes toward and perception of risk, future orientation, and impulse control." This developmental immaturity leads many researchers to discourage the use of zero tolerance policies for teen lapses in judgment.

There have been many controversial and well-publicized cases of zero tolerance policies gone awry. Students have been suspended or expelled for taking Tylenol or Advil during the school day (even when mom or dad gave the okay); students have been suspended or expelled for things like having plastic knives in their lunch boxes or nail clippers in their purse; and students have been suspended and expelled for essays they wrote or pictures they drew that contained hostile words or violent images.

This is not to say that zero tolerance policies are inherently bad, but it is important to carefully consider whether or not zero tolerance punishment allows administrators the leeway to exercise fairness and common sense. Every instance of bullying should have some consequence, but that doesn't mean it is fair for every offense to be met with the harshest punishment possible. A much more effective anti-bullying policy would have zero tolerance for bullying, but allow for graduated sanctions to be imposed (except in extreme cases where there is concern for the safety of the victim).

Some schools with zero tolerance policies have been subjected to lawsuits claiming that the policy is unfair. The parents who file these lawsuits and the critics of zero tolerance punishment believe that a one-size-fits-all or all-or-nothing approach to disciplining children goes against the basic proponents of educating children. They believe that zero tolerance is excessively harsh and children are treated as criminals without further investigation into any existing extenuating circumstances.

The only thing considered with a zero tolerance approach is, "Did this student engage in behavior that is defined as bullying?" If the answer is yes, the punishment is applied. Supporters of zero tolerance policies say this is exactly the point; that if a student bullies another student despite the zero tolerance policy, that student should be punished. If the punishment required is expulsion, then so be it.

There is a middle ground that needs to be considered. Many states have already instituted zero tolerance policies related to bullying. Schools that have these policies should be applauded and supported; but the administration at these schools must be given the opportunity to create graduated, nonpunitive sanctions that give administrators the ability to exercise fairness and sound judgment on a case-by-case basis. Many kids who bully can be taught the error of their ways through education and intervention. And those who don't respond to the graduated school-based sanctions will eventually escalate to the highest possible punishment—expulsion. This way the school isn't arbitrarily punishing students with extreme consequences for every offense, yet those students who do not, will not, or cannot change are eventually removed from the community.

Why Zero Tolerance Actually Decreases Reports

When students attend a school with a strict zero tolerance policy, they are aware of the extreme consequences of certain behaviors. And this can affect their willingness to report bullying incidences. This can be for several reasons:

The Punishment Is Too Harsh

It might be hard to believe that a bullied student would not tell in order to keep a bully at the school, but many bullied children are kind, sensitive kids who, even though being hurt themselves, are reluctant to hurt others.

The Fear of Retaliation

Suspension and expulsion are severe punishments and students know it. If a bully will be suspended or expelled for her actions, bullied kids might be hesitant to tell an adult. They may think it is their fault that the bully was suspended or expelled, and they may have an intense fear that the bully will come after them for revenge.

 Fact

Zero tolerance was created in the late '80s—early '90s as a hard-line approach to drug enforcement. It was meant to deter drug trafficking and drug use by applying a set of predetermined consequences, often punishments of a severe nature, that were applied regardless of any mitigating circumstances (such as the level of seriousness of the violation or in what context the violation occurred).

The Fear of Being Blamed

Most students are savvy enough and have seen enough bullying scenarios to realize that the bully may try to turn the situation around and blame them. They may be afraid that they will be the one to get expelled.

An Adversarial School Climate

Students may feel that administrators enjoy carrying out zero tolerance harsh punishment and that the policy itself has an overtone of vindictiveness. This may strengthen the already strong code of silence that exists between students.

Zero tolerance policies can also affect teachers' willingness to report incidents of bullying. Teachers understand the full implications of removing students from the learning environment. And while reporting every incident and having every offender removed from their classroom might make their lives easier, teachers know that if they report one incident, they must report all, and that in every incident, regardless of the context or motivation, a harsh punishment will be imposed on the student. This rigid one-size-fits-all punishment can be at odds with teachers' educational philosophy.

The goal of a zero tolerance policy is to remove disruptive students in order to create a school climate that is more conducive to learning and safer for all remaining students. Despite the good intentions of this goal, the Zero Tolerance Task Force reports that, "data on a number of indicators of school climate have shown the opposite effect, that is, that schools with higher rates of school suspension and expulsion appear to have *less* satisfactory ratings of school climate, less satisfactory school governance structures, and to spend a disproportionate amount of time on disciplinary matters." Clearly, zero tolerance policies and their effects, both positive and negative, must be re-examined and redefined.

Student Exclusion Policies

At the very heart of the controversy of zero tolerance policies with strict and punitive consequences is the argument that all children have the right to an education. The increase in number of schools employing zero tolerance policies has led to a significant increase in the number of students suspended and expelled from U.S. schools. These students face the loss of educational opportunity, which can increase the risk of negative behavior and the chances of future criminal behavior.

This is not to say that no child should be subjected to severe punitive consequences. A child who poses a danger to the health and welfare of other children due to violent or aggressive behavior should, in fact, be removed from the educational environment. But for students who don't pose a serious threat or for whom violation of a schools anti-bullying zero tolerance policy was minor, manageable, or correctable, suspension and expulsion can be overkill.

Bullies Need Intervention and Positive Role Models

Children who engage in behaviors typically defined as aggressive, harassing, or bullying do so for a variety of reasons. Some kids grow up with extreme violence in the home and become conditioned from an early age to an aggressive relational style. Other kids learn to act aggressively and to be a bully by watching the behavior of various grownups in their lives. Some kids admit to enjoying the feeling of power and control they get when they harass or threaten other, more vulnerable, children. And some children bully as a result of being bullied themselves.

 Essential

It is important to model positive, peaceful problem-solving behavior for your children. Teach tolerance and respect for others. Provide a good example for your children by not using violence or aggressive intimidation when solving problems. Don't use derogatory terms, insult others, or resort to foul language. Behave the way you want your child to behave.

The one thing all these children have in common is the absence of healthy social relational skills and a lack of positive adult role models. Children learn through experience and model their behavior on what they observe from the world around them. Children also learn through positive and negative reinforcement of their behavior. If a child's parent is a grownup bully, should it be surprising when she exhibits the same kind of behavior, and if a child receives positive messages for engaging in bullying behavior such as, "You showed him!" "You're the man!" or "You are the coolest kid in school," is it any wonder he continues to bully?

But do these children deserve to be expelled from school? Or do they deserve to be given a chance to be educated about the harm bullying can cause both victims and bullies? And might it be possible to look past the child's behavior to discover the root cause? Only then can a child be taught a better way to behave and interact with his peers. The other option, zero tolerance, is to hand down strict and rigid punishment, placing all blame on the child (regardless of the circumstances) and remove him from any further interaction with his peers.

Other Misdirected Policies

In the effort to reduce bullying in American schools, numerous programs have been implemented and countless policies have been written. While the effort is laudable, the outcomes have often been less so. With bullying, implementing the wrong program or following a program because it worked for another issue and assuming it will work for this one as well (bullying) can not only fail to work, it can be harmful. Here are a few examples of otherwise good policies that don't work when applied to bullying in schools.

Short-Term or Stop-Gap Policies

A school might conduct a school-wide assembly once a year at the start of school to go over the expectations regarding bullying. Another school might hold a teacher/staff in-service training program about bullying. A third school might hold a PTA meeting for the parents on the topic of bullying. While these programs are all a positive step toward an anti-bullying atmosphere, they are by no means the type of all-inclusive programming that an effective anti-bullying program would require.

Conflict Resolution

Conflict resolution is a common and popular approach to solving many of the issues between students in school. And for many issues, it can be an effective problem-solving strategy. But for bullying, it is not recommended. The three components that define bullying behavior are an imbalance of power between the bully and his victim, the intent to cause harm, and the threat of future harm. When educators require a child who has been victimized by a bully to face his bully and work out the problem, it can be extremely upsetting. And the evidence suggests that this method of intervention is generally ineffective at stopping bullying.

When two kids have a conflict, they are usually both partly to blame for the issue at hand. This is a situation where conflict resolution can be successful. When a child is bullied, he is not at fault. He should be protected, not expected to face his tormentor and be involved in a mediation situation.

Alert!

Group treatment has proven ineffective as a strategy for stopping bullying. When in a group setting, children who bully tend to reinforce and support the bullying behavior of the other group members. So instead of learning anger-management skills and prosocial behavior in group therapy, kids' bullying behavior can actually get worse.

What Policies and Programs Should Be Implemented?

Even though bullying prevention research is still in its early phases, some initial data has provided clues to the direction anti-bullying programs should take. And while we have a long road of trial and error ahead, there have been some encouraging findings. Every school system should research the existing programs and be on the lookout for up-and-coming, new anti-bullying education and prevention programs. Until there is widespread consensus on effective and affordable programs, schools should do everything they can with the available resources and information.

According to the Zero Tolerance Task Force, "There are three programs that have been shown to be effective in reducing the risk of violence or disruption are highlighted: *bullying prevention* (primary), *threat assessment* (secondary) determining the degree to which a given threat or incident constitutes a serious danger to the school, and *restorative justice* (tertiary)." Notice that zero tolerance punishment is not on the list. The task force also reports that, "the controversy over zero tolerance and the concern that increased rates of school removal may decrease educational opportunities have led a number of state legislatures, such as Indiana, Texas, and Virginia, to propose or adopt legislation to modify zero tolerance procedures or expand the range of disciplinary options available to schools."

Since the goal of effective discipline in every school system should be to allow students the opportunity to learn in a safe school climate, some alternative policies should be considered.

Reforming Existing Zero Tolerance Policies

While zero tolerance policies and punishments for certain behaviors or activities (such as weapons, drugs and alcohol, violence, or threats of violence) should remain in effect, anti-bullying policies should be altered to allow more flexibility for lesser offenses that don't compromise the safety of other students.

Adding Additional Programs

If reduction of bullying is a goal, the simple addition of a zero tolerance policy is not enough to correct the problem. Anti-bullying education and prevention programs should be implemented. And programs that improve overall school climate or a sense of community and belonging can go a long way to improving student relationships. Leadership programs, peer counseling programs, and character development programs can all lead to a stronger sense of community and responsibility in a school.

At this time, the jury is still out on what program or combination of programs work best to keep American school children safe from harm. But at least researchers, educators, policymakers, parents, and students are becoming more and more aware of the implications of bullying and school violence. And every day progress is being made in the effort to keep children safe inside and outside of school.

CHAPTER 21

How Students, Parents, Schools, and Communities Can Work Together

Students, parents, schools, and the community at large need to start working with, not against, each other in the battle against bullying. Tolerance for bullying behavior is entrenched in American subculture and nothing short of total involvement will change the current climate in the nation's schools. The time for finger pointing and blame has passed and a decision must be made to work collectively for the benefit of all children. Change can and does happen, but it takes knowledge, understanding, hard work, and dedication.

Identify the Extent of the Problem

A problem can't be fixed until a problem is admitted. A school administration that denies it has a problem with bullying will not be successful in its attempts to stop it. A parent who denies that her child is a bully contributes to the harm that her child will suffer as a result. And a society that looks the other way and allows children to continue to harass each other is a society that will suffer down the line.

School administration and personnel should conduct anonymous student surveys, talk with individual students, discuss bullying with teachers, and gather as much information about the school's overall climate as possible. Once the extent of the bullying problem is clearly identified, steps can be taken to educate the community, reduce the bullying, and improve the school's overall climate.

Essential

Ask the school principal at your child's school whether a bullying assessment survey has been conducted. If one has been conducted, ask to see the data on the results of the survey. If there hasn't been a survey done, ask the principal to consider surveying the students to get an idea of the full extent of the bullying problem in your child's school.

Create an Awareness Campaign

Once a school or educational community understands the full extent of the bullying problem, the next hurdle is to create a public awareness campaign that will notify all members of the school or community about the problem. Full disclosure is necessary for all involved in order to have a true understanding of the nature and scope of the bullying problem. The awareness campaign should identify the problem (bullying), the severity of the problem (types of bullying and how, where, and whom it happens to), have a plan for reducing the problem (implementation of an anti-bullying education and prevention program), and ask for assistance in making attitudinal and behavioral changes (in parents, educators, school personnel, and students).

 **Alert!**

Some schools use creative ways to raise student and public awareness about bullying. Students can have rubber wristbands made that signify the wearer is a supporter of a bully-free environment. Posters can be posted throughout the school. And "Stop bullying" or "Don't bully me" T-shirts can be given to students who sign an anti-bullying contract.

Implement Educational Programs

Bullying prevention in schools won't be successful unless every student, teacher, and administrator is working toward the same goal. In order for that to happen, everyone must first understand what bullying is; how, where, and why it happens; why it happens to specific groups of kids; the difference between bullying among boys and girls; what cyber bullying is and why it is a growing problem; what to do if you are being bullied; what to do if you see or suspect someone else is being bullied; how to report the bullying behavior; and how the teachers and school administration will handle bullying incidents when they occur.

The best way to accomplish this is to find anti-bullying education and prevention programs that have been proven effective and welcome them into schools. Research has shown that the best outcomes occur when the bullying prevention programs are begun at a young age and are continued throughout the school years. For a comprehensive list of existing anti-bullying education and prevention programs, see Appendix C.

 Fact

Go to *www.clemson.edu/olweus/training_staff.html* to check out the details of the widely respected Olweus Bullying Prevention Program. The Olweus program is a comprehensive, school-wide program designed for use in elementary, middle, or junior high schools. The Olweus website provides information on the program content, evidence of effectiveness, training information, program materials, and program costs.

Along with implementing anti-bullying education and prevention programs, the school should incorporate additional strategies to reinforce the whole-school anti-bully approach. One such strategy is to create an anti-bullying contract or pledge for every student to sign at the beginning of each school year.

Here is a sample anti-bullying contract or pledge:

We the students of _____ school agree to work together to stop bullying at our school.

Bullying is defined as intentionally aggressive behavior that can take many forms (verbal, physical, social/relational/emotional, or cyber bullying—or any combination of these); it involves an imbalance of power, and is often repeated over a period of time. The bullying can consist of one child bullying another, a group of children ganging up against one lone child, or one group of kids targeting another group.

Common behaviors attributed to bullying include put-downs, name calling, rumors, gossip, verbal threats, menacing, harassment, intimidation, social isolation or exclusion, and physical assaults.

We believe that no student deserves to be bullied and that every student regardless of race, color, religion, nationality, size, gender, popularity, athletic, academic, or social ability, or intelligence has the right to feel safe, secure, and respected.

I agree to:

► Treat other students with kindness and respect.

► Not engage in verbal, relational, or physical bullying or cyber bullying.

► Be aware of the school's anti-bullying policies and procedures.

► Abide by the school's anti-bullying policies and procedures.

► Support students who have been victimized by bullies.

► Speak out against verbal, relational, and physical bullying and cyber bullying.

► Notify a parent, teacher, or school administrator when bullying does occur.

► Be a good role model for other students.

_____
Student's signature

_____
Parent's signature

_____
Date

The best type of anti-bullying contract or pledge is one developed with input from students. The school could encourage each classroom to come up with a contract or pledge that would represent the students' anti-bullying responsibilities. A school-wide vote could be taken and the best pledge or contract can become the official anti-bullying contract for that school.

Another important (but often overlooked) strategy is to hold bullying prevention programs for parents. Parents are key players in the effort to reduce bullying in and out of schools and they should be included in the school's anti-bullying efforts. Many parents are unaware of the extent of bullying in schools and many more still believe the bullying myths in Chapter 8. When parents have a better understanding of what bullying is and why it is harmful not just to kids who are bullied but to bullies and bystanders as well, they are more motivated to help.

 *Fact*

Books to recommend to school personnel at your child's school: *Bully Prevention; Tips and Strategies for School Leaders and Classroom Teachers* by Elizabeth A. Barton; *How to Stop Bullying and Social Aggression: Elementary Grade Lessons and Activities That Teach Empathy, Friendship, and Respect* by Steve Breakstone, Michael Dreiblatt, Karen Dreiblatt; and *Bullying at School: What We Know and What We Can Do* by Dan Olweus.

Start a Peer-Counseling Program

Another, often successful, anti-bullying strategy is to implement a peer-counseling program. A peer-counseling program trains peers to assist students who are having difficulty with common school and social problems. Peer-counseling programs benefit children in a variety of ways:

- Kids are often more comfortable talking with someone their own age (or close to it).
- Peer counselors provide a positive role model.
- Peer counselors can help kids work out minor problems before they escalate.
- Peer counselors can act as a support and an ally.
- Peer counselors can serve as a link between the students and the administration.
- Talking to a peer counselor can open up a much-needed support network.

Note: Peer counselors should be professionally trained and required to meet stringent confidentiality guidelines. And peer counselors should not be expected to deal with serious bullying situations or situations that involve a threat to students' safety.

 Essential

Here are a few books on the topic of peer counseling: *Youth Helping Youth: A Handbook for Training Peer Facilitators* by Robert D. Myrick and Tom Erney; *A Guide to Peer Counseling* by Jewel Rumley Cox; and *Peer Assisted Learning* by Keith Topping.

Specify Classroom Rules

Consider this scenario: Teacher A has no rules about physical contact in her room. In fact, teacher A encourages the kids to form close friendships. Teacher A allows kids to hug and hold hands, sit close together on the reading mat, and engage in a bit of roughhousing—as long as no one gets hurt.

The following year, many of the students who were in Teacher A's class have Teacher B. Teacher B does not allow the kids in her class to physically touch each other. She teaches every student to respect the personal space of other children and doesn't allow physical contact. Teacher B believes that this rule helps keep classroom conflict to a minimum. In Teacher B's class, there is no pushing, shoving, roughhousing, no doing the hair of your friend, no holding hands, and no sitting close together.

It is likely that the students who had Teacher A will have a difficult time transitioning into Teacher B's class. Teacher A's students will likely get in trouble for inappropriate physical contact during the first few weeks of school.

 *Fact*

Many teachers allow their students to participate in brainstorming the list of classroom rules at the beginning of the school year. Not surprisingly, teachers often find that student-created rules are often stricter than the ones the teacher might impose. This is further evidence that children want and need clear boundaries for classroom behavior.

Every year, your child will be faced with different classroom rules. Is it any wonder your kids are sometimes confused as to what is okay and what is disallowed? It can take a few weeks (or even months) for children to adjust to each teacher's behavioral expectations. This is why researchers have suggested that schools are better off making an effort to specify unified classroom rules. And those schools that incorporate specific policies usually have fewer problems than schools that allow each teacher to set her own rules. Kids need consistency and they tend to feel safer and more secure in environments where they know both what to expect and what is expected of them.

Uniform classroom rules also make it easier for teachers, school personnel, and administrators to enforce school policies. And parents know exactly what to expect from school year to school year.

Practice Cooperative Learning Activities

Classrooms that practice cooperative learning encourage kids to work in small and large groups that foster a working together or team approach to the learning process. Cooperative efforts in the classroom teach kids that when the individuals in a group strive to learn course material and then help other students in their group learn the same material, it creates an atmosphere of mutual achievement. Kids work as one to reach a single goal. Every student learns:

- He succeeds by helping his classmates succeed.
- Every member plays a valuable role in the success of the group.
- Members must work together to succeed or they will fail together.
- The success of the group is more important than the success of the individual.

Alert!

The five essential components of cooperation identified by Johnson, Johnson, & Holubec, 1993, are: positive interdependence (one child can't succeed unless they all succeed); face-to-face promotive interaction (applauding each others efforts); individual and group accountability (each child must contribute to the goal); interpersonal and small-group skills (teamwork); and group processing (examination of the ongoing process).

Cooperative learning activities allow kids to develop social and interpersonal skills, leadership skills, conflict management skills, and decision-making skills. These skills can help children learn to avoid being bullied (or being a bully) and to deal with the dynamics of bullying when it first occurs.

Increase Supervision in High-Risk Areas

Increasing supervision in areas prone to higher levels of bullying is necessary to reduce the overall level of bullying in schools. Schools can and should use anonymous surveys to identify the trouble spots in the school. Areas like the lunchroom, bathrooms, the locker room, hallways, and the playground are frequently cited by kids as areas where bullying is more common and severe. Once identified, the schools should make plans to add additional supervision to these areas.

Due to budget constraints and scheduling issues, schools may need to consider creative solutions. If teachers are unable to rotate additional supervision in their schedules, parents can be asked to be volunteer supervisors, older peer leaders can supervise younger students, or the student council can be utilized as an additional source of supervision.

 Essential

Bullying occurs more often at school than on the way to and from school. Some cases of bullying have occurred on school buses and have, on occasion, garnered national media attention. Schools should include bus drivers in their staff anti-bullying training and provide them with policies and procedures and incident forms to help them handle bullying behavior on the buses.

Some schools have implemented camera surveillance systems to police the trouble spots in schools. If your community schools have problems with bullying and violence, look into the school budget and approach the town government about taxpayer support for increased safety technology in the schools.

Whole-School Policies

Most educators want to do the right thing when it comes to bullying in schools. Most believe that bullying is wrong and would be willing to do their part within a school system that has policies, procedures, and an administration that is willing to follow through with fair and common-sense sanctions in order to create a safe school environment.

But it is not enough to simply write up anti-bullying policies and procedures. And it is not enough to carry out those policies in a vacuum devoid of human compassion. In order to say that a school is anti-bully, all the members of the school community must believe that the school is an anti-bully environment. All members must be working toward a singular goal—that every child has the right to be treated with dignity and respect. The culture of the school must adopt an attitude of "this is who we are and this is how we do it." Every member of the school community must be treated with respect and every member must treat others with respect.

 *Fact*

Bullying prevention efforts seem to work best when they are coordinated by a group that consists of representatives from all facets of the school community. An effective team might consist of: the principal or another top-level administrator; a teacher from each grade level; a member of the teaching support staff; a nonteaching staff member (cafeteria worker, bus driver); a school counselor; and a parent.

The only way this can happen is for parents, teachers, school personnel, and members of the overall community to believe that children's social and emotional growth is just as important as their academic growth. Parents and educators must adjust the antiquated and outdated thinking patterns that allow bullying behavior to be dismissed as unavoidable or part of growing up. No child deserves to be bullied; therefore, every adult needs to do her part to identify bullying when it occurs and put a stop to it as quickly as possible. And this should be done in a way that respects the dignity of all involved. Bullied children need to be protected and supported, kids who bully need to be taught more positive and effective ways of interacting, and bystanders need to be guided and given strategies that empower them to get involved.

Parents need to tune in to their children's social and emotional lives. They need to have discussions about bullies and bullying early and often. And they need to make an effort to be more involved in their children's schools. The schools must make an effort to communicate openly with parents and students. And if every member of the school community supports what everyone else is doing, you will be working your way to creating a whole-school policy. A whole-school policy is one in which no single member of the school community is solely responsible for enforcing that policy; each member does her part to ensure the safety and well-being of all.

Glossary

Abuse:
Repeatedly hurting someone or treating him badly.

Adolescence:
The period of physical, emotional, and psychological development in the years between puberty and maturity.

Aggression:
Feelings of hostility and anger that can fuel a physical or verbal attack.

Anger:
A strong negative emotion experienced in response to an upsetting event.

Anti-bullying program:
A program intended to reduce bullying behavior in school-age children.

Anxiety:
A mental state of worry, apprehension, nervousness, or fear.

Appearance:
An outward or external representation or visible part of a person or thing.

Assault:
A verbal or physical attack.

Assertive:
Behavior that ensures one's needs are met without being aggressive.

Assessment:
The process of gathering information.

Authoritative:
To act in a confident, self-assured manner in order to get what you need.

Avoid:
To stay away from, steering clear of, or actively shunning.

Blog:
A journal that is written online.

Body language:
Gestures, mannerisms, and expressions one uses to communicate.

Bullied:
A child who is the victim of bullying is termed a "bullied child."

Bully:
A person who is intentionally cruel and hurtful to others.

Bullying:
When a child intentionally and repeatedly causes verbal, relational, or physical harm or humiliates another child.

Bystander:
A person who bears witness to an event, but does not participate.

Cell phone:
A portable, wireless telephone.

Chat room:
A virtual online space to "chat" with other people.

Child:
A person from birth to puberty.

Climate:
A condition or prevailing state over time.

Clique:
A small, exclusive group of people who have shared interests and patterns of behavior.

Collaborative school strategy:
A school that works together with internal personnel and outside entities (parents and community).

Communication skills:
Communication requires a collection of skills to get a message successfully conveyed.

Computer:
An electronic device capable of storing and processing data.

Confidence:
The ability to believe in yourself and your abilities; to feeling capable.

Conflict:
A clash or struggle between individuals with opposing viewpoints.

Confrontation:
A face-to-face disagreement or argument.

Counseling:
When a person obtains advice, support, and guidance.

Culture:
A set of values and standards that give meaning and significance to a group.

Cyber bullying:
Bullying that is carried out via electronic means (cell phone, text message, e-mail, instant message, webpage).

Denial:
To refute the validity of a statement.

Depression:
A debilitating mood disorder that interferes with ones ability
to function.

Disability:
A physical, mental, or emotional deficit that interferes with normal
functioning.

Discipline:
Used by parents to teach their child skills to regulate behavior.

Educational program:
A program intended to teach a certain skill or competency.

Electronic devices:
Cell phones, computers, televisions, radios, etc.

E-mail:
Mail composed, sent, and received via electronic technology.

Embarrassment:
When a person experiences psychological discomfort or shame.

Emotional bullying:
The intent to manipulate another person's behavior using emotional
blackmail.

Empathy:
The ability to put yourself in someone else's shoes, to understand
what someone else is experiencing.

Empowerment:
In control and able to handle the problem at hand.

Exclusion:
To be left out or rejected.

Family environment:
The internal workings and relationships within a family.

Fear:
Anxiousness, nervousness, or panic over a perceived negative event.

Friendship:
A positive and supportive ongoing interaction between two people.

Gender:
Male or female.

Genetics:
Biological traits passed down from parent to child.

Gossip:
To discuss the behavior and actions of other people in an unkind or malicious manner.

Group mentality:
The tendency of individuals to behave differently when in a group versus when they are alone.

Harassment:
Repetitive, negative behaviors that are considered offensive and that can cause worry, fear, and angst.

Helplessness:
Feeling like no matter what you do, you will be unable to accomplish a goal.

Home schooling:
When a child receives the majority of his education at home.

Humiliation:
Embarrassment so intense that it can lead to a loss of self-esteem.

Instant messaging (IM):
Text communication carried out in real time with two or more people online at the same time.

Internet:
A global network of interconnected computers.

Intervention:
To intervene in order to improve a negative or harmful situation.

Intimidation:
To threaten harm, injure, or damage a person or thing.

Jealousy:
Being envious of another person's qualities or possessions.

Learning disability:
The inability to process information properly or pay attention to necessary stimulus.

Legal action:
A judicial proceeding brought against a person or institution.

Malicious:
Mean or spiteful.

Media violence:
Violence portrayed on television, in movies, and in video games.

Mentor:
A person who provides guidance, support, and leadership.

Message board:
An online bulletin board where messages can be posted.

Nonverbal communication:
All components of communication that do not include the spoken word (eye contact, tone of voice, body language).

Overprotective:
A parent who is protective to the point of smothering.

Parenting:
The process of raising a child from birth to maturity.

Passive:
Letting other's needs and wishes prevail.

Peer group:
A group of people of similar age and social status.

Peer mediation:
A face-to-face problem-solving technique.

Peer pressure:
The positive or negative influence that peers
can have on a person's behavior.

Physical bullying:
Bullying through physical acts of violence (hitting, kicking, punching).

Positive behaviors:
Behaviors considered socially acceptable and that bring acceptance
and approval.

Positive feedback:
Positive messages received about one's actions and behaviors.

Positive self-talk:
Affirmations that, when repeated, increase one's self-confidence.

Post-traumatic stress disorder:
Intense stress reaction experienced after a traumatic event or
series of events.

Principal:
An educator who has power and influence over school personnel
and students.

Relational bullying:
Bullying carried out by threatening a person's social standing or status.

Relationship:
An intimate connection or enduring interactive pattern of behavior
between two people.

Resilience:
The ability to adapt and recover from a setback.

Respond:
To react to an event or person.

Retaliate:
To seek revenge for a perceived hurt or harm.

Revenge:
Retaliation for a perceived wrong.

Role model:
A person with admirable qualities.

Rumor:
A story that isn't true.

Sanctions:
The consequences or punishments for violating a rule or law.

School personnel:
The people who work inside a school.

School shooting:
A shooting that occurs within or close to a school.

Secrecy:
The intent to hide or conceal something from others.

Self-centered:
A person focused solely on himself.

Self-esteem:
How a person feels about herself.

Sexual harassment:
Unwanted and unwelcome verbal or nonverbal behavior of a sexual content directed toward another person.

Shame:
A sense of guilt or inadequacy.

Social bullying:
Bullying carried out by one person, harming another's relationships and social status.

Social skills:
Skills necessary for positive interpersonal communications and relationships.

Students:
Children who attend school.

Suicide:
Taking one's own life; killing yourself.

Supervision:
Overseeing or watching over someone or something.

Target:
A person who is under attack.

Task force:
A special group created to work on a specific issue or problem.

Teacher:
A person whose occupation is to teach; a conveyor of knowledge.

Teamwork:
A group of people working together to achieve a common goal.

Teasing:
To make fun of a person in a mocking way; can be playful or hurtful.

Temperament:
An inborn set of personality traits.

Text message:
A written message sent between cell phones.

Threat:
A source of danger or imminent harm.

Training program:
An education program that trains participants to handle a problem or situation.

Unconditional love:
To love another without judgment or restraint.

Verbal bullying:
Bullying through the spoken word; taunts, teasing, rumors, and gossip.

Victim:
A person who has suffered harm.

Video games:
Electronic games played on the computer or television.

Violence:
To physically injure, harm, or abuse.

Website:
An online site that contains web pages, images, or videos.

Whole-school policy:
A policy that the entire school community enforces and embraces.

Witness:
A person who is present during an action or event between others.

Zero tolerance:
A policy strictly enforced with specific, often severe, punishment.

APPENDIX B

Resources

Books

Beane, Allan L., PhD. *Protect Your Child from Bullying*. (San Francisco, CA: Wiley, 2008).

Cohen, Cathi, LCSW. *Raise Your Child's Social IQ*. (Washington, DC: Advantage, 2000).

Coloroso, Barbara. *The Bully, the Bullied, and the Bystander: From Preschool to High School—How Parents and Teachers Can Help Break the Cycle of Violence*. (New York: HarperCollins, 2004).

Dellasega, Cheryl and Charisse Nixon. *Girl Wars: 12 Strategies That Will End Female Bullying*. (New York, NY: Fireside, 2003).

Eisen, Andrew R., PhD. *Helping Your Socially Vulnerable Child*. (Oakland, CA: New Harbinger, 2007).

Haber, Joel and Jenna Glatzer. *Bullyproof Your Child for Life: Protect Your Child from Teasing, Taunting, and Bullying for Good*. (New York: Penguin, 2007).

Kowalski, Robin M., PhD, Limber, Susan P., PhD, and Patricia W. Agatston, PhD. *Cyber Bullying*. (Malden, MA: Blackwell, 2008).

Kraizer, Sherryll, PhD. *10 Days to a Bully-Proof Child*. (New York, NY: Marlowe & Company, 2007).

Olweus, Dan. *Bullying at School: What We Know and What We Can Do.* (Cambridge, MA: Blackwell, 1993).

Ross, Dorothea. *Childhood Bullying, Teasing, and Violence: What School Personnel, Other Professionals, and Parents Can Do* (2nd ed.). (Alexandria, VA: American Counseling Association, 2003).

Simmons, Rachel. *Odd Girl Out: The Hidden Culture Of Aggression In Girls.* (Fort Washington, PA: Harcourt, 2003).

Willard, Nancy. *Cyberbullying and Cyberthreats: Responding to the Challenge of Online Social Aggression, Threats, and Distress.* (Champaign, IL: Research Press, 2007).

Wiseman, Rosalind. *Queen Bees and Wannabes: Helping Your Daughter Survive Cliques, Gossip, Boyfriends, and Other Realities of Adolescence.* (New York, NY: Crown, 2003).

Websites

About Bullying
The United States Department of Health and Human Services, Substance Abuse and Mental Health Services Administration's (SAMHSA) National Mental Health Information Center.
www.mentalhealth.samhsa.gov

ACT (Adults & Children Together Against Violence)
Provides education materials for adults to use to teach young children (ages 0 to 8) nonviolent problem solving. This site was developed by the American Psychological Association and the National Association for the Education of Young Children.
www.actagainstviolence.apa.org

Bullying.org
Find information and resources about the prevention of bullying. This is a Canadian website.
www.bullying.org

BullyingUK

This is a British website about bullying prevention. It is an interesting comparison to American anti-bullying websites.
www.bullying.co.uk

BullyPoliceUSA

Find information and resources about the prevention of bullying. This site was created by the mom of a bullied child who committed suicide as the result of being bullied.
www.bullypolice.org

Center for the Study and Prevention of Violence

Find useful information and resources on violence prevention.
www.colorado.edu/cspv/index.html

Exploring the Nature and Prevention of Bullying

This site contains information and resources for teachers, counselors, and school administrators. It was developed by Education Development Center, Inc., for the U.S. Department of Education.
www.ed.gov/admins/lead/safety/training/bullying/index.html36

Eyes on Bullying

Bully prevention information and resources. This site is funded by the IBM Global Work/Life Fund.
www.eyesonbullying.org

Fight Crime: Invest in Kids

A national nonprofit organization that analyzes and reports on bullying.
www.fightcrime.org

National Youth Violence Prevention Resource Center

Information and links to resources on bullying and violence prevention for parents and students. Sponsored by the U.S. Centers for Disease Control and Prevention.
www.safeyouth.org

PACER National Center for Bullying Prevention

Find bullying prevention resources with a special focus on children with disabilities.
www.pacer.org

PREVNet

Find information and resources on bullying prevention. Created by a national network of researchers and organizations in Canada committed to stopping bullying and sponsored by the Networks of Centres of Excellence, Queen's University, and York University.
www.prevnet.ca

Stop Bullying Now!

Find information and resources about bullying prevention and intervention. Sponsored by the U.S. Department of Health & Human Services, Health Resources & Services Administration (HRSA).
www.stopbullyingnow.hrsa.gov

Cyber Bullying Websites
Center for Safe and Responsible Internet use

Provides research and outreach services to address issues of safe and responsible use of the Internet.
www.cyberbully.org

Cyberbullying.us

This site provides research, news, events, and resources on cyber bullying.
www.cyberbullying.us

i-SAFE

i-SAFE is a nonprofit foundation dedicated to protecting the online experiences of youth.
www.i-safe.org

MindOH!

This site provides cyber bullying prevention tips and tools.
www.mindoh.com

Existing Anti-Bullying Education and Prevention Programs

Bully Busters (developed in 2000)
The curriculum has two levels and is designed for students in grades K–5 and 6–8. The focus is on reducing aggression and bullying in the classroom while establishing a positive classroom climate.
www.stopbullyingnow.net

The Bully Free Classroom (developed in 1999)
A comprehensive research-based program designed to develop school-wide campaigns against bullying for K–12 students.
www.bullyfree.com

Bully-Proofing Your School (developed in 1993)
A three-phase comprehensive bully prevention program designed for elementary and middle schools. Bully-Proofing Your School offers a system-wide approach for handling bully/victim problems.
www.bullyproofing.org

BullySafeUSA (developed in 1999)
BullySafeUSA is a comprehensive anti-bullying program that offers student empowerment sessions, staff training, parent and community-leader seminars, and a Train the Trainer Institute. The program is targeted for grades 3–8.
www.bullysafeusa.com

Club Ophelia (developed in 2002)

An afterschool program for middle school girls designed to reduce relational aggression. There is also a five-day nonresidential Camp Ophelia program.

www.opheliaproject.org

Don't Laugh at Me (developed in 2000)

Operation Respect, a nonprofit advocacy organization whose purpose is to assure children safe and respectful school climates in which to grow and learn, offers this curriculum for grades 2–5 and 6–8.

www.operationrespect.org

Get Connected (developed in 2002)

This comprehensive bully prevention program is provided by STOP Violence! It is geared toward K–8 students and focuses on issues related to peer abuse and violence in schools.

www.stop-violence.org

The Incredible Years

This program aims to prevent behavior problems from developing in young children. The program is designed to promote children's social and emotional competence.

www.incredibleyears.com

LIFT (Linking the Interests of Families and Teachers, developed in 2000)

This program is designed for students in grades 1-5 to prevent conduct problems. The main goal is to decrease antisocial behavior and increase prosocial behavior.

www.oslc.org

MetLife Foundation Read for Health Program (Taking Action to Stop Bullying: A Literacy-Based Curriculum Module developed in 2004)

This comprehensive anti-bullying program is designed to be taught by English language arts and/or health education teachers. The program targets middle school students.

www.hhd.org

Olweus Bullying Prevention Program (developed in 1991)
A comprehensive research-based bullying prevention program designed for students in grades 3–10. The program components are implemented at the school-wide level, the classroom level, the individual level, and the community level.
www.clemson.edu/olweus

Safe School Ambassadors (developed in 2000)
This school safety program focuses on school climate and how students can build safer schools from the inside out. Designed for grades 6–12.
www.safeschoolambassadors.org

Steps to Respect: A Bullying Prevention Program (developed in 2002)
This comprehensive research-based bullying prevention program was designed by the Committee for Children. It targets bullying in elementary schools with programs for grades 3–5 or 4–6.
www.cfchildren.org

STOP Violence, A Program of Synergy Services (developed in 2005)
STEP up is a bullying prevention program designed for middle school girls in grades 5–9. The focus is on reducing relational aggression.
www.stop-violence.org

Anti-Bully Pledge
for Use in the Classroom

Here is a sample anti-bullying contract or pledge:

We the students of _____ school agree to work together to stop bullying at our school.

Bullying is defined as intentionally aggressive behavior that can take many forms (verbal, physical, social/relational/emotional, or cyber bullying—or any combination of these); it involves an imbalance of power, and is often repeated over a period of time. The bullying can consist of one child bullying another, a group of children ganging up against one lone child, or one group of kids targeting another group.

Common behaviors attributed to bullying include put-downs, name calling, rumors, gossip, verbal threats, menacing, harassment, intimidation, social isolation or exclusion, and physical assaults.

We believe that no student deserves to be bullied and that every student regardless of race, color, religion, nationality, size, gender, popularity, athletic, academic, or social ability, or intelligence has the right to feel safe, secure, and respected.

I agree to:
- Treat other students with kindness and respect.
- Not engage in verbal, relational, or physical bullying or cyber bullying.
- Be aware of the school's anti-bullying policies and procedures.
- Abide by the school's anti-bullying policies and procedures.
- Support students who have been victimized by bullies.

▶ Speak out against verbal, relational, and physical bullying and cyber bullying.
▶ Notify a parent, teacher, or school administrator when bullying does occur.
▶ Be a good role model for other students.

_____

Student's signature

_____

Parent's signature

_____

Date

Index

Abuse, 2, 85, 86, 87, 89
Age-appropriate discipline, 45
*Aggression in the Schools: Bullies
and Whipping Boys* (Olweus), 4
Alexander, Duane, 6
Alexander, Jenny, 174
Allergy bullying, 221
Alpha dog, 32, 38, 39, 40
Americans with Disabilities Act, 224
Anaphylaxis, 223
Anti-bullying laws, 229, 232
Anti-bullying programs/education, 178
Assault, 233
Assertiveness skills, 170–72
Attention deficit hyperactivity
disorder, 35, 36
Awareness campaigns, creating, 251

Bad Girls (Voigt), 175
Bandura, Albert, 74, 75
Beane, Allan L., 175
Behavior, bullying, 73–87
abuse and, 85, 86, 87
child abuse and, 76–78
domestic violence and, 74, 75–76
environment, 73
family environment and, 80

family violence and, 73
friendships and, 86
genetics and, 80
observational learning and, 75
parental influence and, 73–74, 75
peer rejection and, 86
positive role models and, 78–79
prior victims and, 84–85
school climate/environment
and, 86–87
school failure and, 85
social learning theory and, 74–75
violent television and, 79–81
violent video games and, 82–84
Best Enemies (Leverich), 175
Best Friends, Worst Enemies
(Thompson, Cohen,
and Grace), 135
Blubber (Blume), 3
Blume, Judy, 3
Body language, 163–66
Borba, Michele, 156
*Boys Adrift: The Five Factors
Driving the Growing
Epidemic of Unmotivated
Boys and Underachieving
Young Men* (Sax), 125

The Breakfast Club, 98
Breakstone, Steve, 254
Brown, Laurie Krasny, 158
The bullied, 13, 53–63
    becoming a bully and, 63
    characteristics/traits of, 53–55
    home schooling and, 58
    making of a victim and, 56–59
    parents and, 62
    passive/provocation
        victims, 55, 60–61
    signs of, 54
    the triad and, 55
    why victims don't tell, 61–62
Bullied, warning signs, 100–110
    educational clues and, 103
    emotional/social
        vulnerabilities and, 104
    intervention and, 101, 109
    likely targets and, 104
    parental actions and, 107–10
    parental influences and, 105–07
    physical clues/symptoms
        and, 100–102
    psychological clues and, 102–03
Bullies, boy, 119–28
    androgens and, 124
    biology/environment and, 121
    boys bullying girls and, 126–27
    boy-will-be-boys myth and, 119–22
    bullying other boys and, 127
    danger of stereotypes and, 112–23
    dominant skills and, 120
    intervention and, 125
    intimate skills and, 120
    masculinity and, 119–20
    parents and, 125–26, 128
    physical aggression and, 123–26
    power/domination and, 124, 127
    sexual bullying and, 127

social dominance and, 126
social learning theory and, 124
stereotypes and, 121
violence and, 123, 124
Bullies, girl, 129–40
    bullying other girls and, 136–37
    developmental stages and, 130
    emotional bullying and, 131
    exclusion/social isolation and, 135
    family violence and, 133–34
    girl power and, 133
    good-girl persona and, 137
    group bullying and, 134–35
    indirect bullying and, 130
    neighborhood violence and, 134
    parents and, 137–40
    peer violence and, 133
    physical aggression and, 130
    popularity and, 136
    relational aggression and, 130,
        131, 132, 137, 140, 141
    relational bullying and, 131
    school violence and, 134
    social bullying and, 131
    verbal bullying and, 129–32
    violence and, 132–34
    warning signs and, 138
Bullies, types of, 32–39
    bullied bully, 36–37
    bunch of bullies, 38
    confident, 32–33
    detached, 34–35
    dominant male, 33
    gang of bullies, 38–39
    hyperactive, 35–36
    mean girl, 33
    social, 33–34
The bully, 12, 40–52
    age-appropriate discipline and, 45
    authoritarian parenting

style and, 45–47
characteristics of, 40–43
mean, 49–50
meaner, 51
meanest, 52
permissive parenting
style and, 44–45
social conditioning and, 43
stereotypical, 47–48
the triad and, 47
where bullying occurs, 48–49
why kids bully, 43–47
youngest, 49
Bully, my child as a, 204–16
approach to discipline and, 208
behavior modification
and, 213–14
child's psychological
health and, 209–10
constructive activities and, 214–15
friendship skills and, 212
graduated sanctions and, 211
having and open mind
and, 205–06
interpersonal skills and, 213
intervention and, 206–11
media violence and, 215–16
motivation and, 207
parenting style and, 208–09
school climate and, 211
signs of, 204–05
social behaviors and, 211
social environment and, 210–11
social skills and, 213
your relational style and, 209
zero tolerance policies and, 211
The Bully, the Bullied, and the
Bystander (Coloroso), 11, 57
"Bullycide," 7
Bullycide, 109

Bullycide: Death at Playtime
(Marr and Field), 7
Bullying
behaviors, 1
common markers of, 8–10
definition of, 1–2, 15
direct vs. indirect, 24–25
emotional, 23
facts/statistics and, 5–8
history of, 2–5
impact of, 11
nonverbal, 21
physical, 19–20
psychological, 21
relational, 21–23
research studies and, 4–5
social, 20–21
verbal, 15–18, 129–32
vs. normal conflict, 10
.See also Behavior, bullying
Bullying, a crime, 229–39
anti-bullying laws and, 229, 232
assault and, 233
bodily injury/threat of bodily
injury and, 233–34
bullying laws and, 232–33
complaint procedures and, 236–38
cyber bullying and, 237
e-mail campaigns and, 230
prevention programs and, 239
public awareness and, 231
resolutions and, 238–39
seeking support and, 231–32
state laws and, 229
uncooperative school
officials and, 234–36
Bullying, consequences of, 111–18
educational effects and, 114–15
emotional effects and, 113–14
long-term effects, 117–18

Bullying, consequences
of,—*continued*
parental support and, 118
physical effects and, 111–12
short-term effects, 115–17
Bullying, cyber, 26–31
bash boards and, 28
cell phones and, 29
chat rooms and, 27
cyberspace and, 26
digital photos and, 29
e-mail and, 27–28
Internet and, 26
online exclusions and, 28
peer abuse and, 27
technology and, 30–31
text messages and, 29
videotape and, 30
websites and, 28
Bullying, special needs
children and, 217–28
anti-bullying legislation and, 218
first line of defense and, 225–27
food allergies and, 220–24
legal action and, 227–28
legal rights and, 225
parental involvement and,
219–20
school's role and, 217–18
vulnerabilities and, 218–19, 221
Bullying, types of, 15–31
cyber, 26–31
direct vs. indirect, 24–25
emotional, 23
extortion, 23–24
physical, 19–20
relational, 21–23
social, 20–21
verbal, 15–18
Bullying assessment survey, 251

*Bullying at School: What We Know
and What We Can Do* (Olweus), 4
Bullying laws, directives in, 232–33
Bullying myths .*See* Myths, bullying
Bullying prevention, 178–85
assessment of problem
and, 179–80
character education
programs and, 182
climate of tolerance and, 180
continued education/
intervention and, 185
enforcement of sanctions
and, 184–85
graduated sanctions and, 183–84
integrated, 180–81
programs, 239
reporting procedures and, 182–83
school climate change and, 180
supervising trouble spots and, 185
supportive parents/school
personal and, 181–82
zero tolerance policies
and, 183–84
Bully Police USA, 230, 231
Bully prevention, 42
The bystander, 13–14, 64–72
alternate solutions and, 71
as assistant, 65–66
as avoider, 67–68
characteristics of, 64
defined, 64
empathy/compassion and, 71
as encourager, 66–67
getting help and, 71–72
as hero, 68
innocence and, 69–70
need to tell and, 71
not telling and, 68–69
roles of, 65–68

showing support, 71
stopping the bullying and, 70–72
the triad and, 65

Child abuse, 76–78
Classroom rules, specify, 255–56
Cleary, Beverly, 175
Cohen, Lawrence J., 135, 209
Coleridge, Georgia, 209
Coloroso, Barbara, 11, 47, 57
Columbine High School, 82
Conversational skills, 167–68
Cosby, Bill, 175
Cyber bullying, 186–203, 237
    anonymity and, 195
    consequences of, 196
    defined, 186
    denigration and, 189
    educating against, 200–202
    exclusion and, 192
    exposure and, 192–93
    flaming and, 188
    griefers and, 188
    harassment, 186–88
    hurtful communications
        and, 201–02
    impact of, 195–96
    impersonation and, 189–90
    intervention and, 200
    outing and, 190–91
    parental involvement and,
        198–99, 200–201
    problems of, 193–95
    protection from, 198–99
    reasons for, 194–95
    relational aggression and, 193, 195
    responding to, 200–202
    signs of, 197–98
    social networking sites and, 199
    trickery and, 190–91

types of, 186–93
Cyberspace, 26
Cyberthreats, 7–8

Dear Mr. Henshaw (Cleary), 175
Depression, 6, 42
Dickens, Charles, 3
Disability harassment, 224–25
Doherty, Karen, 209
Domestic violence, 74, 75–76
Do-overs, 153
Dreiblatt, Karen, 254
Dreiblatt, Michael, 254

Educational programs,
    implementing, 252–54
Eisen, Andrew, 174
Elman, Natalie Madorsky, 156
Emotional bullying, 131
Engler, Linda B., 174
Epinephrine, 223
Extortion bully, 23–24

Fab Friends And Best Buds
    (Karres), 158
Families and Work Institute
    studies, 21, 22
Family environment, 80
Family violence, 133–34
Fear reaction, 56
Federal Bureau or Investigation
    report, 132
Field, Tim, 7
Food allergies, 9, 220–24
Food Allergy & Anaphylaxis
    Network (FAAN), 221, 222
Fox, Michael J., 3
The Friendship Factor (Rubin), 156
Friendship-making skills, 143
Friendships, 86

Friendship skills, 154–57, 168–70, 212

Garbarino, James, 134
Gardner, Howard, 162, 172
Genetics, 80
Golding, William, 3
A Good Friend (Herron
 and Peter), 158
Grace, Catherine O'Neill, 135
*Grand Theft Childhood: The
 Surprising Truth about Video
 Games and What Parents Can
 Do* (Kutner and Olson), 83
Gurian, Michael, 120

Harassment
 cyber bullying and, 186–88
 disability, 224–25, 227
 lawsuits, 228
 online, 27
 peer, 217
 sexual, 133
 special needs children and, 220
 teen suicides and, 109
Harm, intent to, 9
Harris, Eric, 82
Heathers (movie), 34
*Helping Your Socially Vulnerable
 Child* (Eisen and Engler), 174
Herron, Ron, 158
High, Brenda, 230, 231
High-risk areas, supervising, 258
Hinton, S. E., 3
Home schooling, 58
Home violence, 37
How to Be a Friend (Brown) , 158
*How You Can Be Bully
 Free* (Beane), 175
Humiliation, 20–21
Humor, 154

The Incredible Years, 181
Inner discipline, 46
Internet, 26
Internet slang, 202
Interpersonal relationships,
 160, 162, 167
Interpersonal skills, 213
Intervention, 4, 16, 42, 43, 50, 101,
 109, 124, 125, 200, 206–11
Intrapersonal intelligence, 172

Josephson Institute of Ethics, 6
*The Journal of the American
 Medical Association*, 5

Kaiser Foundation, 2, 6, 7, 79
The Karate Kid, 3, 98
Karres, Erika V. Shearin, 138, 158
Kennedy-Moore, Eileen, 156
Kindlon, Dan, 125
Klebold, Dylan, 82
Kraizer, Sherryll, 174
Kutner, Lawrence, 83, 84

Lane, Marilyn L., 209
Language, hurtful, 17–18
Learning activities, cooperative, 257
Learning difficulties, 58
Learning disabilities, 35
Leverich, Kathleen, 175
Linking the Interest of Families
 and Teachers (LIFT), 181
Lord of the Flies (Golding), 3

Maine Project Against Bullying, 93
Manipulation, 23
Marr, Neil, 7
*Mean Chicks, Cliques, and
 Dirty Tricks* (Karres), 138

The Meanest Things to Say (Cosby), 175
Mean Girls (movie), 34, 98
Mehrabian, Albert, 165
Myths, bullying, 88–99
  afraid of retaliation and, 92
  bullied children always tell and, 92–95
  bullies are loners and, 97–98
  bullying doesn't happen and, 96–97
  fears, 92–95
  learned behavior and, 95–96
  normal rite of passage and, 88–90
  people are born bullies and, 95–96
  a school problem and, 98-99
  self-defense and, 90–92
  tattletales and, 94

National Center for Education Statistics, 58
National Crime Victimization Survey, 132
National Institute of Child Health and Human Development (NICHD), 6
National Institute of Mental Health, 80, 138
National Mental Health Information Center, 54
National Youth Violence Prevention Center, 1, 178
Nobody Liked, Everybody Hates Me (Borba), 156
Nonverbal learning disability (NLD), 161

Odd Girl Out: The Hidden Culture of Aggression in Girls (Simmons), 130, 135
Oliver Twist (Dickens), 3

Olson, Cheryl, 83, 84
Olweus, Dan, 4, 47, 53, 89, 97, 179, 254
Olweus Bullying Prevention Program, 181, 183, 252
The Ophelia Project, 140–41
The Outsiders (Hinton), 3

Parental responsibility, enacting change and, 173–85
  awareness of situation and, 175–76
  being overprotective and, 176
  being supportive and, 177
  embarrassment and, 174
  fear, 173–74
  honoring child's wishes and, 175–76
  reporting bullying and, 177–78
  .*See also* Bullying prevention
Parenting with Purpose (Reasoner and Lane), 209
Parents Television Council, 80
Peer abuse, xiv, 27
Peer-counseling programs, 254–55
Peer pressure, 38
Peer violence, 133
Peter, Val J., 158
Pew Internet & American Life Project, 190, 194, 199, 200
Physical aggression, 19, 47, 123–26, 130
Physical violence, threat of, 20
Playful Parenting (Cohen), 209
Pollack, William, 125
Posturing, 20
Preschool, 15, 16
Problem, identifying, 250–51

Queen Bees and Wannabes (Wiseman), 34, 131

*Raising Cain: Protecting the
Emotional Life of Boys* (Kindlon
and Thompson), 125
*Real Boys: Rescuing Our
Sons from the Myths of
Boyhood* (Pollack), 125
Reasoner, Robert W., 209
Rehabilitation Act, 224
Relational aggression, 130, 131,
132, 137, 140, 141, 193, 195
Relational bullying, 131
Relationships, 22
Rubin, Kenneth H., 156

Sadler, Marilyn, 175
Sax, Leonard, 125
School Psychology International, 91
School violence, 134
Schwartz, David, 59
See Jane Hit (Garbarino), 134
Self-esteem, 6, 144–54
    areas of improvement and, 150–52
    areas of strength/competence
        and, 147–48
    behaviors and, 144–45
    being helpful, 156
    being positive and, 155
    blending in and, 155
    damaging statements, 149–50
    definition of, 144
    do-overs and, 153
    friendship, 157
    friendship skills and, 154–57
    humor and, 154
    improvement plans and, 151–52
    improvement strategies, 147–54
    joining clubs/groups and, 158
    learning from mistakes
        and, 152–53
    physical activity and, 150

positive body language and, 155
positive self-talk and, 152
praising/encouraging, 148–50
prevention skills , 158–59
self-affirmation and, 152, 153
self-defense classes and, 158–59
similar interests and, 155–56
temperament and, 146–47
traits and, 146, 148
Seven Secrets of Successful Parenting
    (Coleridge and Doherty), 209
Sexual intimidation, 20
Shootings, 7
Simmons, Rachel, 130, 135, 136
Slam book, 33–34, 133, 189
Social behaviors, 211
Social bully, 33
Social bullying, 131
Social environment, 210–11
Social/interpersonal skills, 143
Social isolation, 42
Socialization, 151
Social learning theory, 74–75, 124
Social networking sites, 199
Social skills, 160–70, 213
    attitudes and, 166
    body language and, 163–66
    conversational skills and, 167–68
    essential, 161–63
    eye contact and, 164
    facial expressions and, 165
    friendship skills and, 168–70
    greeting and, 167–68
    interpersonal relationships
        and, 160, 162, 167
    introductions and, 168
    joining in, 169
    making compliments and, 169
    making friends and, 161
    nervousness and, 167

offering help and, 169
play activities and, 161
posture and, 164–65
resiliency and, 162–63
self-confidence and, 162
showing appreciation and, 170
sustaining conversations and, 168
teaching, 142–43
voice quality and, 166–67
Southern California Center
of Excellence on Youth
Violence Prevention, 37
Superheroes, 119–20

Technology, 30–31
Teen suicides, 109
Temper tantrums, 43–44, 46
*10 Days to a Bully-Proof
Child* (Kraizer), 174
Thompson, Michael, 125, 135

The Unwritten Rules of Friendship
(Elman and Kennedy-Moore), 156
U. S. Secret Service/Department
of Education, reports of, 7, 96

The Very Bad Bunny (Sadler), 175
Violence, 37, 123, 124, 132–34, 215–16
Virginia Tech massacre, 82
Virginia Tech Review Panel, 82
Voice quality, 166–67
Voigt, Cynthia, 175

*What Stories Does My Son
Need? A Guide to Books and
Movies that Build Character
in Boys* (Gurian), 120
When Your Child Is Bullied
(Alexander), 174
Whole-school policies, 259–60

Wiseman, Rosalind, 34, 131
Workplace Bullying Institute, 98

Youth violence, 7

Zero tolerance policies, 240–49
conflict resolution and, 247
decreasing incidence
reports and, 242–44
description, 240–41
goal of, 244
graduated sanctions
and, 183–84, 242
intervention/positive role
models and, 245–46
lawsuits and, 242
policies/programs to be
used and, 247–49
school and, 211
short-term/stop-gap
policies and, 246
student exclusion policies
and, 244–45